Underwriting Democracy

Encouraging Free Enterprise and
Democratic Reform Among the Soviets
and in Eastern Europe

Underwriting Democracy

Encouraging Free Enterprise and Democratic Reform Among the Soviets and in Eastern Europe

GEORGE SOROS

PublicAffairs
New York

Library of Congress Cataloging-in-Publication data
Soros, George
Underwriting democracy: encouraging free enterprise
and democratic reform among the Soviets and in
Eastern Europe / George Soros.
p. cm.
Hardbound ed. published c1991.
Rev and expanded ed. of: Opening the Soviet system. 1990.
Includes index.
ISBN-10: 1-58648-227-0   ISBN-13: 978-1-58648-227-5 (pbk.)
1. Soros Foundation. 2. Endowments—Program related investments—United States. 3. Europe, Eastern—Politics and government—1989- 4. Soviet Union—Politics and government—1985–1991. 5. Soros, George. 6. Capitalists and financiers—United States—Biography. I. Soros, George. Opening the Soviet system. II. Title.
HV97.S67S67 2004
361.7'632'092—dc22
2003068952

To the people of the Soviet Union and Eastern Europe
whose aspirations I sought to support

▢ CONTENTS ▢

□ PREFACE □

The rise and fall of the Soviet system is a strange story in which the unreal has been rendered credible and the real has become incredible. In its heyday the Stalinist regime managed to impose a totally distorted view of the world on its subjects through a combination of physical terror and mental indoctrination. Now that that regime is in its final throes, the rate of change in the Soviet Union has accelerated to a point where it exceeds most people's imagination. Comprehension cannot keep pace with events, and the gap between them is, in turn, part of the reason that events are spinning out of control. The divergence between perception and reality plays a crucial role both in the success and in the failure of the Soviet system.

We are baffled by the course of events because we lack a frame of reference in terms of which we could understand it. We are witnessing a revolution; but we do not even have a theory of history. A better understanding is desperately needed if an orderly transformation of the Soviet system is to be achieved. The purpose of this book is to fill that need.

I have been both a participant and a close observer of the opening of the Soviet system, and my involvement has grown with the process itself. I started out some ten years ago by trying to create small cracks in the monolithic structure that goes under the name of communism in the belief that in a rigid structure even a small crack can have a devastating effect. As the cracks grew, so did my efforts, until they came to take up most of my time and energy. I have been active on at least three fronts: I have established a series of foundations throughout the Communist world with the purpose of opening up these closed societies

ix

and helping them make the transition to an open society. I have also become involved in the political process by proposing and helping to develop economic reform programs. Finally, I have tried to understand the process of change in which I was participating. This book is both an account of that understanding and a brief report of my own activities.

I began to write this book in November 1989, after the fall of the Berlin Wall and around the time of the rather disappointing meeting between Presidents Bush and Gorbachev in Malta. I felt a tremendous sense of urgency. Here is what I wrote then:

We are at a crucial decision point in history. The political landscape as we have known it since the end of the Second World War is undergoing a radical transformation. Communist dogma has lost its sway over people's minds and the Soviet empire, which had been based on that dogma, is collapsing. A process that has been gathering momentum over decades has accelerated to a point where it qualifies as a revolution. Events are happening so fast that it is hard to keep up with them. East Germany is transformed from one day to the other, followed by Bulgaria and Czechoslovakia in quick succession. The demise of the Communist system in Eastern Europe has become an accomplished fact in the space of not much more than a month. What is now at stake is the fate of the Soviet Union itself. And that, in turn, will help to shape the political future of the whole world.

There are two possible outcomes. Either the Soviet Union will become integrated into the free world or it will continue to disintegrate. The events of the next few months will, in my opinion, have a decisive influence on the ultimate outcome. In any case, the pace of events cannot continue to accelerate much further, so that much more is likely to happen in the next few months than in the years and even decades to come.

We have seen similar historical decision points in the past. The year 1945 was one; 1919 was another. But the closest parallel is with 1848, because that was the last time a revolutionary fervor swept from country to country and the raw manifestation of the people's will had a major impact on the nature of government. There is another similarity with 1848: the people's will manifests itself in the form of nationalism.

Yet there is a common goal which unites the various manifestations: the desire to get rid of an oppressive system of government. This gives national movements a universal character: there is a sense of brotherhood that connects them.

The destruction of the old system is more or less assured. What is at stake is the shape of the new one. Will it be possible to replace the old structure with new ones so that people of various nationalities can live side by side and among each other in peace, or will the process of disintegration continue until it deteriorates into civil war? Unfortunately, the line of least resistance leads to the latter alternative. It takes time and energy to construct a new system and both are in short supply. It is my firm conviction that only the deus ex machina of Western assistance can tip the scales in favor of a constructive solution. That is the conviction that has guided me in my actions and that is the case I want to argue here.

My forebodings were fully justified. Western policy continued to lag behind events, and the Soviet Union continued to disintegrate. If the Western powers had been willing in 1988 to devote the resources they were prepared to provide in assistance to the Soviet Union in 1990, events might have taken a different course; but to reverse the trend now would require much larger resources than the West is ready to consider. The lag persists. Needless to say, the failure of Western policy is only one of the elements in the impending economic and political breakdown. The internal political turmoil is a more important factor. The old Soviet political center is moribund, but it refuses to lie down and die. And a new political center has not yet emerged. The Shatalin plan—a recent Soviet scheme for transforming the economy—was a last, desperate attempt to create a new center on a Union-wide basis, but it was subverted by the bureaucracy it was destined to destroy.

In my judgment, the chance of replacing the Soviet Union with a new kind of union capable of generating popular support has been irretrievably lost. Popular support is crystallizing around local or national centers, and the attempt to preserve the union

will have to take a dictatorial turn. We can hope that the dictatorship will have progressive intentions, but it is safe to say it will
not be able to resolve the underlying economic and political
problems. The prospects are for repression or chaos or a succession
or combination of both.

Propelled by a sense of urgency, I wrote what I called an
"instant" book, *Opening the Soviet System*, published in London
in June 1990. It served a useful purpose. It enabled me to communicate my views to policy-makers at a time when they were
beginning to consider economic assistance to the Soviet Union.
It also gave me an opportunity to clarify my own thinking.

Now that the revolution of 1989 has begun to subside, there
is a little more time to take stock and draw some conclusions.
Needless to say, I emerge from the experience with a somewhat
different perspective from the one with which I entered it. But
my basic idea, that the interplay between perceptions and events
provides a clue to the understanding of history, has been powerfully reinforced.

I had approached the crisis in Eastern Europe with a well-
developed set of ideas about how societies work and how they
change. But that framework was getting old. I formulated it
first as a student at the London School of Economics in the
1950s. At that time, I had just left Hungary, which had come
under Soviet domination, and I was preoccupied with the differences between the closed social system I wanted to get away
from and the open one I had chosen to live in. I was greatly
influenced by the philosophy of Karl Popper and to a lesser
extent by the free-market views of Friedrich Hayek. I had finished
my courses in two years and I had a third year to wait before
the degree was conferred on me. I used that opportunity in
1952–53 to submit some essays to Popper, and I continued to
develop my ideas while working first in London and then in
New York. Eventually, I gave up philosophy and devoted myself
to making money. But the urge to try to understand societies
and how they work did not disappear, and I kept returning to

it in various ways at various times. Eventually I managed to come up with a way to explain how historical change occurs, but by that time I was thoroughly engaged in trying to make money in financial markets. I used the financial markets as a laboratory for testing my ideas. The results were rather encouraging: one thousand dollars invested in my fund, the Quantum Fund, at its inception in 1969 has grown to more than half a million dollars by now. I was acclaimed by the *Institutional Investor* as the "best money manager in the world," and this renown provided me with a platform from which I could expound my views. My first book, *The Alchemy of Finance*, published in 1987, explained how financial markets are propelled by the reflexive relationship between economic fundamentals and the investors' biases. All that time, the distinction between open and closed societies had stayed with me and eventually served as both inspiration and guiding principle behind my foundation, the Open Society Fund, and everything that followed from it.

But during 1989, as the disintegration of the Soviet system accelerated, my framework for understanding the convulsive changes became increasingly inadequate. At the time I conceived them, in the 1950s, the concepts of the open and the closed society appeared as alternative principles of social organization, each with its own strengths and weaknesses, vying for supremacy. I was a partisan of open society, but I could not take its superiority for granted because communism had conquered half the world and democracies were hard pressed to resist its encroachments. The two systems were locked in deadly combat, and the outcome was far from assured. Now that the communist system has collapsed, I have a lot more historical evidence to support my preference for an open society. At the same time, recent experience has taught us all a bitter lesson: it is not enough to destroy a closed society in order to bring about an open society. While this is obvious to me now, I cannot claim that I was equally conscious of it at the time when I started the Open Society Fund. I defined the foundation's objectives as helping to open up closed societies and helping to make open societies more viable. What has become my main objective—namely, helping to build the infrastructure and the institutions that are lacking in a closed society but are indispensable to the functioning of an open society—was not part of my original program. Fortunately Gorbachev did not realize either how difficult it is to bring an open society into existence; otherwise he might never have embarked on his course. Open society is a very sophisticated form of organization. Its creation will take much longer than the destruction of an oppressive regime.

Clearly, the framework I constructed in the 1950s is badly in need of revision. I started the process in the "instant book" published in June 1990, but writing in the heat of the moment I could not fully integrate the recent experiences into a coherent interpretation. I have made a lot more progress since then and have had an insight which amounted to a breakthrough in my thinking. As a result I have arrived at what I believe is the beginning of a coherent theory of history. It is based on the divergence between thinking and reality which has played such a crucial role in both the rise and the fall of the Soviet system. The participants' perceptions never correspond to reality—that is what sets human history apart from natural phenomena—but the extent of the divergence and of its consequent influence on the course of events vary greatly. Herein lies the key to a better understanding of history.

My new insight comes from a body of thought variously called evolutionary systems theory, theory of complexity, or simply chaos theory. This so-called chaos theory has not yet had time to permeate public consciousness, yet it offers a useful vocabulary for discussing revolutions. I have in mind particularly the concept of "far-from-equilibrium conditions" that was introduced by the Nobel physicist Ilya Prigogine. The generally accepted view is that conditions tend toward equilibrium. The idea that the tendency ceases to prevail when conditions are sufficiently far removed from equilibrium is novel and in some ways shocking, because it seems to contradict the very concept of equilibrium. Yet it provides a clue to the understanding of the revolution currently unfolding. What is even more interesting, it also throws light on the rigid Stalinist system that preceded it, because, as I shall try to show, closed societies and revolutions are both far-from-equilibrium situations—only the time scale is different: in closed societies nothing changes over an extended period, in revolutions everything changes in a very short period. There are many situations like these in the phenomena studied by evolutionary systems theory: the history of the universe itself is probably the prime example.

By borrowing the concept of "far-from-equilibrium conditions" from chaos theory, I arrive at a challenging theory of history. The relationship between thinking and reality can take one of three forms: dynamic equilibrium (open society); static disequilibrium (closed society); or dynamic disequilibrium (revolution or the boom–bust pattern familiar from financial markets). This framework supersedes my earlier one, which distinguished only between open and closed societies.

The pattern of revolution closely resembles the boom–bust pattern of financial markets. There are many ifs and buts about this pattern, but I shall not go into them at this point; that would risk losing the reader who is more interested in the specifics of the current situation than in abstract theory. I have organized the book into three parts. Part One contains the historical narrative that formed part of my book *Opening the Soviet System*; it brings the reader up to the spring of 1990. Part Two covers events—especially those in which I personally participated—after that time. Part Three is devoted to my theory of history. The advantage of this arrangement is twofold. On the one hand, the reader is offered an interpretation of current events that benefits from a coherent point of view without the theory itself intruding; on the other hand, the theory can be presented to those who are interested in it without any pressure to make it particularly relevant to the present moment. After all, theories are supposed to be timelessly valid.

The arrangement is less than perfect—in particular, some seams are showing between Part One and Part Two; and who knows how anachronistic Part Two may become by the time the book is published. But that is unavoidable in a book which deals with a revolution while it is unfolding. While reading Part One the reader should bear in mind that it was written between November 1989 and April 1990. It serves as a prelude to Part Two, where many of the themes introduced in Part One will be developed further. Revisions in Part One have been deliberately kept to a minimum.

□ PART ONE □

The Revolution of 1989

□ 1 □

Cracking the
Communist Structure

I began my work directed at opening up closed societies about ten years ago. I was a successful manager of an international investment fund and I was making more money than I had use for. I began to think about what I should do with it. The idea of setting up a foundation appealed to me because I had always felt that one should do something for other people if one could afford it. I was a confirmed egoist but I considered the pursuit of self-interest as too narrow a base for my rather inflated self. If truth be known, I carried some rather potent messianic fantasies with me from childhood which I felt I had to control, otherwise they might get me into trouble. But when I had made my way in the world I wanted to indulge my fantasies to the extent that I could afford.

As I looked around for a worthy cause, I ran into difficulties. I did not belong to any special community. I was born a Jew in Hungary. Having escaped Nazi persecution by living under assumed names during the German occupation, I went to England in 1947 and then to the United States in 1956. But I never quite became an American. I had left Hungary behind,

3

and my Jewishness did not express itself in a sense of tribal loyalty that would have led me to support Israel. On the contrary, I took pride in being in the minority, an outsider who was capable of seeing the other point of view. Only the ability to think critically and to rise above a particular point of view could make up for the dangers and indignities that being a Hungarian Jew had inflicted on me. I realized that I cared passionately about the concept of an open society in which people like me could enjoy freedom without being hounded to death. Accordingly, I called my foundation the Open Society Fund, with the objective of making open societies viable and helping to open up closed societies.

I had considerable reservations about charitable activities. I had had a formative experience as an impecunious student in London. I had gone to the Jewish Board of Guardians to ask for financial assistance, but it turned me down. The explanation was that it did not support students, only young men who took up a trade. One Christmas vacation, while still a student, I was working on the railroad as a porter and broke my leg. This is the occasion to get money out of those bastards, I decided. I went back to the Guardians and lied to them. I told them I was working illegally when I broke my leg and therefore was not eligible for National Assistance. They could not refuse me, but they gave me a hard time. They made me climb up three flights of stairs, on crutches, every week to collect my money. At the same time a friend of mine was also receiving assistance from them. He was playing them along; he was willing to learn a trade but kept losing his job. After a while, they refused to help me any more. I wrote the chairman of the Board of Guardians a heartrending letter. I shall not starve, I said. It only hurts me that this is how one Jew treats another in need. The chairman replied by return mail. He offered to send me the weekly allowance without my having to come to the office. I graciously accepted and, long after the plaster had come off my leg and I had taken a hitchhiking trip to the south of France, I informed the Guardians that I was no longer in need of their assistance.

I learned a lot from this experience, which stood me in good stead when I had a foundation of my own. I learned that it is the task of the applicant to get money out of a foundation and it is the task of the foundation to protect itself. The Jewish Board of Guardians had investigated me thoroughly but had failed to discover that I was also drawing National Assistance benefits. That permitted me to write with such moral indignation to the chairman although I was cheating. I also discovered that charity, like all other human endeavors, can have unintended consequences. The paradox of charity is that it turns the recipients, like my friend who pretended to be learning a trade, into objects of charity. There are two ways to overcome these difficulties. One is to become very bureaucratic like the Ford Foundation, and the other is not to be visible at all—to make grants without inviting applications and to remain anonymous. I chose the latter alternative.

My first major undertaking was in South Africa in 1979, where I identified Capetown University as an institution devoted to the ideal of an open society. I established scholarships for black students on a scale large enough to make an impact on the university. The scheme did not work as well as I had hoped, because the university was not quite as open-minded as it claimed to be and my funds were used partly to support students already there and only partly to offer places to new students. But at least it did no harm.

I became moderately active in human rights as a member and supporter of Helsinki Watch and Americas Watch. My newly created Open Society Fund also offered a number of scholarships in the United States to dissident intellectuals from Eastern Europe, and this was the program that led me to establish a foundation in Hungary. Selecting candidates became a problem after a while, because we had to go by word of mouth, which did not seem to be the fairest arrangement. It occurred to me that it would be advantageous to set up a selection committee in Hungary and have a public competition. I approached the Hungarian Ambassador in Washington, who contacted his government. To my great astonishment I got a positive reply.

When I went to Hungary to negotiate, I had a secret weapon at my disposal: the recipients of Open Society scholarships were ready and eager to help. On the government side, my negotiating partner was Ferenc Barta, who was at the time concerned with foreign economic relations and looked on me as an expatriate businessman whom he was anxious to accommodate. He introduced me to the Hungarian Academy of Sciences, and we concluded an agreement between the academy and the newly established Soros Foundation in New York. (Open Society Fund was considered too controversial a name by the Hungarian government, so I had to set up a special foundation to deal with them.) We established a joint committee with an official of the academy and me as co-chairmen. The rest of the members were independent-minded Hungarian intellectuals, approved by both parties. Both parties had the right of veto over the decisions of the committee. There was also to be an independent executive director operating under the aegis of the academy.

I was very lucky in the selection of my associates. I engaged as my personal representative Miklos Vasarhelyi, who had been the press representative of the Imre Nagy government of 1956 and had been tried and sentenced together with Nagy. He was currently working as a researcher in an academic institute. Although he could not be an official member of the committee, he was accepted as my personal representative. He was an elder statesman of the unofficial opposition but at the same time enjoyed the respect of officials. His involvement sent a clear signal to society where the foundation stood in relation to the communist regime. I also had a very good lawyer, Lajos Dornbach,* who

* Now vice-president of the Hungarian Parliament.

6

was completely devoted to the cause and was one of a number of people who understood the purpose of the foundation better than I did.

Some very hard negotiations took place both before and after the signing of the agreement. The officials thought they were dealing with a well-meaning expatriate, the proverbial American uncle, whom they could humor and take advantage of. But they soon learned otherwise. My requirement that the foundation be headed by an independent executive became a particular sticking point. The officials' idea was that the committee would make its decisions and the director would take notes, then pass on the decisions to the relevant authorities for execution. The relevant authorities were, of course, an integral part of the internal security system. Matters came to a breaking point. I went to see Gyorgy Aczel, the unofficial cultural czar of Hungary and General Secretary Kadar's close adviser. I told him, "I can't accept; I am packing up." He said, "I hope you are not leaving with bad feelings." I replied that I could not help being disappointed, having put so many months into the negotiations. We were at the door when he asked, "What is it you really need to make the foundation work?" "An independent executive director," I answered. "Let me see what I can do," he said. We arrived at a compromise: the foundation could have its independent director, but the academy also had to be represented, and communications had to be signed both by the academy's representative and our director.

When I interviewed the candidate put forward by the academy, I said to him, "You will have a tough job serving two masters." "Only two?" he replied, which I understood (mistakenly, as it later turned out) to imply that he also had to report to the security agencies. After that, we had a good working relationship. One of the people I had engaged to work in the foundation had lost his job because of his political activities. The official side protested against employing him, saying he had a "spot" on his character. But they allowed him to remain on a temporary basis. After a

7

year, he was promoted to executive director, and he has worked together with the academy's representative as a coequal ever since.

The foundation announced a number of grant opportunities, including an open invitation for independent projects of an innovative character. We supported a wide range of activities as long as they were not state controlled: amateur theaters, ecological projects, historical restorations, family therapy, sociological research, voluntary associations, summer schools, and myriad other projects.

To finance these grants, we looked for ways to convert dollars into Hungarian currency. Perhaps our most successful program was providing photocopy machines to public libraries and academic institutes against payment in Hungarian forints. We then used the forints to give grants locally. We established local scholarships for writers and social scientists but, ironically, were not allowed to give out grants for foreign travel. That was the monopoly of an official scholarship committee, tightly controlled by the security agencies. I continued to award scholarships through the Open Society Fund, and I made no secret of it. At the same time I announced in the annual report of the Soros Foundation that we were unable to offer scholarships for study abroad because of official objections. Eventually, the Ministry of Education, which controlled official scholarships, capitulated. We agreed that applications would have to be submitted in duplicate and the grants awarded by our independent scholarship committee would be approved automatically by the official one.

Luckily for us, the propaganda apparatus of the Communist party put a ban on publicity concerning the activities of the Soros Foundation. We were allowed to advertise in newspapers and publish an annual report in accordance with our agreement, but that was all. As a result, the public became aware of our existence only gradually, and then only in connection with some activity that we were supporting. We made a policy of supporting practically any initiative that was spontaneous and nongovernmental. The name of the Soros Foundation kept on cropping up in the most unexpected places. The foundation attained a mythical quality exactly because it received so little publicity. For those who were politically conscious, it became an instrument of civil society; for the public at large, it was manna from heaven.

We carefully arranged our activities so that programs considered constructive by the government outweighed those that would be regarded with suspicion by the authorities in charge of ideology. The attitude of the authorities was divided. Those concerned with economic matters were generally in favor and those with culture against. Only rarely did we run into serious objections. When we did, it merely spurred us on. Doing good may be noble, but fighting evil can be fun.

One such conflict occurred in the fall of 1987. Apparently, General Secretary Kadar himself became angry when he read about one of our grants in a weekly newspaper that had taken it on itself to publish our awards regularly. It was for a historical study that might have showed him in an unfavorable light. The weekly was forbidden to continue reporting our activities. At the same time, the Minister of Culture sent out a circular forbidding educational institutions to apply to the foundation directly without checking with the ministry first. I protested both those actions. When I received no satisfaction, I announced that I would not visit Hungary and the foundation would make no new awards until the matter was settled. The stock market crash of October 1987 occurred in the meantime, and a reporter from the Hungarian radio asked me in a telephone interview whether I was closing the foundation because I had lost my fortune. I explained to him why I was refusing to go to Hungary. It was a misunderstanding, I said, which was sure to be cleared up soon. The interview was broadcast, and the authorities were embarrassed. I gained my points and paid a visit to Hungary. While I was meeting with the Prime Minister, the head of the Party's propaganda department, Mr. Berec, personally imposed a ban on any interviews with me. The ban was broken within

9

the week when Moscow TV reported my visit to President Gromyko in the Kremlin and, according to communist etiquette, Hungarian TV replayed it in Budapest. I was amused.

With the passage of time we developed a keener sense of priorities. Miklos Vasarhelyi laid particular stress on youth programs. We supported a number of self-governing student colleges (faculty dormitories where students instituted their own educational programs). They became the incubators of FIDESZ (Association of Young Democrats), which later spearheaded the transition to democracy and is currently one of the two major opposition parties in Parliament. Several members of our first group of scholars at Oxford later became leaders of FIDESZ.

It is not for me to evaluate the social and political significance of the foundation. I can only give a subjective judgment. It succeeded beyond my wildest expectations. It became an efficient, smooth-working organization full of spirit. After the initial startup period, I did not have to spend much time on it at all; it ran all by itself. It was a real pleasure to make decisions in the knowledge that they would be carried out. It was an even greater pleasure to encounter the foundation at work in ways of which I was not even aware. Once, on a flight from Budapest to Moscow, I sat next to a gypsy who was unusually well-educated. He was an ethnographer collecting gypsy folk dances. When I mentioned my name, he told me he was traveling on a foundation scholarship. At the airport in Moscow I met eighteen Hungarian economists who were on the way to China on a foundation-sponsored study tour. It made my day.

Encouraged by the success of the Soros Foundation in Hungary and aware of the reform movement in China, I put out feelers in the spring of 1986 to find out whether China might be ready for a foundation similar to the Hungarian one. I met Liang Heng, author of *The Son of the Revolution,** just before he returned to China for a visit. He established good contacts among the reformers and, as a result, the Hungarian foundation invited

* Alfred A. Knopf, Inc., 1983.

10

eighteen Chinese economists to come and study the reform process in Hungary and Yugoslavia. The visit was very successful
because the real contacts were arranged outside official channels,
and the Chinese economists gained very good insights. I met
them in Hungary and discussed the concept of a foundation
with Chen Yizi, head of the Institute for Economic Reform.
Subsequently, I went to China with Liang Heng, who became
my personal representative, and set up a foundation on the Hungarian model with Chen Yizi's institute as my partner. Bao Tung,
Communist party General Secretary Zhao Ziyang's reform-
minded principal secretary, cut through the red tape and approved
the foundation on the spot.

Both Bao and the foundation ran into a lot of trouble subsequently when his political enemies tried to use the foundation
as a vehicle for attacking him. They prepared an elaborate dossier,
which named me as a CIA agent and an anti-Communist conspir-
ator. Bao Tung counter-attacked with voluminous information
about my other foundations to prove my good faith. That was
not too difficult because I had always been very open about
my intentions; by 1987 I had also established a foundation in
Moscow. President Gromyko himself had put the seal of approval
on it by officially receiving me in the Kremlin. Nevertheless,
in China, some high party council decided to liquidate the foundation and refund the money. It took the personal intervention
of Zhao Ziyang to rescind the decision. He arranged for Chen
Yizi to resign as co-chairman and for the International Cultural
Exchange Center, whose chairman turned out to be a high-
ranking official in the security service, to take over as our host
organization.

I was not fully aware of those behind-the-scenes maneuvers.
I had not been satisfied with the way the foundation was operating
and had been giving poor Chen Yizi a hard time for keeping
too much of the money for his own institute, so I was naïve
enough to be pleased when he relinquished control. But the
foundation did not function any better under the new regime.

I was taken to visit one of our projects, a mobile library unit

11

operated by the Young Pioneers, and was appalled. It was a formal affair, the children in uniform, the instructors making stiff, meaningless speeches, the children forming a *tableau vivant* to demonstrate the use of the library. Worst of all, the secretary of the foundation was so pleased that she had tears in her eyes.

I began to hear some adverse comments from people who had dealings with the foundation. Finally, a Chinese grant recipient told me that the foundation was being run by the security agency. Soon thereafter, Zhao Ziyang was removed from power, and I used that excuse to suspend operations in China.

After the crackdown in Tiananmen Square, the foundation figured prominently in the accusations against Zhao Ziyang and Bao Tung. There were three charges against Zhao: "bourgeois deviationism," for being too soft on the students; betraying state secrets, for telling Gorbachev that Deng Xiaoping still wielded the ultimate power; and, finally treason, for allowing the foundation to operate. Treason is always a capital charge. When I heard about this from Chen Yizi, who had escaped,* I wrote Deng Xiaoping a letter offering to clear my name by going to China or providing them with any information they might need. I wrote in part as follows:

In its first year (1986–87), the China Fund received more than 200 applications for funding and approved a total of forty grants. In its second year (1987–88), the China Fund received more than 2,000 applications and approved a total of 209 grants. All the grants were publicly disclosed in the annual reports of the China Fund. I think it will be clear to anyone who examines the grants made by the China Fund that they were not intended to promote subversion. Rather, they were intended to promote the publicly stated aims of the China Fund. Those who associated with the China Fund did so in the belief that they were furthering the interests of the Chinese people and participating in an activity sanctioned by the Chinese Government.

* Chen Yizi gave an account of the history of the foundation in an interview with Lu Keng on October 1, 1989, in Paris: "Chen Yizi Exposes the Plot of Overthrowing Zhao Ziyang—the Whole Story of the Soros Event," *Pai Hsing*, No. 203 (November 1, 1989).

I understand that rumors have circulated in China that I am associated with the CIA or some other U.S. government agency. There is no truth to such rumors. The funds that I donated to the China Fund, and to the other foundations I have established, are entirely my own. My financial status can be easily checked and verified. Having benefited greatly from an economic system that is capable of generating considerable wealth, I am eager to assist the Chinese government in reforming its economy so as to produce wealth for the whole country.

For now, I have ended my support for the China Fund. I am eager to resume support, however. If the Chinese Government indicates its desire to pursue a policy of economic reform and openness, and makes it clear that those associated with the China Fund will not suffer any adverse consequences for their association, I would like to begin again to provide support for the activities of the Fund. Nothing would please me more than to be able to resume a friendly and productive association with your government.

My letter was printed in the widely circulated *Digest of Party Documents*, which indicated that the charge was dropped. It was a relatively happy ending to a very unpleasant experience.

It became clear to me in retrospect that I had made a mistake in setting up a foundation in China. China was not ready for it because there were no independent or dissident intelligentsia. The people on whom I based the foundation were members of a party faction. They could not be totally open and honest with me because they were beholden to their faction. The foundation could not become an institution of civil society (that is, society independent of state and party) because no such society existed. It would have been much better to make an outright grant to Chen Yizi's institute, which deserved support.

Conditions have changed since the revolt of 1989. Prior to the Tiananmen Square massacre, anybody who wanted to change society had to operate within the party. There was little room for a dissident, independent intelligentsia because society was totally subservient to the party and ostracized those who incurred its disapproval. But after the massacre the party lost the confidence of the people. Those who are expelled from the party or lose their jobs are able to survive because society supports them. That is the beginning of an independent intelligentsia.

Seen from this perspective, the Chinese revolution of 1989 was the equivalent of the Hungarian revolution of 1956. I hope it will not take as long in China for the revolution to bear fruit as it did in Hungary. Hungary was closed to the outside world, but China remains open. With fax machines and foreigners around, it will not be possible to re-establish the rigid thought control that prevailed previously. China has become too dependent on foreign trade and foreign investment to return to a closed society. The hard-liners cannot last very long.

Not long after China, I also established a foundation in Poland. The Open Society Fund had been operating a very successful Polish scholarship and visiting fellowship program at Oxford University under the direction of Dr. Zbigniew Pelczynski, and it was also supporting other Polish causes. Pelczynski, who visited Hungary regularly to select students for our Oxford scholarship programs, persuaded me to try my hand in Poland.

I thought it would be easy: Pelczynski was ready to negotiate with the government, and I had my own contacts with the Solidarity underground. It did not work out that way. The Polish participants insisted that the foundation be totally independent of the government, and I respected their wish. The foundation was established, but it could not function; it could not even find office space. The members of the board attended meetings, but very little was accomplished. There was also a deep disagreement within the board about the direction the foundation ought to be taking. Some members wanted to concentrate on academic activities; others envisioned a broader role. Without clear direction, the foundation failed to establish itself as an instrument of civil society.

I was aware of the problem, but I did not have the time or energy to deal with it. When Solidarity came to power, I asked the board to resign and put the foundation into the hands of a new team headed by Zbigniew Bujak, erstwhile leader of Solidar-

14

ity in Warsaw, and since then the foundation has worked much better.

I visited Warsaw only occasionally, for a day or two at a time. Almost instantaneously, I established close personal contact with Walesa's chief adviser, Bronislaw Geremek. I was also received by General Jaruszelski, the head of State, to obtain his blessing for the foundation. We had a very interesting conversation. I suggested that he sit down and negotiate with Solidarity. He said he was willing to talk with practically anybody and was, in fact, trying to arrange a dialogue through the Church, but because the leaders of Solidarity were traitors who had persuaded the Western powers to impose economic sanctions on Poland, he would have nothing to do with them. I told him that I had met Geremek, who had shown a very positive attitude toward reaching some kind of compromise exactly because the economy was in such bad shape and people were becoming disaffected. He knew a great deal more about Geremek than I did. "He changed his religion when he was a mature man; he could not have done that out of conviction," he said. "I had changed my views too, but I did it when I was a youth." It was a great pity that the general had such strong personal feelings, I answered, because it would prevent him from reaching a compromise. In a democracy, you can govern with less than 50 percent of the vote, but when you have no democracy you must have the entire population with you. Without Solidarity that was not possible. I remarked that Solidarity would be taking a tremendous risk if it entered into negotiations, because any economic program would involve severe cutbacks in heavy industry and would hurt the workers who provided Solidarity's muscle. Nevertheless, they were willing to take the chance because they were concerned with the future of Poland as a country. The argument about the political risks that Solidarity would be running made an impression on him. As I found out later, he repeated it at the Politburo meeting the next day.

My foundation was named the Stefan Batory Foundation,

after a Hungarian nobleman who became King of Poland and defeated the Russians in war. On the way out of my audience with Jaruszelski, the interpreter told me about a famous saying of Stefan Batory's: "You can do much for the Poles, but you cannot do much with the Poles." I felt the foundation was aptly named.

❑

The amount of time, money, and energy I devoted to the transformation of Communist systems increased tremendously when I decided to set up a foundation in the Soviet Union. I took my cue from Gorbachev's telephone call to Andrei Sakharov in Gorky in December 1986 asking him "to resume his patriotic activities in Moscow." (Sakharov told me later that the telephone line had to be installed especially for the purpose the night before.) The fact that he was not sent abroad indicated to me that a significant change had occurred in the Soviet Union.

I was hoping to base my foundation on Sakharov as my personal representative. I went to Moscow in early March 1987 as a tourist. I had two introductions from Franz Alerdinck, a Dutchman who had set up a foundation in the Netherlands to sponsor media contacts between East and West. One was to a high-ranking official in the Novosti news service and the other to the free-lance Soviet journalist Michael Bruck, who was the late Armand Hammer's contact in the Soviet Union. I also had the names of a number of dissidents and independent-minded people who were willing to talk to foreigners. Conditions were not much different then from what they had been ten years previously, when I had gone to the Soviet Union for the first time. The phone rang practically the moment I entered my hotel room. Michael Bruck was on the line. I wondered how he knew I had arrived. He spoke perfect English and acted as my interpreter at Novosty. The man at Novosti mentioned the Cultural Foundation of the USSR, a newly formed organization which had Raisa Gorbachev as its patron. It sounded good and

16

I asked for an appointment. The Novosti official picked up one of the several telephones on his desk and arranged it right away. At the Cultural Foundation I was received by the deputy chairman, Georgy Myasnikov, an older man with a large, craggy, handsome face and very smooth manners. I explained to him how the foundation in Hungary operated and showed him the documents. He was very receptive. Within an hour we were discussing details. I told him that if his people wanted me to proceed he should send me an official invitation.

I also had some interesting unofficial meetings. The late Politburo member Anastas Mikoyan's grandson took me to meet his best friend, who had been a brilliant academic historian but had dropped out. He called himself a *spekulant* and lived on the fringes of society. A Soviet emigré gave me the name and phone number of a young scientist friend of his. When I called him at his institute, he asked me to meet him at a busy subway station. I also met with such leading dissidents as Sakharov, Grigoyants, and Lev Timofeyev, but they were rather doubtful about my project. Sakharov said that my money would only go to swell the coffers of the KGB. He refused to participate in the foundation personally but promised to come up with some suggestions for possible members of the committee.

After a while I received an official invitation. I found out later that the authorities had checked me out with the Hungarian authorities and had received good references. I was met at the airport by the newly apointed vice chairman of the Cultural Foundation, Vladimir Aksyonov. He was a younger man with whom I established a good rapport almost immediately. He was a fan of Mihajlo D. Mesarovic, a leading figure in complex systems theory and a friend of mine. This put us on the same wave length. He became an enthusiastic supporter of the foundation. "If you had not come along, we would have had to invent you," he said. I made the rounds of prospective committee members, but I felt uneasy. It did not seem to me I was finding people who were independent enough to qualify as members

17

of civil society and at the same time would be acceptable to the authorities as members of the foundation. Indeed, I came to doubt whether civil society existed at all, apart from a few outspoken dissidents like Sakharov.

The breakthrough came in August, when a large delegation from the Soviet Union was passing through New York on the way to the Chautauqua Conference of Soviet–American friendship. Among them was Tatyana Zaslavskaya, a leading sociologist and one of Gorbachev's early advisers, whom I was anxious to meet. I extended an invitation to the entire delegation, and my wife, Susan, arranged a sitdown dinner for 150 people on short notice. It was quite a scene. There was hardly any room to move, but everyone had a great time. Only the head of the delegation, a lady astronaut, was annoyed that, instead of her, I had Tatyana Zaslavskaya on my right. Zaslavskaya and I arranged to see each other again in Chautauqua, where we had a long conversation and a wonderful meeting of minds. When we discussed the composition of the foundation committee, I felt I was getting somewhere. I had also met the future executive director of the New York office, Nina Bouis, a well-known translator of Russian literature, at my own party.

The committee, when it was finally constituted on September 22, 1987, consisted of Yury Afanasyev, the historian; Grigory Baklanov, the editor of *Znamya*; Daniil Granin and Valentin Rasputin, writers; Tenghiz Buachidze, a philologist from Georgia; Boris Raushenbakh, a space scientist and religious philosopher; and Tatyana Zaslavskaya. Myasnikov and I were co-chairmen, both with the right of veto, and Aksyonov and Nina Bouis were our respective deputies.

From the start, the people on the committee have been wonderful. They have become leading figures in Soviet society, always in the limelight, always overworked, some of them despite frail health. Nevertheless, they have come to the meetings regularly and have put in long hours. Some of our meetings were held on Sundays because that was the only time the members had

18

available. They represented a wide range of views. Baklanov and Rasputin were at opposite poles; our committee meetings were the only occasion when they were willing to sit at the same table. Eventually their antagonism became intolerable because Rasputin increasingly identified himself with an extremist Russian nationalism. We were relieved when Gorbachev nominated him to the Presidential Council and he had to resign. At any rate, in the early days it was very useful to have him on the committee, because with him there it could not be labeled cosmopolitan or left-wing.

Myasnikov was a problem from the beginning. He was the quintessential bureaucrat. He turned hostile early on when I told him that I wanted to rely on the advice of dissidents in selecting the members of the committee. "Grigoryants is not a man of culture," he told me. We had quite a scene, with some harsh words, but he was more friendly than ever at lunch afterward. Unfailingly polite, he used every opportunity to create obstacles, yet he always yielded in the end because he did not want to take the responsibility for our failure.

I tried to find someone more in tune with my ideas. I went to Leningrad to meet with the Chairman of the Cultural Foundation, Academician Pyotr Likhachev, a wonderfully cultured man of eighty-two who had been through the labor camps under Stalin. He looked to me like a much better choice for co-chairman than Myasnikov. When I asked him to consider the office, he immediately phoned somebody in the Central Committee. When the party official called back, I asked Nina to translate Likhachev's responses for me. But Likhachev never said anything but brief words of assent. Obviously it was one of those famous Kremlin phone calls in which the recipient may use only the earpiece. When he hung up, he said, "Nothing doing. Myasnikov must be the co-chairman."

We got started anyhow. We created our own rubles by donating some computers. I was visiting the head of the Institute for Personal Computers, who told me about his grandiose plans to

19

produce millions of computers for the schools. He mentioned in passing that he had permission to import one hundred IBM ATs and the license was about to expire, but he did not have the dollars to pay for them. I volunteered to supply the dollars if he would give me rubles. "How many?" he asked. I took a chance: "Five rubles to the dollar." The black market rate for tourists was about three rubles at the time. "Agreed." We had a written agreement within twenty-four hours. I then flew to Paris and called IBM. IBM refused to deal with me, as it had a company policy against dealing with intermediaries. So I bought two hundred IBM clones from Taiwan in Vienna for the same amount of money, but I ran into difficulties with the license. We, as an American foundation, were subject to the licensing requirements of the Coordinating Committee on Export Controls (COCOM), even though the Taiwanese manufacturer and the Viennese intermediary were not. I could not get a ruling in Washington, even though ATs were supposed to be coming off license. Eventually I called John Whitehead, Deputy Secretary of State. After that I received both the license and a letter stating that no license was required. Lest I give the impression that American bureaucracy is worse than the Soviet, I must mention that my Soviet counterpart had great difficulty in paying me the rubles. The exchange rate of five rubles to the dollar was unacceptable to the authorities, and a government institute is not allowed to make donations to a foundation. But finally, after some high-level interventions, we got our money.

Finding office space was another adventure. We ended up in an eighteenth-century merchant's palace, an architectural monument in need of renovation. It belonged to the Cultural Foundation, and Myasnikov did his best to restrict our use of the building. My friends in the Soviet Union devised an ingenious scheme for getting rid of Myasnikov. Fortunately, he was quite lazy and did not realize what we were up to until it was too late. We established an independent foundation under Soviet law, called the Soviet–American Foundation Cultural Initiative,

20

and both Myasnikov and I were promoted to its Board of Trustees without any right to interfere with the decisions of the committee, now renamed the Board of Directors. Aksyonov and Nina Bouis took our places as co-chairs of the board.

Myasnikov is no longer directly involved in the foundation, but he continues to make trouble from a distance. The Peace Foundation came in as the money partner from the Soviet side, offering to put up five rubles for each of my dollars. This also led to untold complications: we made our agreement in May 1988 but got our first contribution from them only in the very last days of 1989.

Undaunted, we started to operate. We invited applications. Out of 2,000 received, we announced our first forty awards. They included two oral history projects dealing with the Stalinist period; an archive of nongovernmental organizations; an alternative town planning group; an association of legal advocates; a consumer group; a cooperative for manufacturing wheelchairs; and a number of research projects dealing with disappearing Siberian languages, gypsy folk songs, the ecology of Lake Baikal, and so on.

Getting an official charter for the foundation was not easy, either. There was another foundation with prestigious backing, the International Foundation for the Survival and Development of Humanity, which refused to operate without a charter and, after a year's struggle, obtained one. We asked for a similar charter, but even so it took the approval of thirty-six ministries and several months' work to get it. But it was worth the wait. It gives us so many powers that I compare it to the charter of the East India Company. By the time we received it, in February 1989, we were ready to publish our first annual report.

Our progress has been laborious. Every little thing presented a big problem. But it has also been fun. I have met a lot of wonderful people. I don't know why, but I feel a great empathy for Russian intellectuals. My father had lived through the Russian Revolution, mostly in Siberia as an escaped prisoner of war, and through him I must have imbibed some of the Russian spirit. I could communicate very well despite the fact that I do not speak Russian. I have a wonderful guide and interpreter in Nina Bouis. She has great good humor and makes my businesslike American approach more acceptable. In a way, I find better human contact in the Soviet Union than in the United States. We seem to share the same values. My article on Gorbachev's vision, published in the periodical *Znamya*, made me one of the best-liked nonfiction writers in the Soviet Union at one stroke, and I was proud of that status.

After a lot of time and effort, the foundation took root. Our rundown eighteenth-century palace hummed (and is humming still), even at nine o'clock at night. The executive director, Sergei Chernyshov, regularly put in sixteen-hour days. Some very capable new people joined the staff, and Nina spent three months in Moscow. By the end of 1989 I felt that the Hungarian foundation was not the only one that worked.

We started to branch out to the republics. I visited Kiev in the late spring of 1989. I timed my visit so that an expatriate Ukrainian business school professor whom I had gotten to know previously, Bohdan Hawrylyshyn, would also be there. On the first evening the leaders of intellectual life assembled at a meeting to put forward their ideas. I had to discourage most of them and felt quite bad about being so negative. But afterward they told me they loved it. "A Soviet official will never say no. You said no ten times in ten minutes; it was so refreshing." In the evening they took me to the sixtieth birthday celebration of the Ukrainian poet Dmytro Pavlychko. Several hundred people gathered in a big hall to listen to poetry and songs, and then Pavlychko began to answer questions. It reminded me of what it must have been like in 1848.

Subsequently I made Bohdan Hawrylyshyn my personal representative on the Ukrainian–American Foundation "Ukraine Renaissance" which was officially inaugurated on April 18, 1990. I believe Hawrylyshyn will be as successful in the Ukraine as Miklos Vasarhelyi has been in Hungary.

CRACKING THE COMMUNIST STRUCTURE

In the fall of 1989 I visited Estonia and Lithuania. It was more like a state visit than a business call: I arrived everywhere by private plane with the crew of 60 *Minutes* trailing me. I was the first foreigner ever to land at Tartu in Estonia. Nevertheless, much was accomplished. We established autonomous branches in two of the three Baltic republics. At present we are also setting up offices in Sverdlovsk, Leningrad, and Irkutsk, so that the Russian republic should not be neglected.

My involvement with the foundation has given me a unique vantage point to observe the evolution of civil society in the Soviet Union. When I went there in March 1987, I could not locate civil society at all, and not only because of my inexperience. Soviet intellectuals themselves did not know what other people thought outside their own intimate circle. Independent thinking was carried on underground. All this has changed. Everybody knows where everybody else stands. Positions have been drawn and differences clarified by public debate. The transformation has the quality of a dream.

There is always a gap between thought and reality. It occurs whenever participants seek to understand the situation in which they are involved. The gap, in turn, shapes the situation in a reflexive fashion, because participants base their decisions not on facts but on beliefs and expectations. Thus the divergence between thought and fact is both an essential feature of the human condition and a driving force of history.

The Soviet system was based on the systematic denial of such a divergence. Dogma was supposed to dominate both thought and reality, and thought was not allowed to be adjusted to reality directly but only through the mediation of the prevailing dogma. That made adjustments difficult and rendered both thought and reality extremely rigid. It gave rise to a different kind of gap: there was a formal system where both thought and reality were governed by dogma, and then there was a private world where the divergence between dogma and reality could be acknowledged. There were two kinds of people: those who accepted the

23

dogma as it was presented to them, and those who had a private world. There was a sharp dividing line between the two kinds, and I could generally sense almost immediately whether I was dealing with a real person or an automaton.

When Gorbachev introduced *glasnost*, he shattered the formal system of thought. Thinking was suddenly liberated from dogma, and people were allowed to express their real views. The result was the reappearance of a gap between thinking and reality. Indeed, the gap became wider than ever because, while intellectual life blossomed, material conditions deteriorated. There was a discrepancy between the two levels, which endowed events with a dreamlike quality. On the level of thought, there was excitement and joy; on the level of reality, the dominant experience was disappointment: supplies were deteriorating and one disaster after another struck. The only characteristic common to both levels was confusion. Nobody was quite sure what part of the system was in overhaul and what was still in operation. The bureaucrats did not dare say either yes or no, and therefore almost anything was possible and almost nothing happened. That is another way to describe a dream.

The Cultural Initiative Foundation had the same dreamlike quality. Almost everything was permitted, but almost nothing could be accomplished. Having learned to operate within definite limits in Hungary, I was shocked to find that there seemed to be no external constraints on what the foundation in Moscow might do. A representative of the Central Committee attended some of our meetings, but he was a great admirer of Afanasyev, the most radical member of our committee. It was too good to be true but, of course, I had not been to Hungary lately.

☐

There was a period of about nine months when I was so involved in the Soviet Union that I neglected my Hungarian home base. When I visited Hungary again in the fall of 1988, I found that the country had leapfrogged the Soviet Union. Political parties were forming, and the Communist party was visibly disintegrating. The foundation enjoyed such favor with the authorities that the Ministry of Education offered to match my contributions in excess of $3 million a year, presumably to establish its own legitimacy. I accepted.

The Soros Foundation found itself in an entirely new situation: its moral capital far exceeded my financial contribution. This opened up possibilities that previously could not have been contemplated. At the same time, the original objective of the foundation had been accomplished. It had set out to demolish the monopoly of dogma by making an alternate source of financing available for cultural and social activities. Dogma had indeed crumbled. It was one thing to work toward that end, but quite another to see it happen before one's own eyes.

I was reminded of a stone that once was removed from my salivary gland. The operation had been quite painful, and I wanted to keep the stone as a memento; but after it had been exposed to the open air for a few days, what had been a stone-hard object and a source of great discomfort crumbled into dust.

It was time for radical rethinking of the objectives of the foundation. We had been effective in working outside the established institutions; now it was time to help in reforming or transforming the institutions themselves. Whether we could be effective remained to be seen, but it was a risk worth taking; otherwise we would ourselves become an institution whose time had passed.

We already had some experience in institution building. We had assisted Karl Marx University of Economics in Budapest in a program to reform its curriculum. Over a three-year period, we sent some sixty lecturers, representing about 15 percent of the teaching staff, abroad to attend a business course, which they would then teach after their return. I was also a founder of the International Management Center in Budapest.

We decided to tackle the humanities first. The teaching of humanities was still largely in the hands of party hacks chosen for ideological reasons. The task would be much more difficult

25

than had been the case at Karl Marx University, because there the initiative came from the university itself, while here we would have to overcome considerable internal resistance. We formed a task force and made a number of grants throughout Hungary's highest education system; it remains to be seen how successful they will be.

I identified two other objectives: one was business education, and the other, much closer to my heart, the promotion of open society throughout the region. Specifically, I wanted to promote greater contacts and better understanding with the other countries of the region. Programs involving neighboring countries had been strictly taboo; now nothing stood in the way of greater cooperation with Soros-sponsored foundations in other countries. We established our first joint program, a series of seminars at the Dubrovnik (Yugoslavia) Inter-University Center, which took place in April 1989. It will be expanded in 1990 with participants from several more countries.*

❑

After the Gentle Revolution in Prague in November 1989, the Charter 77 Foundation of Stockholm, which I had supported since 1981, sprung into operation inside Czechoslovakia fully armed like Pallas Athena. Frantisek Janouch, founder and executive director, flew to Prague, and I joined him a week later on December 13. We set up committees in Prague, Brno, and Bratislava, and I put $1 million at their disposal. With the help of the newly appointed Finance Minister, Vaclav Klaus, we put up $100,000 in the next official currency auction. It went for eight times the official rate and, even more surprisingly, almost triple the black market rate. The first grants were paid out within the week, allowing such newly emerging underground organizations as the Civil Forum (now the government party)

---

* This was the kernel of the proposed Central European University. See p. 129.

and the newspaper *Lidove Noviny* to pay their staffs. I was very proud of this performance but, ironically, the foundation ran into criticism from the very people it benefited. They were jealous of Janouch because he controlled the purse strings. It was a case of what I call the paradox of charity.

Together with Prince Kari Schwarzenberg, another supporter of the Charter 77 Foundation (and now *chef de cabinet* of President Havel), we went to see Marian Calfa, who was then acting president. It was meant to be a courtesy visit but it turned into a moving occasion. Calfa opened his heart. He said that the last three weeks had really shaken his view of the world. He had not realized how far out of touch his party was with reality. He had had an intimate conversation with Jiri Dienstbier, the former political prisoner and newly appointed Foreign Minister, and that is when he found out that dissidents' children had been regularly denied the right to be educated in Czechoslovakia. (Dienstbier's daughter had managed to get to Switzerland.) He was deeply ashamed and determined to establish democracy in Czechoslovakia. We all agreed that it was imperative to have Vaclav Havel elected president by the current rubber-stamp parliament; to organize a plebiscite would delay matters and create uncertainties. Havel as president would consolidate the Gentle Revolution. "Unfortunately, the leaders of the party do not agree with me but, as acting president, I have certain prerogatives and I intend to use them," Calfa said. He sounded sincere, and we were impressed. It was an unbelievable situation: the head of an apparatus of repression that only a few weeks before had routed a student demonstration was voluntarily abdicating in favor of a dissident without an organization who would have trouble winning a plebiscite.

As I began writing this account (January 11, 1990), I was about to go to Romania, meaning to visit Bulgaria shortly afterward. My intention was to sponsor a network of foundations whose main mission would be to promote better understanding and greater cooperation in the region. They would be fully autonomous: it would be up to them to decide how they wanted to cooperate. If they failed to do so, I would stop supporting them. I shall update the story of the foundations later in the book.

❑

My personal involvement has followed the same revolutionary course as the events themselves. It now extends well beyond my foundations to the issues of economic policy and international affairs. Until quite recently I kept a very low profile: I could be much more effective by not taking a public stand. The fact that I was under wraps in Hungary and did not give any interviews in the Western press was important to the success of the foundation. But all this has changed in the last few years. I became a public figure; indeed, I began to act almost like a statesman. It was a somewhat anomalous situation, because I had no state to represent, but I soon got used to it. My father, who had lived through the Revolution of 1917, had told me that in revolutionary times anything is possible. I was guided by his advice.

The story began at a conference on East–West security concerns in Potsdam in June 1988. I presented a grandiose plan for a mutual security pact between NATO and the Warsaw Pact, coupled with large-scale economic assistance to the Soviet bloc. My proposal was greeted with laughter, as the *Frankfurter Allgemeine Zeitung* duly reported. The reader will note that, in retrospect, it would not have been such a bad idea.

The Soviet Ambassador in Washington, Yury Dubinin, said that my ideas were too visionary. "Tell us what we can do by ourselves," he said. That set me to thinking, and during the summer I developed the concept of a market-oriented open sector that would be implanted within the body of the centrally planned economy. Dubinin liked the idea and forwarded it to Moscow. I received an invitation from the Chairman of the Council on Foreign Economic Relations, Kamintsev, who passed me on to his deputy, Ivan Ivanov. We agreed to form an international task force to develop the concept. The team that the Soviet side wanted to field, however, was inadequate. When Dubinin came to see me one morning for breakfast before leaving for Moscow, I told him that nothing would come of my idea unless it was taken up at a higher level. He agreed and got Prime Minister Ryzhkov to issue an order requiring all the relevant agencies to cooperate.

Our team, consisting of Wassily Leontief, the Nobel economist; Ed Hewett from the Brookings Institute; Phil Hansen from Birmingham University; Marton Tardos, the Hungarian economist; and me, went to Moscow in November 1988 and met with a fairly high-powered Soviet team, including Valentin Pavlov, who later became Prime Minister. Our meetings culminated in a four-hour session with Ryzhkov in the Kremlin. He seemed favorably impressed. "It looks like a good way to go, once you have decided you want to get there," he said. "The trouble is we can't make up our mind. There is a lot of resistance to new ideas." It was agreed that the idea should be developed further and that six subgroups should be set up to study separate aspects of the concept. But underlying this agreement was a conflict between Ivanov's interest in geographically designed free trade zones and our interest in using the open sector to convert the entire economy gradually to market principles.

Ed Hewett took charge of organizing the task force from the Western side. The first series of meetings was arranged for late January 1989 in Moscow. The task force comprised some twenty people from Western countries and a slightly larger number from the Soviet Union. I insisted on a plenary meeting, because I did not want the subgroups to go off at tangents until the basic principles had been agreed upon, but Ivanov kept the plenary very short. It soon became obvious that some of the Soviet participants were genuinely interested and eager to further the cause while others were attending out of bureaucratic duty or were downright hostile to the idea.

One of the "good guys" privately suggested that we ask for a meeting with the economic section of the Central Committee.

This was arranged, and several of our group were received by Vladimir Mozhin, head of the section. We presented our concept. I told Mozhin that we needed some direction from the Soviet authorities; otherwise the groups would just go over the same ground again and again. In response Mozhin went through an hour or so of what I call "automatic speaking," until his assistant, who had obviously been briefed by the "good guy" who had suggested the meeting, asked some pertinent questions. We then had a good discussion, but we never got the guidance we asked for. It was a lesson in the ways of Soviet bureaucracy I have never forgotten. I realized that our recommendations would not lead to action.

I told Ivanov that I myself would not take any part in further discussions, but the Cultural Initiative Foundation would continue to sponsor them financially. The meetings continued for a few months but, as I had predicted, they were deteriorating into tourism. We were supposed to present our final report in May in a series of meetings involving first the academics, then the government, then the party, and finally the press. That did not come about because Ivanov asked for a postponement, citing the pressure of other business. I was glad. After my experience with the task force, I no longer thought the concept was viable. I recognized that the decision-making center was paralyzed and the body of the centrally planned economy had decayed too much to be able to nurture the embryo of a market economy. Nevertheless, I did not consider either the time or the money wasted. I had learned a lot about the disintegration of the Soviet economy and the paralysis at the decision-making center. Besides, some of the Soviet participants learned a lot about market principles. I also got to know some people who would become influential later on. Petrakov, who became Gorbachev's personal economic adviser and one of the authors of the Shatalin plan, was a member of the task force. I came away with the conviction that the Soviet economy cannot be turned around any time soon. The best that could be hoped for was to slow down the process of disintegration so as to give a chance for a much slower process of learning to start producing positive results.

◻

I felt much more hopeful about Poland, where the process of disintegration had reached a climax and the elections had produced a clear-cut break with the past. That is the kind of discontinuity that permits a new departure. Poland was also a country for which the Western assistance necessary to give the economy an upward momentum could be mobilized. I considered it essential to demonstrate that the political transformation could result in economic improvement: Poland was the place where this could be accomplished.

I prepared the broad outlines of a comprehensive economic program. It had three ingredients: monetary stabilization, structural changes, and debt reorganization. I argued that the three objectives could be accomplished better in combination than separately. That was particularly true for industrial reorganization and debt reorganization since they represented opposite sides of the national balance sheet. I proposed a kind of macroeconomic debt-for-equity swap.

I showed the plan to Geremek and Professor Trcziakowski, who headed the economic roundtable in the talks that preceded the transfer of power, and they were both enthusiastic. I started to drum up support in Western countries, but there I was less successful. The so-called Paris Club debt (money owed to government institutions), which accounted for three-quarters of the Polish total, was an untouchable subject. Concessions made to one country would have to be extended to all the others; therefore no concessions could be made. Moreover, there was general incredulity that Poland would be willing to switch to a market economy in one bold move.

I joined forces with Professor Jeffrey Sachs of Harvard University, who was advocating a similar program, and sponsored his work in Poland through the Stefan Batory Foundation. He created

31

a tremendous stir with his ideas and became a very controversial figure, but he succeeded in focusing the debate on the right issues. I also worked closely with Professor Stanislaw Gomulka, who became adviser to the new Finance Minister, Leszek Balcerowicz, and was in the end more influential than Professor Sachs.

I visited Warsaw the week after the new government took office. It was my first experience of history in the making. I could see clearly the clash between two contending approaches. The President of the Central Bank, Bakka, who had been appointed by President Jaruszelski and was not responsible to the new government, advocated a policy of continuity. It would have meant piecemeal reforms and would have made the new government dependent on the present power structure, because only they knew which levers to pull. Balcerowicz was committed to a radical approach, but he was overwhelmed by the magnitude of his task. He had brought in with him only two new people to the ministry; otherwise he had to depend on the existing staff—not the best conditions for establishing discontinuity. But Balcerowicz stuck to his guns and presented a radical program of monetary stabilization at the International Monetary Fund meeting in Washington. The IMF approved, and the program went into effect on January 1, 1990. It was very tough on the population, but people were willing to take a lot of pain in order to see real change. The program was prepared in such haste that some serious administrative mistakes were made. I shall give an example.

On December 2, 1989, I took an illustrious group of foreign economic advisers to Warsaw to discuss the Polish plan. When the budget minister outlined the budget for 1990, we were shocked to hear that it was based on an anticipated inflation rate of 140 percent. This was incompatible with the Balcerowicz plan, which called for a virtual wage freeze after the initial adjustment period. But it was too late to rewrite the budget. Fortunately, the inflation rate came in much higher than expected in November so that, by introducing indexation at the rate of 20 percent of the cost of living, the plan could be fitted to the budget. It would have been much cleaner to fit the budget to the plan and to have no cost-of-living escalation.

❑

After the collapse of the East German regime, my focus shifted back to the Soviet Union. Events were speeding up tremendously, and I was afraid that there was no time to wait for the Polish experiment to succeed. Only the promise of large-scale Western assistance to the Soviet Union could prevent a descent into the abyss. I summarized my views in an article published in the *Wall Street Journal* on December 7, 1989. I tried desperately to reach President Bush before his meeting with Gorbachev in Malta, but I got only as far as Under Secretary of State Lawrence Eagleburger. That is when I decided to write *Opening the Soviet System*.

□ 2 □

The Collapse of the
Soviet System

We are witnessing the disintegration of a closed system as embodied by the Soviet Union. The disintegration affects all aspects of the system, notably an ideology, a system of government, an economic system, and a territorial empire. When the system was intact, all those elements were integrated; now that the system is falling apart, the various elements are decaying in various ways and at various speeds, but events in one area tend to reinforce developments in the other.

The decay started a long time ago, with the death of Stalin. A totalitarian regime needs a totalitarian at the top. Stalin fulfilled that role with gusto. Under him the system attained its maximum extension, in both ideological and territorial coverage. There was hardly an aspect of existence that escaped its influence. Even genetics obeyed the Marxist doctrine. Not every science could be subjugated with equal success, but at least the scientists could be tamed and their contact with youth restricted by confining them in the Institutes of the Academy and preventing them from teaching at universities. Terror played a large part in making the system work, but the cover of ideology successfully concealed the underlying coercion and fear.

34

It is a testimony to Stalin's genius that the system survived him by some thirty-five years. There was a brief moment of hope when Khrushchev revealed some of the truth about Stalin in his speech before the Twentieth Congress, but eventually the hierarchy reasserted itself. A twilight period began when dogma was preserved by administrative methods, without any belief in its validity. Interestingly, the rigidity of the system increased even further. As long as there had been a live totalitarian at the helm, the system enjoyed some maneuverability: the party line could be changed at the whim of the dictator and the previous one excised. Now that flexibility was lost, and the system became rigid. At the same time the terror abated and a subtle process of decay set in. Every enterprise and institution sought to improve its own position. Since none of them had any autonomy, they had to barter whatever powers they had for the resources they needed for their own survival. Gradually an elaborate system of institutional bargaining replaced the central planning and central control that had prevailed while the system had been in totalitarian hands. Moreover, an informal system of economic relationships evolved to supplement and fill the gaps left by the formal system. The inadequacy of the system became increasingly evident, and the pressure for reform mounted.

Now comes a point that needs to be emphasized: reform accelerated the process of disintegration. It introduced or legitimated alternatives at a time when the system depended on a lack of alternatives for its survival. Alternatives raise questions; they undermine authority; they not only reveal discrepancies in the existing arrangements but reinforce them by diverting resources to more economic uses. A command economy cannot avoid a misallocation of resources: introduce a modicum of choice, and the shortages are bound to become more pronounced. Moreover, the profits that can be earned by diverting resources from the command economy are much greater than those that can be earned from productive activity; it is therefore not at all certain that overall production will benefit.

The fact remains that in every communist country, with the

notable exception of the Soviet Union itself, there has been an initial improvement when economic reform has been introduced. The reason is that a command economy is so wasteful that any change is initially for the better. Only later does the damage done to the rigid structure of the centrally planned economy begin to outweigh the initial benefits obtained.

The Chinese reformers concluded, after a study tour of Hungary and Yugoslavia in 1986 sponsored by my foundations, that reform enjoys an initial "golden period" during which an improvement in the allocation of existing resources gives people a definite sense of progress. Only later, when existing capacity has been redeployed and new investments are necessary does the reform process run into insuperable difficulties. At that point, political reforms are needed to make further economic reforms possible.

The communist system suffers from a fatal flaw, which cannot be remedied by reform: investments are hopelessly inefficient because capital has no value. It is understandable why this should be so: communism was meant as an antidote to capitalism, which had alienated the worker from the means of production. Communism claimed to protect the interests of the worker; therefore, the interests of capital could receive no representation. All property was taken over by the State, and the State was an embodiment of the collective interest, as defined by the party. That placed the party in charge of the allocation of capital. The party's allegiance, however, was with the workers, so it could not even recognize that capital also needed to be looked after. It was not just a matter of state ownership; it was a case of having no ownership at all.* Capital is a scarce resource, just like labor or land, and needs to be allocated among competing uses. This basic principle of economics was ignored by the system of central planning as it evolved under Stalin.

A closed society calls for distortions that would be inconceivable

---

* C.f. Roman Frydman and Andrzej Rapaczynski, *Markets and Institutions in Large-Scale Privatizations* (New York: New York University, C. V. Starr Center, 1990).

in an open society. What better demonstration could one ask for? Economic activity under the Soviet system is simply not economic; it is better understood as the expression of some kind of quasi-religious dogma. Perhaps the best analogy is with the pyramid-building of the pharaohs. This interpretation explains why the portion of resources devoted to investment is maximized, while the economic benefit derived form them remains at a minimum. It would also explain why investment takes the form of monumental projects. We may view the gigantic hydroelectric dams, the steel plants, the marble halls of the Moscow subway, and the skyscrapers of Stalinist architecture as so many pyramids built by a modern pharaoh. Hydroelectric plants do produce energy, and steel plants turn out steel, but if the steel and energy are used simply to produce more dams and steel plants, the effect on the economy is not very different from that of the construction of pyramids.

That is why there is so much room for putting existing resources to better use. Redirecting existing resources is relatively easy, but when it comes to investment decisions, much more profound changes are needed. Capital must be treated as a scarce and valuable resource. A price must be put on capital and the rate of interest used as a guide in its allocation. This means, in effect, that the party must be removed from its role as the guardian of capital. It is on this issue that every reform is bound to come to grief: only a change that goes beyond reform and qualifies as a transformation of the system can hope to be effective.

This line of argument is well supported by the historical evidence. Both in Hungary and in Yugoslavia, and later in China, reform initially produced positive results. Its greatest success was in agriculture, where decentralization and the introduction of incentives led to higher output within a relatively short time. This gave the reform movement credibility on which it could draw later. The allocation of capital was not much of an issue, particularly in China, where practically no machinery is employed in agriculture. People just worked harder because they

37

were allowed to enjoy the fruits of their labor. Outside of agriculture, reform consisted mainly of introducing a more realistic price structure and a more flexible plan, giving enterprises a greater degree of autonomy. In China, for instance, the plan called for the production of four items: bicycles, watches, sewing machines, and radios. Greater availability of those products gave people a sense of progress and helped maintain the momentum of reform.

Reform was a gradual process, directed from above. The difficulties also arose gradually. They had to do with the weakening of the center and the imperfect autonomy of the decision-making units. It is difficult to trace the process in general terms, because reform followed a somewhat different path in each country; it was intricately interwoven with political developments and took many twists and turns. I am not well qualified to provide a historical account, because I was not paying any particular attention until the last few years. But that may be an advantage, because it allows me to concentrate on the salient features.

Although enterprises were given increasing latitude, they were not converted into truly autonomous units. They remained responsible to the state or, more exactly, to the party, which was in charge of the state. Managements were members of the *nomenklatura*, the party system by which appointments were made to specific posts. Their appointment, as well as their removal, depended on the party apparatus. Direct commands from the ministry may have been replaced by indirect rules couched in monetary terms, but the lines of command remained the same. As a result, what was proclaimed as a market-oriented system was not really dependent on the market but remained oriented toward the sources of power.

There is always a divergence between the system as designed and the system as it really functions. When market-oriented reforms are introduced, the gap does not disappear, it merely changes shape. Direct commands are replaced by rules couched in monetary terms, but in practice the supposedly fixed market rules are subject to administrative adjustment.

Enterprises operate under what Janos Kornai called "soft budgetary constraints": there are no real penalties for breaking monetary rules. Being members of the party–state hierarchy, managers find it more rewarding to try to change the rules in their favor than to play by the rules as given. This leads to the emergence of a small group of successful entrepreneurs, the "red barons," whose success depends on their ability to manipulate the system. One need only look at Hungary as recently as 1989 to see how complex such a system can become: almost every large enterprise had a special set of taxes and subsidies that applied to it. Ostensibly, these were associated with trading within COMECON (Council for Mutual Economic Assistance); be that as it may, they affected the fortunes of the companies concerned more profoundly than any other factor.

In a quasi-market system, enterprises are not allowed to fail. Reformers may clamor for the introduction of bankruptcy procedures, but bankruptcy would generate unemployment, and unemployment would be an admission of the failure of the system. The political center, as long as it retains any power at all, resists bankruptcies, especially among the noneconomic pyramids of heavy industry.

Hungary has by now established quite a sophisticated two-tier monetary system, in which the central bank is supposed to exercise monetary control through commercial banks. Hungary is a member of the International Monetary Fund. Its agreement with the IMF calls for strict limits on the amounts of money in circulation and credit outstanding. But the limits cannot be enforced: enterprises simply do not pay each other. Suppliers have to wait in line to be paid when a debtor company receives money on its own account. Since the suppliers' debtors are also standing in line, the phenomenon has spread throughout the economy, until now, in mid-1990, it affects some 60 percent of all enterprises. The nonexistent credit outstanding (in the form of accounts receivable) equals seven weeks of national production. No wonder monetary controls are ineffective! All this would change if companies were forced into bankruptcy: creditors standing in line would then lose money and so would be much more reluctant to supply goods on credit. Not until December 1989, when Hungary was on the verge of passing from reform to transformation, was the decision made to put fifty-one companies into bankruptcy—and, of course, it was never executed. There has been remarkably little progress even to this day.

In less advanced reform economies, institutional bargaining is all-important because there is no price put on capital and no penalty for its inefficient use. As a consequence, the demand for capital is practically unlimited. The allocation of capital, which in theory is the function of the central planning agency, is in practice determined by pulling strings within the bureaucracy. Even so, there is never enough to go around. Two outstanding facts about the Soviet Union during the stagnation period: the average time of construction of an industrial plant was around eleven years, and inventories amounted to almost a full year's production. No investment can be economic in such circumstances, in the sense of producing returns that would allow paying a realistic rate of interest. In other reform economies the situation was not half as bad as in the Soviet Union, but the problem of capital allocation remained the root cause of chronic macroeconomic imbalance.

China is a particularly clear-cut case. Before the crackdown, reform had made considerable headway. Production was soaring, but investment demand was growing even faster. Every province wanted its own bicycle factory, and every department along the Yangtse River its own container port. As a result, inflationary pressures became unsustainable. The reform faction of Zhao Ziyang pressed for changes in the management of enterprises but lost out, and political repression followed.

Inflation is the bane of reform. The system prides itself on stability. Yet as soon as any kind of market mechanism is introduced, a rise in prices becomes unavoidable on account of the pent-up demand. At first it is gratefully accepted, because a supply of goods at higher prices is much preferable to no supply at all. Prices for basic commodities remain controlled, but the amount the state has to spend on subsidies goes up. This raises the amount of money in circulation, so the pressure of demand on the rest of the economy increases. Because it cannot be satisfied, an overhang of unspent money accumulates. The urge to invest also becomes more pressing. When prices are stable, there is no penalty for investing unwisely; when prices rise, there is a positive inducement, because real interest rates turn negative. When wages are also allowed to rise, all hell breaks loose. It is very hard to prevent that from happening, because as the center weakens, enterprises become increasingly preoccupied with keeping their workers happy. When the workers start to organize, the pressure becomes irresistible.

I call the transformation of latent into manifest inflation the Polish disease, because it is in Poland that it has reached its apogee. But it occurred in Yugoslavia, the land of self-management, much earlier, and the process can also be observed, in various stages of development, in Hungary, China, and the Soviet Union. In Poland it reached fruition in 1989, when the political power center was paralyzed and the enterprises had to fend for themselves as best they could. "Real" wages rose some 30 percent, but of course they were not real, because production did not rise at all. In fact, it fell by about 8 percent. The difference was taken up by the so-called inflation tax, that is, the depreciation in the value of money while it is in the hands of the population. It took an ever rising inflation rate, reaching 1,000 percent near the end, to square the circle. The enterprises subordinated all their other obligations to paying their workers. They stopped investing, they stopped paying taxes, they even stopped paying their suppliers. At the same time, nobody wanted to hold zlotys. When a free market in dollars was legalized, zlotys became practically valueless in dollar terms. With the total value of money in circulation rapidly shrinking, the state had to print more and more to finance the budget deficit. That is why inflation spun out of control.

Once it is recognized that reform is a process of disintegration, it can be seen that the course of reform bears a remarkable

41

similarity to the boom/bust pattern one can discern in stock markets. It starts off relatively slowly. At first it satisfies some of the aspirations attached to it and is thus reinforced. But when results begin to diverge significantly from expectations, the divergence also serves to reinforce the process: the shortcomings of the system become more apparent and its ability to resist change erodes, while the desire for change gains momentum. Political and economic changes mutually reinforce each other. As the economic influence of the decision-making center is weakened, its political authority is also undermined. It is bound to resist— after all, the primary instinct of every bureaucracy is to preserve itself—but its resistance will engender further attacks until the political objectives come to overshadow the economic ones, and destroying the center of power becomes the primary goal. At that point reform is superseded by revolution.

There is another factor that tends to play an important part in the process: foreign debt. Reforming regimes often try to alleviate the problem of scarcities by borrowing from the West. Unfortunately, they waste the borrowed assets just as they waste their own, because they do not have a proper system of capital allocation. Both Poland and Hungary borrowed heavily in the 1970s, but their investment plans were ill-conceived and inefficiently executed. Projects not only failed to pay for themselves but left the countries heavily encumbered by hard currency debt. Cause and effect are hard to disentangle in a reflexive process, but there can be no doubt that in each case a reform regime sought to justify itself by creating the illusion of progress. There is a positive correlation among economic reform, foreign debt, and subsequent inflation. This can be seen by comparing Poland, Hungary, and Yugoslavia on the one hand with Czechoslovakia, Romania, and East Germany on the other. The first group followed the route of reform, debt, and inflation; the second resisted reform and avoided debt and inflation, but remained hopelessly rigid and misshapen. Bulgaria combined the disadvantages of both.

With the advent of *perestroika* in the Soviet Union, the process of disintegration entered its terminal phase, because the reform was primarily political and, as I mentioned before, the "golden period" was missing. As living standards started to decline, public opinion turned against the regime, leading to a catastrophic acceleration which is culminating in the total collapse of the system.

❑

The question poses itself: did the reformers anticipate the consequences of their policies? The answer is rather complicated. Undoubtedly, party and government reformers were motivated primarily by a desire to change the system and were willing to advocate half-measures, knowing full well that eventually further measures would be required. At the same time they probably did not fully anticipate the negative consequences, or they could not have advocated the policies so effectively. Of course, the policies enacted fell short of the policies advocated in many respects, and reformers could always claim that their prescriptions had not been followed. At any rate, they all got sucked into the process whether they supported the government or opposed it, because they came to believe that every problem had a solution even if the solution engendered a new problem. In other words, they became participants and as such were committed to the reform process. Even if they had reservations, they could not voice them; their only course was to remain silent.* Thus the reform debate came to be dominated by an unspoken belief in the efficacy of a continuous process of reform, even though that belief, judged from today's perspective, was clearly wrong.

Reform must be equated with the disintegration of a rigid, closed, changeless system. The farther it proceeds, the more thorough the disintegration becomes. A continuous process must lead to indefinite decay. Only if there is a moment of discontinuity

---

* The outstanding practitioner of silence was Janos Kornai, who, after writing the most incisive theoretical analysis, meticulously kept himself above the fray until quite recently.

can the trend be reversed and a new system brought into existence. As I shall argue later, indigenous forces are not strong enough to reverse the trend by themselves. The process of disintegration must be superseded by a process of integration into Western society, and that process cannot be accomplished without assistance from the West. Lacking that, the process of disintegration will continue, and the universal closed society of the Soviet Union will break up into its component parts, but it will not be able to acquire and maintain the institutions or even the frame of mind of an open society.

Here I am concerned only with establishing the first step in this argument: I want to show that reform, both economic and political, is connected with the decay of the system in a reflexive fashion: decay invites reform and reform hastens decay. The point is obvious, once we look at reform from the standpoint of the system: the weakening of the center constitutes a deadly threat. But the point is far from generally recognized; indeed, it has hardly ever been made. Perhaps the only ones who recognize its full import are the hard-liners who oppose reform in any shape or form, and they are fighting a losing battle. The reformers see it far less clearly, which is not surprising. Until recently, it would have been detrimental or downright dangerous to emphasize this point. To equate reform with disintegration would have doomed reform. Even today it may give intellectual ammunition to the hard-liners in the Soviet Union, not to mention China. But we are too far along in an accelerating sequence to be concerned about it. It is exactly because reform is bound up with decay that the process cannot be reversed. There may be repression, as in Tiananmen Square, but the status quo cannot be re-established. The monopoly of dogma has been well and truly broken, and there is no point in paying lip service to it.

Reformers have had a hard time adjusting to changing circumstances. Until recently all discussion had to be couched in Marxist terms. Even today it is not really acceptable in the Soviet Union to question Lenin. Fortunately, Lenin went through many phases. One of them—the New Economic Policy (NEP) in which private enterprise was encouraged—provides a suitable ideological base for the current debate. Terms like "private property" are suspect: as recently as 1990 it was more politic to speak of "individual property," as a major proposal submitted to the Supreme Soviet did. This is now no longer true.

The pace of events has accelerated tremendously, and it is hard enough to keep up with them without having to watch one's words. But mental patterns developed over a lifetime are difficult to break. Having to abandon the dogma one has been trying to reform can be a disorienting experience. Reformers are doomed to disappear; they will be replaced by radical transformers on the one side and hard-liners on the other. A younger generation will come along, no longer burdened by the intellectual luggage of past struggles.

I know from personal experience how difficult it is to adjust one's rhetoric to changing circumstances. When I started my foundation in Hungary in 1984, it was considered unnecessarily provocative to call it the Open Society Fund; in the second half of 1988 that probably would have ceased to be true. When I set up the Fund for the Opening and Reform of China in 1986, I was at pains to point out the connection between my concept of reflexivity and the Marxist concept of dialectics. Today people are singularly uninterested in the issue. In the Soviet Union I could truthfully present myself as an avid supporter of Gorbachev's new thinking, but I could not have said many of the things I am saying in this book. I may in fact become persona non grata when it is published. Events have moved at different speeds in different countries. In order to be able to function with my foundations I thought it best to keep my opinions to myself as an observer. Only in the last year or so did I begin to speak out; only since the collapse of the Soviet Empire in Eastern Europe have I been less concerned with the fate of my foundations than with making my views known and influencing Western policy. Hence this book.

When reformers become radicalized they must revise and reverse their attitude toward the center of power. As reformers, any step that weakened the center and distributed power seemed a step in the right direction. But radical transformation requires a functioning executive power. It is not enough to destroy the central power of a closed society; a new authority must be established that is strong enough to bring open society into existence. That is the main obstacle to the transformation of a communist system. How can the old center be destroyed and a new one, concerned with the development of a market economy, created concurrently? How can people switch from subversive to constructive activity or—even more difficult—carry on both at the same time? This became the central issue of the Shatalin Plan. (See Chapter 5.)

❏

Now we come to one of the most interesting questions in our inquiry: where does Gorbachev fit into the picture? There can be no doubt that he played a crucial role in bringing about the present situation. Without him, events in Eastern Europe would not have accelerated the way they did. He deliberately set about dismantling certain features of the Soviet system. Did he want to destroy the whole system? If so, why? And what did he want to put in its place? Did he want to change only certain elements of the system? If so, which ones and for what reason? Did he know what he was doing? To what extent do the results correspond to his expectations? We need some answers in order to understand what has happened in the Soviet Union and what is to be expected.

We shall probably never know the truth. Historical research will be able to establish many facts, but the facts will be subject to many interpretations. Participants act on the basis of imperfect understanding. Their views are both inconsistent at any given time and subject to change in the course of time. In the case of Gorbachev, the situation is complicated by the fact that he is not at liberty to say what he thinks at any given moment.

His rhetoric has changed remarkably over time. Did his thinking change, or did the conditions change that influenced the way he expressed himself? For instance, he asserted in December 1989 that he was a committed communist. That he made the statement is a fact. What did it mean? That is a matter for conjecture. The conjecture can then be checked against other facts already known or yet to be established. It is in this spirit that I shall offer my interpretation.

Just as man created God in his own image, until recently I was inclined to do likewise with Gorbachev. I believed that Gorbachev's view of the world was not very different from my own. Specifically, Gorbachev considered the distinction between open and closed society to be the critical issue. In his mind, the transformation of the Soviet Union into an open society took precedence over all other objectives. That was the central point on which he and I were in agreement. We differed on many other issues. For one thing, he did not understand economics; for another, he was a Russian and imbued with its culture, which includes both the Soviet period and the epoch that preceded it. He was probably deeply committed to communism as an ideal of social justice and was not aware of the fatal flaw in its construction. We differed in all those respects, but I suspected that he shared my view of history as a reflexive process, or else he could not have moved as boldly as he did. He was also a good example of the participant with imperfect understanding; otherwise he might not have embarked on his adventure in the first place. Specifically, he did not realize that dismantling the Stalinist system was not sufficient to bring about a free society. He was driven by a desire to remove constraints, and his vision did not extend far enough to foresee the problems he would encounter at that point. That was not surprising. Who would have thought he would get as far as he did in destroying the old regime?

I realized that my interpretation would be difficult to reconcile with certain preconceived notions that were widely held, especially in the United States. We tend to believe that a leader's primary objective is to gain and hold power. Gorbachev, with his brilliant maneuvers in consolidating his position, seemed to fit the mold. Yet I did not believe that Gorbachev wanted power at any price, as witness his behavior over the Armenian issue when it first arose. In my view Gorbachev was almost as squeamish about spilling blood as President Carter. Admittedly, he had a hot temper—he showed it by arresting the Nagorno-Kharabakh committee when they insulted his wife—and his temper was running short. But I could not see him turning into a despot in the manner of Peter the Great. In particular, I could not see him presiding over the use of force in the Baltics.

Another of our cherished notions is that the primary concern of a leader is for the national interests of his country. We have been greatly influenced by the doctrine of geopolitics, holding that national interests are largely determined by objective factors, which exert their influence over whatever government is in power. The doctrine does not hold up when a superpower radically redefines its national interests. Nevertheless, established patterns of thought tend to linger, and it was still widely believed until quite recently that Gorbachev was trying to change the system in order to regain the power the Soviet Union would otherwise lose. Recent events have put the lie to this contention: by no stretch of the imagination can it be argued that the upheaval in Eastern Europe served to strengthen the geopolitical position of the Soviet Union, yet it was a push from Gorbachev that made the dominoes tumble. Events have reinforced my interpretation.

Gorbachev's primary goal was the internal transformation of the Soviet Union. His recipe for accomplishing it was to break the isolation into which the Soviet Union had fallen under Stalin's rule and to integrate it into the community of nations. Thus, Gorbachev's foreign policy has been guided by internal considerations rather than the other way around. This is a point that foreign policy experts in the West, well grounded in geopolitics, found difficult to grasp.

Gorbachev's views on international relations were much better developed than the rest of his program. Indeed, the expression "new thinking" applied only to this sphere. It was also in this sphere that he could count on the most competent professional support. It is not an exaggeration to say that the foreign ministry was the only bureaucracy in the Soviet Union that was unreservedly committed to Gorbachev's policies. I was shocked when a foreign ministry official proudly told me some time in 1987 that "everything that has been done with regard to human rights has been done by our department." I felt it should have been done by the interior ministry. As recently as the summer of 1989, the foreign ministry set up an economics section, recognizing that the officials charged with foreign economic relations were not doing their job.

The vision of the world that guided Gorbachev can be an inspiration for us all. It is based on the concept of an open society. He spoke of belonging to a "European house." His remarks were badly misinterpreted. Where are the frontiers of Europe, people wanted to know, in the Ural mountains, or at Vladivostok? It seemed more convenient to draw the line at the Western frontier of the Soviet Union. But that is not what Gorbachev had in mind: he thought of Europe as an open society, where frontiers lose their significance. That is a thought worth cherishing. It envisages Europe as a network of connections, not as a geographic location. The connections are open and manifold. They encompass every aspect of thinking, information, communication and exchange, not just the relationships between states. Being open-ended, its scope extends beyond the continent of Europe: it includes the United States as well as the Soviet Union, not to mention the more recent members of Western civilization such as Japan.

This conception turns Europe into the ideal of Western civilization, the ideal of mankind as an open society. Within this conception there is a need for closer association between sovereign states, but the states do not define or dominate the activities of people. It stands in contrast with the concept of Fortress Europe.

49

It is an extension of the concept of civil society to the international arena.

All this may sound very idealistic to Western ears, but it holds great appeal for people who have been deprived of the benefits of an open society. Whether people in the West can also resonate to it will have considerable bearing on the future shape of the world.

There have been previous attempts to translate similar ideas into reality, notably the League of Nations and the United Nations. In both cases, the institutions foundered because they could not protect themselves against totalitarian regimes: Mussolini and Hitler in the first case, Stalin in the second. It is noteworthy that one of Gorbachev's first gestures was to pay up the Soviet Union's arrears with the United Nations.

Perhaps because he attached such high hopes to his foreign policy, Gorbachev had much less clearly defined objectives in internal politics and economics. He wanted to give people an opportunity to express their will and had a ready-made instrument for the purpose: the people's councils, called Soviets, from which the Soviet Union derived its name. But he failed to think through the relationship between the Soviets and the Communist party. When the issue arose, at the Party Congress that reactivated the Soviets, he improvised a makeshift solution. He was even more vague in his plans for the economy.

Gorbachev ran into insuperable difficulties almost from the start on two counts: the economy proved incapable of reform, and the desire of the various nationalities for increasing autonomy could not be assuaged. One might add a third difficulty—the inability of the Soviet Union to maintain its hegemony over Eastern Europe—but because Gorbachev refused to treat it as a problem he did not have to contend with it. The first two were not so easily dismissed.

Gorbachev had great confidence in his own ability to lead. Therefore he did not feel the need for well-developed strategic plans. That was just as well. Had he considered all the difficulties in advance, he might not have had the temerity to embark on his course. Early on, in 1987, the Columbia University sovietologist Seweryn Bialer could argue convincingly that the Soviet Union could never follow China along a path of economic and political reform, because China was homogeneous while the Soviet Union was both internally and externally an empire that needed a repressive regime to hold it together. His analysis was valid, but Gorbachev was so determined to change the regime that he was not deterred by it.

Much has changed since I formulated this view. My own opinion of Gorbachev is less adulatory in 1991 than it was a year ago, but my criticism relates to his recent actions, not to his historical merit. Gorbachev has reached the limit beyond which he cannot keep up with the revolution he has unleashed. The turning point came when he narrowly missed the opportunity to throw his weight behind the Shatalin Plan. Before that, he had always managed to regain the initiative by taking a radical step forward, surprising the progressives who were about to give up hope and keeping the *apparatchiks* off balance just as they were about to close in on him. But Gorbachev was too deeply rooted in his own past to make the radical break that the Shatalin Plan demanded of him. He had qualms about introducing private ownership, especially where land is concerned, and he could not give up the territorial integrity of the Soviet Union. As he had indicated in many of his utterances, he could go back to an ideological Lenin but no farther. Most important, he could not escape the *apparat* he was trying to abolish, because he had failed to develop a new method of administration, appropriate to administering change.

The failure was not personal but generational. It applies to practically all the progressives whether or not they support Gorbachev. Boris Yeltsin, for instance, is much less able to transcend the milieu from which he stems than Gorbachev. Significantly, the Shatalin Plan was the work of people under forty. It is the tragedy of the revolution that it did not allow enough time for

51

people of that age group to come to the fore. By contrast, Zhao Ziyang in China, whose economic reforms were much more successful, relied heavily on young people. It is a historic achievement for Gorbachev to have stayed in the forefront of the revolution he started as long as he did.

Gorbachev has lost his vision; he is floundering. It is possible to argue that he never had a vision, that he was simply seeking power, just as he is now clinging to it. In my opinion that would be a mistake, because it would imply that his view of the world remained constant while the world around him changed out of all recognition. I view history as an interplay between events and perceptions, and it fits that view much better to recognize that Gorbachev's thinking has changed in the course of events.

❑

I shall consider the problems of the economy and of the nationalities separately but, of course, they are intrinsically connected. I shall first try to answer the question, why was the "golden period" of reform missing in the Soviet Union?

There are several factors at play. One is the almost total lack of comprehension about elementary economics that permeates the country and reaches the highest echelons of leadership. The contrast with China is striking. There, former Communist party General Secretary Zhao Ziyang was an accomplished economist, and he had a "think tank" of brilliant young intellects at his disposal. There is nothing comparable in the Soviet Union. A member of the Soviet top leadership, Alexander Yakovlev, told me in 1988, "We do not understand economics and we are afraid to ask any questions because we would betray our ignorance. We thought that our economists would know what to do because they were so good at pointing out the shortcomings of the system, but we have been bitterly disappointed."

Closely related to the lack of understanding was the lack of concern with economic issues. Gorbachev was primarily preoccupied with politics, partly because he had to capture the levers of power and partly because he believed, correctly, that political change is a precondition of economic change. He exploited brilliantly every instance of failure and used it for replacing people in power with his own nominees until he reached a position within the party which by traditional standards would be considered impregnable. Only then did economic issues come to the forefront of his attention. He could no longer blame others for the failures, yet his own nominees were not much better than the people they replaced. Thus, he had to start taking the blame. Moreover, the traditional yardsticks were no longer applicable in determining how secure his position was. An impregnable position within the party was no longer sufficient to protect him when the party itself was losing power.

Gorbachev made a serious error in failing to recognize that political change was merely a necessary condition, not a sufficient condition, of economic change. He had a rather naïve belief in democracy: allow people to make their own decisions and they will make the right decisions. But business cannot be run on consensus. Within each organization there must be a well-defined chain of command. In the absence of autonomous business organizations, there must also be a chain of command for the economy as a whole. If the economy is to be restructured, someone must be in charge of the restructuring. No attempt was made to establish an authority suited to the purpose.

Managing change requires an institutional setting different from the kind needed to manage a system that aims to be changeless. For managing change Japan had the Ministry of International Trade and Industry; Korea had the Economic Development Agency; even China had the State Commission for Economic Reform. But the Soviet Union did not establish an appropriate organ. The existing structures of command were retained; only some of the faces were changed. The most important error, the one that can be held responsible for the breakdown of the economy, was the decision to decentralize prematurely. State enterprises were given greater autonomy before they were reconstituted as autonomous entities, and new forms of economic activity were authorized before their scope and mode of operations were properly defined. As I have mentioned before, reformers learned to regard any step that distributed power as a step in the right direction. Events proved how wrong they were.

The bureaucracy was totally unprepared for functioning in the new environment. They were adept at taking their cues from above. They had learned to watch which way the wind was blowing at the top and to position themselves accordingly. Gorbachev told them that the system had changed and they had to take responsibility for their own decisions. At first they mouthed the slogans of *perestroika* without really believing them, but then they discovered that the system had indeed changed and they were not subject to the harsh discipline of the past. They did what any bureaucracy would do in the circumstances: they avoided responsibility. The result was a paralysis in the decision-making process. Decisions took even longer to reach than before, and the gap between decisions and their execution grew even wider. Reinforcing the paralysis was the issue of nationalities and the desire of the republics for greater autonomy. The writ of Moscow simply ceased to rule in the outlying regions of the empire.

Several other factors can be cited in the failure of *perestroika* to produce any initial benefits. There was no residual knowledge of free enterprise to draw upon. Nor was there a large emigré community to provide support. Private enterprise, insofar as it got started at all, could derive much greater profits from exploiting the anomalies of the system than from incremental production. I know of a fertilizer company selling its production for hard currency in Finland, only to have it sold back to a Soviet agricultural complex at a higher price without even changing the label. I have met the head of a successful cooperative, Artem Tarasov, who shocked public opinion by paying 90,000 rubles one month as his Communist party dues (members are supposed to pay 2 percent of their income to the party every month). He told me how his enterprise bought surplus raw materials from state enterprises at a discount, then sold them abroad in a barter deal for computers, which they could resell in the Soviet Union at thirty times the official rate of exchange—giving them an overall profit margin of 90 percent!

On balance, incremental benefits from newly authorized forms of economic activity have amounted to less than the harm done by the disruption of the established forms. If you shake a rigid structure, it will collapse. That is what happened in the Soviet Union. The only reason economic life did not come to a complete standstill is that it had not relied purely on the formal structure in the first place. There have always been many informal arrangements, and they are becoming even more pervasive. I have heard of an unofficial trading organization that has some three thousand state enterprises as members.

Economic restructuring is sorely in need of a concrete experience of success. If only some desirable new product were to become widely available! People would have at least one piece of tangible evidence of what the future might bring. For instance, sanitary napkins manufactured by Johnson & Johnson would bring considerable relief to women still using primitive methods of protection to cope with their monthly period. Johnson & Johnson is, in fact, part of the consortium of U.S. firms that is trying to arrange a series of interconnected joint ventures. Negotiations went on for two years before the first deal (involving Chevron), which would produce the oil that would provide the hard currency for the other products, was finally concluded with the Republic of Kazakhstan. It is unlikely therefore that locally manufactured sanitary napkins will become available any time soon. Unfortunately, not much relief can be expected from any other quarter either in view of the long lead times involved. There is only McDonald's in Pushkin Square with its mile-long lines.

In the absence of positive results, public opinion has reacted adversely to the manifestations of free enterprise. There is a strong streak of egalitarianism in Russia whose roots go back before communism to the rural communes, called *obshchina*, which flourished after serfdom was abolished and which, in turn, harked back to the halcyon days of organic society before serfdom was introduced.

Since there is no understanding of economics, people confuse profits with profiteering. They do not realize that it is only the distorted price structure that makes the windfall profits possible. Instead of pressing for the abolition of price controls, they clamor for the suppression of private enterprise. There has been a severe backlash. Many of the rights given to cooperatives have been subsequently rescinded; *perestroika* is almost dead. There is now an attempt to revert to the way things were. But Humpty-Dumpty cannot be put together again; the economy is drifting into chaos.

❑

Let me now turn to the issue of nationalism. This goes to the very heart of the Soviet Union. The ideological base of the Union is the universal creed of communism, but its territorial base is the Russian empire. After the Revolution of 1917 the empire fell apart, a number of autonomous republics were established, and a civil war ensued in the course of which power was consolidated in communist hands and the outlying regions were once again brought under central control. It is possible to view the civil war as Moscow's reassertion of authority over its dominions.

Stalin, of course, became an absolute ruler with more power than the czars ever had. During and after World War II, he enlarged the territory of the Soviet Union by annexing the Baltic states and taking over parts of Poland, Romania, and Czechoslovakia, not to mention Konigsburg (Kaliningrad) and the Kurile Islands. In addition, he extended the sway of the Soviet Union over Eastern Europe. In speaking of the Soviet empire, we usually mean the countries that the Soviet Union used to dominate outside its own borders, but there is a patchwork of nationalities within the boundaries of the Soviet Union that were also subjugated by the Stalinist system.

This is not the place to review Stalin's policy toward nationalities. Suffice it to say that he had no more respect for nationality than for any other human attribute. His only concern was to make his system work, and he would not hesitate to move people around on a very large scale. A high proportion of the population was deported from the Baltic states to other parts of the Soviet Union and replaced by ethnic Russians. Similarly, hundreds of thousands of ethnic Koreans were moved from the maritime areas of Siberia to locations farther inland, ethnic Ukrainians replaced Poles in Lvov, Germans were deported from Kaliningrad to Saratov Province, and so on.

When Gorbachev loosened the constraints, various national resentments and aspirations began to find expression. That was what Gorbachev was hoping for: nationalist movements were his natural allies in shaking up the rigid power structure. He wanted to release spontaneous forces, but in Armenia and Azerbaijan they turned against each other and posed a deadly threat to his policy of liberalization. Gorbachev was mentally unprepared for the process he unleashed.

Nationalism has two faces. It is easy to distinguish between them. One is benign, cultural, seeking self-expression, and supportive of the aspirations of other nationalities. It is the nationalism that swept Europe in 1848. The other is primitive, violent, and directed against other nationalities. It is the stuff civil wars are made of. The benign form fits in well with the concept of open society; the vicious form is the breeding ground of closed societies. What is difficult to understand is the way the two faces are related to each other.

There can be no doubt that nationalist movements during the Gorbachev era started with a benign face. They gave rise to the popular fronts, which came to dominate political life in most of the republics. The popular fronts formed an alliance among themselves, the Interregional Group, that became, in

THE REVOLUTION OF 1989

effect, a parliamentary opposition pushing for more radical reforms (they qualify as left-wing in Soviet parlance, but right-wing in Western terminology). At the height of the Nagorno-Karabakh conflict in September 1989, when Gorbachev issued an ultimatum threatening military intervention in order to lift the economic blockade of Armenia, the Interregional Group arranged an armistice. Once again, at the end of January 1990 the Armenian and Azerbaijani popular fronts got together in Riga, Latvia, under the auspices of the Baltic movements to try to resolve their differences. But to no avail.

Nationalism in the Baltics has quite a different character from that in the Caucasus and the Asian republics. The Ukraine is yet another story. The leaders of the Ukrainian nationalist movement in Kiev, the republic's capital, are artists and intellectuals, while the principal city of the western Ukraine, Lvov, is inhabited by people who were allowed to take over the apartments of Poles after the war; nationalism has taken a more violent form in Lvov than in Kiev.

One can try to draw a distinction between different forms of nationalism according to the cultural traditions of the people involved. I believe, however, that there is a more interesting historical connection to be found between the two faces of nationalism. I suspect that nationalism is following the same boom—bust pattern as economic reform, and for much the same reason. The failure of the benign, 1848-type of nationalism to produce positive results is what tends to lead to a radicalization of the movement. Well-meaning artists and intellectuals get pushed aside, and bigots and roughnecks take over. This holds true in the Baltics as well as in the Caucasus.

Failure is the feature that connects the nationalist movements with economic developments. If they produced positive results, nationalist movements would remain benign; similarly, if it were to satisfy national aspirations, *perestroika* would have a chance to succeed. As it is, economic failure and nationalist bigotry reinforce each other. To be specific, the Baltic states are clamoring for independence. Having their own currency is an essential

58

ingredient in that demand. But as long as the rest of the Soviet Union does not have a currency that fulfills the functions of money, introducing money in one part of the Union would cause tremendous disruption in economic relations with the rest of the Union. It is because these disruptions cannot be tolerated by the central authority that the demands for autonomy cannot be fulfilled. If the Soviet Union had a real currency, the legitimate aspirations of the Baltic countries could be fulfilled, and *perestroika* could proceed at different speeds in different parts of the country. That is perhaps the only hope for *perestroika* to succeed at all. Unfortunately, the Soviet Union is not in a position to turn the ruble into a real currency. (These ideas will be developed further in Chapter 7.)

I want to emphasize that there is nothing inevitable about the boom–bust pattern. It merely represents the course that events are most likely to take, the line of least resistance. If sufficient resistance can be mustered, the line can be interrupted at any point. Discontinuity is an inherent feature of reflexive patterns; otherwise, developments based on some kind of bias would be reinforced forever. In the normal course of events a trend has to go quite far before sufficient forces are generated to correct the bias that sustains it. But trends can be broken at any time, especially if exogenous forces come into play. In this case, where could such forces come from? In my opinion, only from the West.

I shall try to be more specific and sketch out a particular path that the line of least resistance is likely to take in the absence of Western assistance. Needless to say, it is only one of many possibilities, but it happens to have greater probability than others have. As events climb the decision-tree, the odds may shift. So there is no historic inevitability about my prediction.

The clamor for autonomy and independence in the republics and the desire of the center to maintain the integrity of the Union are on a collision course. The center will find it difficult to resist the demands of the republics. Gorbachev showed himself

59

reluctant to use force at the time of the first Armenian–Azerbaijani conflict. That was a watershed: the rule of terror was over, and it was replaced by persuasion. Gorbachev is a master of persuasion, but arguments cannot suppress the legitimate demands of the people—and the revelation of the secret clauses in the Molotov–Ribbentrop pact, which ceded the Baltic republics to the Soviet Union, has rendered the demands of the Baltic republics legitimate. Gorbachev has gone on record as saying that the Soviet Union cannot countenance the independence of the Baltic states. This puts him into an untenable position. Whatever compromise he manages to work out, it is bound to result in a further weakening of central authority. In my opinion, Gorbachev is more vulnerable in the Baltic republics than in Azerbaijan and the other Asian republics. In Asia he can use force, but in the Baltics he cannot. Even if he were replaced by a hard-liner, Soviet rule cannot be maintained by force, because the soldiers cannot be counted on to follow orders. There is simply not enough force in the Soviet Union today to cow the Baltic people into submission. What hard-liner wants to be in charge if he cannot use force? Therefore Gorbachev's position is more secure than it seems, but at the same time the authority attached to his position is likely to erode. A weakening of central authority would merely accelerate the process of disintegration. Gorbachev's disappearance would make it final. It is impossible to predict how far the process will go, but it is quite likely to culminate in a breakup of the Soviet Union. After all, the Russian empire also broke up when the czarist regime collapsed.

The more independent the constituent republics become, the more likely it is that a reactionary nationalist regime will take over in the Russian republic. Such a regime will have a century-old anti-Western and anti-Semitic intellectual tradition behind it. The similarity with Nazism is not incidental: they have common philosophical roots* and will have a similar sense of national

---

* See Alexander Yanov, *The Russian Challenge* (Oxford: Basil Blackwell, 1987).

injury to draw on. With the economy in shambles, the regime will have no choice but to follow a revanchist, expansionist policy. With atomic weapons widely deployed, one is tempted to conclude that a new Russian nationalist regime would pose a greater threat to the world than the Soviet Union ever did. The Soviet Union, as we can now see, was essentially moribund; while it managed to maintain a threatening posture, it was very careful how it moved, because it was aware of its own fragility. The new regime would be out to prove itself, and the only means at its disposal would be military force. Fortunately, atomic arsenals become useless after a while (it has to do with the half-life of tritium), so the threat may be regional rather than global.

There is nothing inevitable about this scenario, but if nothing is done to prevent it, it is what is most likely to happen. What should the West do? That is the question I shall address in the next chapter.

□ 3 □

Europe as an Open System

I concluded the previous chapter on a pessimistic note. It appears as if the Soviet Union, left to its own devices, will be unable to convert itself into an open society. I have reached this conclusion despite my postulate (now outdated) that Gorbachev regards the transformation of the Soviet Union into an open society as his primary goal, one that takes precedence over all other objectives including his own survival, let alone the survival of the Soviet empire. But if there is anything to be learned from the experience of the last few years, it is that there is no easy transition from closed to open society. It is not enough to remove the constraints of a closed society; it is necessary to construct the institutions, laws, habits of thought, and yes, even traditions of an open society. An open society is a complex system, more complex than a closed society, exactly because its structures are not rigid but so flexible that they are hardly perceived. In a closed society there is room for only one conception, the prevailing dogma, which maintains its supremacy by suppressing dissenting views. But an open society not only allows but requires all participants to act as autonomous decision-making units. It also relies on sophisticated mechanisms for keeping the participants' biases within bounds. The construction of such a complex system takes time and energy. The process that Gorbachev has unleashed affords neither.

Revolutions are destructive in nature. They may serve to bring about a transition from an open society to a closed one—as happened in Russia after 1917—but they cannot, by themselves, accomplish the opposite. It usually requires a long period of gestation before the positive results of a revolution bear fruit. In Hungary, the Revolution of 1848 was followed by the Reconciliation of 1867, and the Revolution of 1956 by the first tentative reforms in 1968 and the establishment of a fully democratic government in 1990.

What is missing from our current understanding of how history works is a proper theory of the growth of self-organizing complex systems. The concept of reflexivity provides the rudiments of such a theory, but it lacks some vital ingredients, most notably a theory of learning (and forgetting). Without it, the transition from a closed to an open society cannot be understood, let alone master-minded.

Learning is not the simple amassing of information in the manner of an entomologist collecting butterflies. It involves the organization of information, the creation of mental structures ("frames" in the terminology of computer science). These mental structures interact reflexively with the subjects to which they relate to produce a complex system which we call society. An open society is a much more complex system than a closed one. A closed society requires only one complete frame (the "mainframe" in computer language), and individuals who develop their own frames are a source of complications, which is why they must be suppressed. In an open society each autonomous unit needs its own frame—that is what makes them autonomous. Such units cannot be bought in shops, so here the analogy with computers breaks down. How do such units evolve? That is where my own framework is deficient. One thing is certain: their evolution takes time, and the lack of time creates chaos. (*Smutnoye vremya*, or troubled times, is the expression Russians use.)

My timeless model of open society is deficient because it disregards the process of learning. It is a mistake to believe that a complex system can spontaneously spring into existence, even though it is the distinguishing feature of the system that it both allows and requires spontaneous, self-generated activity from its participants. There is an important lesson here about the nature of open societies: they represent a more advanced form of social organization than closed societies. Gorbachev is not the only one who has to learn this. Western political thought is also deficient on this point.

When I first formulated my theoretical framework in the 1950s, I could not insist on the innate superiority of open society, because it would have been too much like special pleading. The Soviet system at that time seemed invincible, and the Western alliance appeared relatively weak. The only basis for my contention would have been the theory itself, and that would not do. Today there is convincing historical evidence. But we are also discovering that the superiority of open society has a negative aspect: it is not as easy to pass from closed to open society as the other way round. Here is the flaw in my original framework: it drew a distinction between open society as an ideal and as fact, but it failed to recognize the difficulty of turning the ideal into fact. It is a strange oversight, but I have not been alone in committing it. I believe it applies to practically all dissidents and reformers, Gorbachev included, not to mention Western thinking on the subject. I have corrected the error in practice during the evolution of my foundations, but it required this book to identify it in theory.

The point needs to be emphasized because it has far-reaching implications for policy. It is a widely held view that the transformation from a totalitarian to a pluralistic society must be accomplished by the people concerned and that any outside interference is not only inappropriate but probably counterproductive. This view is false. People who have been living in a totalitarian system all their lives may have the desire for an open society, but they lack the knowledge and experience necessary to bring it about. They need outside assistance to turn their aspirations into reality.

The idea of assistance runs counter to the principle of laissez-faire that is so widely accepted in the English-speaking world today. That only goes to show that there is something wrong with the principle of laissez-faire. Free competition does not lead to the optimum allocation of resources unless there are functioning markets. That is so even though the absence of free competition leads to a woeful misallocation of resources. Markets are institutions; they have to be established. Moreover, as human constructs, they are bound to be flawed.

I have argued the point, in a different context, in *The Alchemy of Finance*. I demonstrated there that financial markets are inherently unstable and that stability must be recognized as an objective of public policy if a breakdown is to be avoided. Here I claim that the pursuit of self-interest, by itself, will not produce a viable political system. Only an unselfish dedication to the principles of open society can bring it into existence. Outside assistance must also be at least partially motivated by a genuine desire to make the system work. Otherwise it will not be effective. When we look at history we find that such unselfish energies are, in fact, generated at critical moments. The American Revolution is a case in point.

But open societies, such as Europe and the United States, often suffer from a deficiency of purpose. Now we can see that flaw from the other side of the fence. Here are the Soviet Union and its erstwhile satellites seeking to become open societies but lacking the time and money needed to construct the necessary infrastructure; are the open societies of the West willing and able to help them over the fence? The response to this challenge will determine the fate not only of Eastern Europe but also of the open societies of the West.

We are indeed at a critical decision point. We have seen what lies ahead if the line of least resistance is allowed to prevail.

Let us consider what could be accomplished if the required energies could be mobilized. I must restrain myself from getting carried away, but this much must be said: practically all the political aspirations of mankind are within its grasp. Not only could the cold war between two opposing systems of social organization be brought to an end, but the nagging flaw of open society, its deficiency of purpose, could be overcome, at least for our generation. The concept of Europe as an open society in which a multiplicity of connections prevail and frontiers lose their previous significance would provide Western society with what it lacks: an ideal that fires people's imagination and engages their creative energies. It would fill in what is missing above the bottom line of self-interest. It would also allow mankind to address, in a spirit of cooperation, the ecological issues that are beginning to threaten its survival.

All this may sound like sentimental mush, but that is only because we have been too often disappointed to allow ourselves to hope. People who have seen the United Nations fail to bring about a just world order cannot easily be roused by Gorbachev's vision, especially when the failure of the United Nations is due to his predecessor, Stalin. Even so, people did respond to the breaching of the Berlin Wall, to the idealism of the gentle revolution in Prague, and to the heroism of the bloody uprising in Romania. There *is* a new spirit aboard on the continent, and it could be harnessed for constructive purposes. Even if it fails, the effort is well worth making.

❏

I shall now descend from the lofty heights of rhetoric and spell out what can be done. We must draw a distinction between Eastern Europe and the Soviet Union, just as Gorbachev has done. He has cut Eastern Europe loose and wished it bon voyage toward democracy, but he is trying to hold together the Soviet Union as best he can.

There is only one way in which the Soviet Union could

become a viable entity: if it were converted into a confederation. The example of the British Commonwealth comes to mind, because it evolved out of the British Empire and granted progressively greater autonomy to its constituent parts. Of course, the British Commonwealth did not hold together at all in the end, and the same might happen to the Soviet Union. But chances are that the Soviet Union would show much greater cohesion, because it is geographically contiguous and economically interdependent. That is all the more reason for the constituent parts to learn to live with each other.

The conversion of the Soviet Union into a confederation would be of great benefit to the West. It would significantly reduce the military threat that the Soviet Union presents as a cohesive power; even more important, it would lessen the danger that civil conflict within the Soviet Union constitutes for the entire region. Such an outcome is worth a great deal, and the West must be prepared to pay for it. Taking the savings on military expenditures into account, the bargain would be highly attractive.

The question will be asked, what can the West do to promote a confederate solution? What is the use of economic assistance when the Soviet economy is such a hopeless mess? There is an answer, although the specifics will be extremely difficult to work out. As we have seen, the Soviet Union lacks a real currency, one that can be converted into goods within the country, let alone being convertible into other currencies. There is little prospect of the Soviet Union's establishing such a currency on its own, but it might be able to do so with Western assistance.

The introduction of a sound currency would improve the efficiency of the Soviet economy out of all recognition. Barter is a very ineffective way of exchanging goods to begin with, but in the barter arrangements that predominate in the Soviet Union today, people are exchanging goods that belong to the state for goods that they need personally. Such bargaining borders on pilfering and is extremely wasteful. If goods were bought and sold for money, the waste could be greatly reduced. Moreover, the various political units that go to make up the Soviet Union could be given any degree of autonomy without disrupting the economy: the exchange of goods and services would be conducted on the basis of a common currency.

As I argued in an article published in the *Wall Street Journal,* * as little as $25 billion might have been able to do the trick. The budget deficit in 1990 was in excess of 100 billion rubles, and the so-called monetary overhang—money in the hands of the population that it is unable to spend because there are no goods to be bought—was variously estimated between 200 and 250 billion rubles at the time. This is an enormous amount in relation to Soviet national output, but it becomes quite modest when converted into Western currency. Using a conversion rate of fifteen rubles to the dollar (the black market was already higher), $25 billion would have covered the shortfall. It may be objected that the black market is a marginal rate, and the rate would have fallen if $25 billion had been made available. That is true; but the marginal rate could have been easily applied to the entire amount, because the population would have been happy to convert its entire overhang at that rate if given the opportunity.

Of course, it is not enough to remove the excess stock of rubles; the constant flow of additional rubles must also be stanched. At present the supply of rubles is totally elastic: they can be created at will if there is anything to be bought with them. A thoroughgoing institutional reform would be required, and that could be decided on and carried out only by the Soviet authorities. The first requirement for a successful transition is a sound currency. In East Germany, where there was a total commitment on the part of the West Germans to make the transformation succeed, the process started with introducing the West German mark as the currency. In the case of the Soviet Union, the specifics would have been extremely difficult to work out, but at least it would have been worthwhile to explore the

* December 7, 1989.

subject. Although the Soviet authorities were in a state of paralysis, the prospect of Western assistance might have galvanized them into action. Once the Soviet Union had a real currency, economic autonomy for the republics would not constitute the threat to the survival of the Union that it is today.

I realized that my suggestion was far removed from the political realities of the day. The West had a hard enough time coming to grips with the need for economic assistance to Poland. But it would have been high time to start thinking about it. The pace of events has speeded up tremendously and it is the unfortunate characteristic of revolutionary developments that they do not tarry until people catch up with them. That is why events spin out of control and one leader after another gets left behind.

The right time to broach the subject would have been at the Malta summit meeting in December 1989. That was the moment when admiration for Gorbachev was at its height in the West because of what he had done in Eastern Europe, while at the same time the problems confronting him in the Soviet Union had become all too obvious. But President Bush was not ready. If Western assistance to Poland had been put into place earlier and had already begun to bear some fruit, a similar initiative for the Soviet Union could at least have been considered. As it was, the auspicious moment was lost, perhaps forever. Until the demolition of the Berlin Wall, the opponents of change could take a wait-and-see attitude; after recent events, they can convincingly argue that it is too late to come to the aid of Gorbachev.

In all candor, I cannot see how the Soviet economy could be turned around in the short term. It will take decades to establish the attitudes, habits, skills, and institutions that are necessary for a well-functioning economy. That is all the more reason why the pace of disintegration must be slowed down.

In the conditions that prevail in the Soviet Union the introduction of a real currency may not be totally successful all at once. There are bound to be many leaks requiring a lot of intervention

69

as well as replenishments of liquidity. It is a process to which the International Monetary Fund is well accustomed. It lacks expertise in centrally planned economies and tends to apply the same methods as in other parts of the world. This is a mistake. To avoid it, it may be advisable to establish a separate international agency for the Soviet Union. But it is also possible that the IMF will have learned from its experiences with Poland and Hungary and from its recent study of the Soviet Union, in which case it would be qualified to deal with the problem. In any case, stabilizing the ruble would be a job for an international monetary agency. Creating a real currency, even if it is not totally stable, is probably the only way to arrest the disintegration; it would give breathing space for the slow process of reconstruction to begin.

The trouble is that there is an unresolved conflict between destruction and construction. One the one hand it is necessary to demolish the structures of a closed society; on the other, the structures of an open society must be brought into existence. How to reverse the trend from disintegration to integration— that is the unsolved question. It requires a reversal of attitudes, which does not come easily. People have learned to regard every-thing that serves to diminish the power of the center as desirable. Now they have to constitute a legitimate government and endow it with sufficient power to bring about a radical and in many ways painful transformation of the economic and social system.

To make matters worse, it is not only central planning but also the fledgling market mechanism that fails to function prop-erly. Without efficient markets, profits turn into profiteering and the rush to privatize deteriorates into looting the store when the master is gone. The transition must be properly organized; that is why a strong government is needed. Even then, a trend reversal could not be achieved without significant outside assis-tance.

External assistance also has its drawbacks. Government aid is slow and bureaucratic. Private initiatives attract people who

70

have failed in their own environment or who nurture harebrained schemes that get no hearing at home. (I fall into the latter category.) The results are bound to fall short of expectations.

But that is no reason to withhold assistance. A helping hand from the West would reinforce those who seek to transform the Soviet Union into an open society. These people are currently in positions of power, but they are fighting a losing battle. Western involvement would give them a new lease on life. Western aid cannot possibly live up to expectations because those expectations are greatly inflated. But that is exactly why it would be so effective. It would raise hopes and slow down the process of disintegration. For instance, it may enable Gorbachev to convert the Soviet Union into a confederation. If it did nothing more, it would serve its purpose.

❑

The situation in Eastern Europe is quite different. The revolution is complete and, with the notable exception of Romania, it has been successful. Communism is well and truly dead. The question is, what will take its place? The answer is not at all assured.

Communism was a universal closed system. Some people opposed it because it was universal and it violated their sense of national identity; others opposed it because it was closed and infringed on their sense of freedom. This is the fault line along which post-communist political life is beginning to evolve. Accordingly, there are now two alternatives. Either the region breaks up into smaller more or less closed units along national lines or it becomes part of the universal open system, which is symbolized by the word "Europe."

It would be only too easy to slip back to the situation which prevailed before the Second World War, with more or less authoritarian regimes, national rivalries, and lagging economies. Eastern Europe would then become a backward area, more backward than it was in the interwar period because the gap in economic

71

conditions has been greatly increased by forty years of communist rule. All the old national antagonisms which were repressed by Soviet domination are still simmering. Indeed, a major new irritant has been added by the fact that Poland has been bodily shifted to the West. Chauvinistic nationalism has therefore good potential to emerge as the dominant political trend, especially if economic conditions deteriorate. It will draw its support from several sources. First, the communist establishment, which has no future in an open society, is ready to change horses now that communism is a dead horse. Look at Yugoslavia, where Milosevich gained popularity by riding the cause of greater Serbia, or look at Romania where the Vatra Romanesca emerged from nowhere and organized the bloody riots of Tirgu Mures. Second, there is also a nationalist streak among the original opponents of communism. And finally, there are some elements in emigration whose thinking is still rooted in the past wherein they left their country of birth. Their influence is most strongly felt in places like Slovakia and Croatia.

All these forces could be easily contained by the prospect of joining Europe. Europe holds a tremendous emotional appeal for East Europeans that outweighs any yearning for the past. The appeal is not only material but also intellectual and spiritual. The people who are currently in power in Poland and Czechoslovakia believe passionately in an open society; and in Hungary, too, a European orientation prevails even though the attitude of the government parties is somewhat more mixed. The situation in Romania and Bulgaria is much more questionable.

Yugoslavia is a particularly interesting case. Even as national rivalries have brought the country to the verge of a breakup, a radical monetary stabilization program, which was introduced on the same date as in Poland—January 1, 1990—has begun to change the political landscape. The program is very much along the Polish lines, and it had greater initial success. By the middle of the year people were beginning to think Yugoslav again, and the federal Prime Minister, Ante Markovich, was going to run for office as a non-Communist in the federal elections. But Milosevich managed to derail the recovery by literally robbing the central bank, and the country is on the verge of civil war. The case of Yugoslavia demonstrates better than any other that the real choice is between chauvinistic nationalism on the one hand and economic progress and stability on the other.

Which of the two tendencies will prevail depends to a greater extent than we like to acknowledge on the attitude of the West. Yugoslavia could implement its stabilization program without major outside assistance because Yugoslavia has been open to the West for the last twenty years; but that is not true of the other countries. They have been devastated by forty years of communist rule and lack the foundations on which a smoothly functioning democracy and a market economy can be built. Hungary and Poland are much better situated in this respect than Czechoslovakia, East Germany, or Bulgaria, not to mention Romania. Hungary and Poland had reform communist regimes and developed flourishing civil societies, but they paid a heavy penalty for this privilege in the form of foreign debt. The other countries are left with hopelessly misshapen economies and inadequate social and political structures. Bulgaria has the added disadvantage of a heavy debt load, and the social and moral degradation of Romania defies description. All these countries need assistance, although they each need to be treated differently.

Take the case of Poland. The government acted very courageously; indeed, the stabilization program had some of the earmarks of a Polish cavalry charge. Inflation has been reduced, but the outcome still hangs in the balance because structural adjustment is slow in coming. Production has fallen by 30 percent, but employment has fallen by only 3 percent. This means that the entrenched management of state enterprises is using the respite it gained from wage claims to improve profit margins and keep the workers employed. There is an unholy alliance between management and labor that will be very hard to break.

73

People talk a lot about privatization, but I personally have come to the conclusion that it is futile to wait for privatization to solve the problem. What is needed now is to impose market discipline on the state enterprises. There have been practically no bankruptcies. If loss-making operations were forced into liquidation, both labor and other resources would become freely available. Western enterprises could then come in and employ cheap Polish labor and other resources in supplying Western markets. It would be much better for them to start afresh than to get bogged down in the existing structure of state enterprises. To attract them, some special incentives are needed, at least to get the process started. That is where Western government aid ought to come into play. West Germany has offered Western enterprises starting up in East Germany a special incentive of 12 percent in the first year and 8 percent in the second. Europe ought to do the same for Poland. Indeed, the percentages ought to be higher for Poland because the outlook for East Germany is more assured. In my opinion, Poland is a test case for Europe. How Europe responds will determine not only the fate of Poland but also the fate of Europe, given the problems raised by a reunified Germany.

❏

Although each country is different, they all have one thing in common: they have recently rejoined Europe. The transformation in the shape of Europe is dramatic. The division between East and West, which rigidly defined everything else, has suddenly disappeared. Europe has re-emerged in very much the same configuration that prevailed before World War II. Admittedly, Poland's frontiers have been shuffled westward. But the shift in frontiers is also reminiscent of the interwar situation: the Versailles and Trianon treaties after World War I also established new frontiers, which acted as irritants and deeply influenced political activities in the interwar period.

I am reminded of an apocryphal Indian story that was one of my father's favorites. A beautiful girl had four suitors. She was so torn among them that she pined away and died. One of the suitors was so distraught that he threw himself on the funeral pyre; the second vowed that he would devote his life to guarding her ashes; the third one went forth to seek an answer for this terrible tragedy. The fourth accepted the inevitable and returned to his village.

After years of wandering, the third suitor learned the secret of life from an old yogi. He rushed back and applied the magic formula to the ashes of his beloved. Lo and behold, the beautiful girl came back to life. But from the same ashes emerged the suitor who had thrown himself into the funeral pyre. The one who was guarding the ashes was, of course, also present. And the one who went back to the village heard about the wondrous news and returned to press his suit. So the girl was faced with the same choice that had driven her to distraction before. * Similarly, the reconstitution of Europe as it was before World War II could confront the world with a familiar set of issues.

It is easy to see how the interwar scenario could be replayed. A united Germany becomes the strongest economic power and develops Eastern Europe as its lebensraum; the French rebuild their old alliances with Poland, Czechoslovakia, and Romania; Great Britain tries (in vain, of course) to move farther out into the Atlantic; issues of nationality poison the atmosphere between—and within—the various East European countries and, of course, the Balkans will be the Balkans. Add to it a new frontier dispute between Germany and Poland and between Poland and the Ukraine, not to mention Kaliningrad and the Baltic states, and you have a potent witch's brew.

What distinguishes Europe today from the interwar period is the existence of the European Community. In Western Europe national borders have lost much of their significance. If a similar

---

* The end of the story is that the suitors went back to the same old yogi, who delivered a Solomonic judgment. The one who found the magic formula should be her father; the one who emerged from the same ashes should be her brother; the one who guarded her ashes, her servant. That left the man who went back to his village to be her husband.

development occurred in Eastern Europe, the danger of national conflicts would be averted. The European Community holds tremendous attraction for the countries of Eastern Europe. The question is whether the wealthy countries of Western Europe are ready to reach out and integrate them into their community.

The solution has great appeal for the West. It provides a context in which a reunited Germany need not upset the balance of Europe. More important, it turns Europe into the embodiment of an open society and, insofar as open society is an ideal, it turns Europe into an ideal. That was the missing ingredient in the Common Market. Eastern Europe brings to Western Europe what is normally lacking in an open society: a sense of purpose, a goal that transcends narrow self-interest.

Fortunately, there is widespread support for this view. The Germans, above all, realize that the situation must not be interpreted in terms of national frontiers, that the issue is the creation of an open society. They are awed by the successful revolution in East Germany—a unique event in German history—and they understand that the choice is between an open and a closed system of social organization. People in other West European countries share this vision to a greater or lesser extent but, understandably, they are more worried about German reunification than the Germans themselves. The French and Italian governments have shown real leadership; only Margaret Thatcher has failed badly to rise to the occasion. It is ironic that the votaries of a free market system—the British and American governments—should be the least willing to help in the establishment of market-oriented economies in Eastern Europe. It shows up a fundamental flaw in their perception of the free market system, namely a belief that the system will function all by itself if left alone.

❑

How can the enthusiasm of the moment be converted into fact? As I have said before, membership in the European Community should be acknowledged in principle. In the near term, however, association must take a more rudimentary form: access to the Common Market, economic assistance from the West, and the multiplicity of cultural and institutional ties that befit a pluralistic society. Equally important is the forging of ties among the East European countries. There is a latent rivalry between the European ideal and nationalist aspirations, which could easily turn into overt hostility. In the only East European country where party politics have already developed, Hungary, the main division is drawn along this line. It is just as important to avoid hostility between the European and national ideals as it is to avoid hostility between the various nationalities. This means that it would be dangerous to propose a Central European Confederation, unless it serves as a stepping stone to membership in the European community. It is up to the West to show leadership in this respect and to deal with Eastern Europe on a regional basis rather than country by country.

An important step in this direction has already been taken. At the instigation of President Mitterand, a European Bank for Development and Reconstruction has been established with a capital of 13 billion ecus ($16 billion). The institution will function as other regional development banks do, and its capital is large enough to make a difference. Unfortunately, however, the institution is bogged down in bureaucratic wrangling that began even before it was born. Jacques Attalie, the intellectual author of the project, made a fatal mistake by insisting on becoming its president. Since then, much more bureaucratic effort has been expanded on making him fail than on making the project succeed. Each of the twenty-four countries that participated was allotted a directorship and vice directorship, so that the board of directors will eat up half the income, not to mention all the extra work this arrangement will inflict on the staff. The United States insisted on all kinds of restrictions in lending and for the longest time failed to nominate a deputy director. Attalie continues to behave as his own worst enemy, creating animosity at

77

every step. It is a tragedy that an institution so badly needed should be so badly mismanaged.

There is another area where action would be required at least as urgently as in financing development: the financing of intraregional trade. The communist trading system, COMECON, is on its last legs, yet it plays a decisive role in the economies of Eastern Europe. The breakdown in trade with the Soviet Union has already begun and threatens to leave the East European economies in shambles. The Sofia meeting of COMECON in February 1990 resolved to design a new trading system as fast as possible, but it is fair to expect that, left to their own devices, member countries would be unable to do so. At best, there will be a series of bilateral arrangements, similar to what happened in Western Europe after World War II. At that time the United States came to the aid of Western Europe by financing the creation of a European Payments Union. That was the foundation of European economic recovery and of the evolution of a European economic community. There is an urgent need for similar assistance in replacing COMECON with a market-oriented institution that would foster trade in the region. That would be an appropriate replay of the Marshall Plan and the European Payments Union.

The problem after World War II was that European countries had an insatiable appetite for imports from America but could not pay. Now the problem is that the East European countries depend on the Soviet Union for their energy and raw material imports, and although the Soviet Union has an insatiable appetite for their exports, production and trade are organized on totally uneconomic lines so that the Soviet Union receives shoddy goods and East European industry remains uncompetitive in world markets.

The present plan is to switch Comecon trade to hard currency. This is bound to cause a virtual collapse in trading. Soviet enterprises will cut back on their imports from Eastern Europe because they have no hard currency, and what they do have they prefer to spend in the West. The East European countries will have to continue buying oil and other raw materials if not from the Soviet Union then from other hard currency sources, causing a significant deterioration in their balance of trade. Eastern Europe will be deprived of its export markets, and the Soviet Union will be deprived of the goods that Eastern Europe supplies, however shoddy they are. That is the road to economic collapse.

There was an alternative, but it would have required Western assistance. An East European Payments Union sponsored by the West could have provided a transition mechanism from uneconomic to market-oriented trade among the Comecon countries. As I envisaged it in 1990, trade would be carried on in local currencies; only the differences would be settled in dollars. That means that each country would have to open its markets to imports, and trade would expand rather than shrink as it would under a direct switch to hard currency settlement. Some of the difference would have to be settled in cash by the deficit country; some would be financed by the surplus country. The Western countries would act as bankers and guarantors of the scheme. Limits would have to be set on the amount of credit available to deficit countries, and remedial steps would be prescribed long before the limits are reached. The steps would include both devaluation and tight money. The participating countries would thus be subjected to the dual discipline of import competition and monetary constraint. They could not escape a full-scale conversion to market economies. Western participation was necessary to give the scheme credibility.

At first, the East European countries would run a deficit vis-à-vis the Soviet Union, because even if the Soviet Union continued to accept shoddy goods, it would pay less for them in hard currency than it does in Comecon barter. But gradually Eastern Europe would increase its exports in both quality and quantity, because the Soviet Union is a natural market for its products. Exporting to the Soviet Union would not be as harmful to East European industries as it is at present because they would have

79

to compete on price if not on quality, and they would earn hard currency. The danger was rather that Eastern Europe would have developed a chronic trade surplus vis-à-vis the Soviet Union. It was at that point that controlling the money supply within the Soviet Union would have become a critical issue. The West could not be expected to subsidize East European exports to the Soviet Union indefinitely. If trade was to be carried on in local currencies, the ruble would have had to be turned into a real currency.

The concept of an East European Payments Union could have been extended to the Baltic States. That would have allowed the Baltic States to maintain their trade with the rest of the Soviet Union while enjoying local autonomy. In this way, Western credit could have directly contributed to the transformation of the Soviet Union into a confederation.

Based on these considerations, a range of policy options toward the erstwhile Soviet bloc could be developed. We may list the various steps according to the degree of difficulty and cost:

1. Economic assistance to East European countries, including facilitating trade among themselves
2. An East European Payments Union including the Soviet Union to replace COMECON
3. Extension of the East European Payments Union to the Baltic States
4. Establishment and funding of a functioning monetary system within the Soviet Union

At the time, the proper place to start negotiations was at the second stage. Neither the West nor the Soviet Union was properly prepared to start any higher; but to start at stage 1 and deliberately exclude the Soviet Union from a proposed East European Payments Union would have been not only an unfriendly gesture toward the Soviet Union but would have also confirmed the economic disaster that was about to overtake Eastern Europe.

If the negotiations had been successful, they would have soon escalated to stages 3 and 4, because within two or three years the East European countries would have begun to develop a trade surplus with the Soviet Union, and a functioning monetary system would have been needed to prevent the Soviet Union from becoming a bottomless pit for East European exports. Settling relations between the republics and the Union was, in turn, a precondition for a functioning monetary system. If, on the other hand, negotiations with the Soviet Union did not make any progress, stage 1 would have become a suitable fallback position.

Poland, Hungary, and Czechoslovakia were in a position to introduce an East European Payments Union almost immediately. All they needed were the financial resources to make their currencies convertible for trade purposes. There would have been quite a shock to the system, especially in Czechoslovakia, where the necessary structural changes had not yet been introduced, but it would have helped to speed up the internal transformation.

One of the main obstacles to the proper functioning of the market mechanism is the monopolistic position of most enterprises: competition from abroad would prevent the monopolies from exploiting their position beyond a certain point. Exports may also provide a safety valve when domestic demand collapses, as is now happening in Poland. Of course, there would have been tremendous dislocations, structural as well as transitional unemployment, and often painful adjustments of relative positions. But Western backing for the scheme would have given some assurance of better days ahead and would have ensured the political will necessary to carry out the adjustments.

The Soviet Union was less well prepared. Of course the internal markets could have been opened up, and they could have absorbed almost any quantity of imports. But how could they be prevented from becoming a bottomless pit? That was where the problem

81

lay. Far-reaching reforms had to be introduced, and the Soviet Union had neither the experts nor the institutions for carrying them out, not to mention the necessary political will. It might be easier to forge a political consensus when the markets are flooded by imported goods than it is now, but it would be impossible to get a monetary system working without foreign technical assistance and, even so, there would be a lot of slippage, making the scheme expensive for the West. In my opinion, the political benefits would render the cost and effort well worth while. Unfortunately, that will become apparent only after the West has failed to act. If and when the disintegration of the Soviet Union turns into civil war, millions die, and a few nuclear accidents occur, the desirability of having prevented these things from happening will be obvious.

I explored these ideas in practice. At my suggestion, the Hungarian government invited the Czech, Polish, and Soviet governments for exploratory talks, and the Bank for International Settlement sent an observer. The discussion, which took place on April 10, 1990, revealed some of the pitfalls in the idea. There was a danger that a payments union could be used to perpetuate the barter techniques of COMECON. More important, the Central European countries, with their eyes firmly fixed on the West, would regard any attempt at integration with each other or, even worse, with the Soviet economy as a retrograde step. This was particularly true of Czechoslovakia. Vaclav Klaus, the Finance Minister, made this point very strongly in a conference we both attended in Washington on May 23. I was amused to learn that, after the Iraqi crisis had caused the price of oil to double, the Czechoslovak government floated the idea that the West should extend credit to the Central European countries to pay for Soviet oil, provided the Soviet Union opens its consumer market to imports from Central Europe. The idea was very close to the one I had proposed. Unfortunately, it came too late. The disintegration of the Soviet economy was too far advanced to make the scheme practical.

❏

Apart from the economic issues, the West ought to engage on a much larger scale in the kind of cultural, educational, and intellectual assistance that my foundations are providing. Many such initiatives are already in various stages of realization, and there is a great untapped potential in both Western Europe and the United States, not to mention Japan. It will take time before these efforts produce visible results; however, if my analysis is correct, time is in short supply. That should not discourage anyone. On the contrary, it is a reason for moving more aggressively. The intellectual capital that is developed in these countries will not be lost, even if actual conditions take a turn for the worse; indeed, it will become more precious, because it cannot be readily replaced. Consider China: the clock cannot be set back, because people have learned about the outside world. Or Romania: Ceausescu created a cultural wasteland, which will make it very difficult for democracy to take root. I shall mention only one example from Hungary: the recent reform of Karl Marx University was spearheaded by a few people who visited the United States on Ford scholarships in the 1960s.

I, for one, decided to go all out with my foundations in 1990 exactly because I was so pessimistic about the outlook. I reasoned that, if my analysis was correct, I would not be able to spend so much money in the Soviet Union in the future; and if everyone followed my example, my analysis would prove incorrect.

□4□

America at the Crossroads

Where does the collapse of the Soviet empire leave the United States? In a profound crisis of national identity. We have learned to think of the world in terms of two superpowers confronting each other and have had no difficulty in casting ourselves in the role of the good guy confronting the evil empire. This way of looking at the world had its pitfalls—it allowed us to engage in certain questionable activities in places like Central and South America that were no better than those of our adversaries—but at least the evil empire confronting us could be used as an excuse for actions that could not be justified in any other way. Now we are losing the most reliable guidepost of our foreign policy, the enemy in terms of whom we can define ourselves. The abominable snowman is melting before our eyes and we are left looking somewhat ridiculous—dressed for the cold war in a warm climate.

The emergence of Europe as an integrated economy is similarly disorienting. We have come to realize that the United States may not be the strongest economy in the world, on account of the rapid rise of Japan, but we have continued secure in the knowledge that it was the largest. Now that is no longer true. The European Community is actually larger than the United

84

States, and with the addition of the other East European countries, it is going to become even larger.

Being the largest economy and a military superpower are key features of the American self-image. It would take a profound and wrenching adjustment to renounce them. We like to be the defenders of the free world; we are used to having the last word with our allies; we have veto power in the international financial institutions and are inclined to downgrade the United Nations exactly because we do not control it.

Our crisis of national identity is much less acute than that of the Soviet Union. But whereas Gorbachev has done some profound "new thinking," especially in the sphere of international relations, we have done hardly any new thinking at all. Our approach to international relations is firmly grounded in the doctrine of geopolitics, which holds that national interests are determined by objective factors like geography, which will prevail in the long run over the subjective views of politicians. I need hardly point out that geopolitics is in conflict with the theory of reflexivity, which holds that the views of the participants, exactly because they are biased, have a way of affecting the fundamentals. The present is a case in point. Gorbachev has redefined the policy objectives of the Soviet Union, and the fundamentals are clearly not the same as they were before.

The doctrine of geopolitics gained ascendancy as a reaction to the well-meaning idealistic approach to international relations that proved so inadequate in dealing with Stalin's Soviet Union. It is ironic that the well-meaning idealistic approach of Gorbachev should now show up the inadequacy of geopolitics. No wonder that the hardheaded professionals of our foreign policy establishment should suspect a ruse! The weight of evidence is gradually forcing them to revise their views, but much valuable time has been lost in the process. As a result, the United States has been reacting to events rather than taking the lead.

That is a great pity. The participants' perceptions always diverge from reality, but it makes all the difference whether they anticipate

85

or lag behind the actual state of affairs. For better or worse, the United States still occupies the leadership position in the world. If it fails to exercise leadership, events are going to follow the line of least resistance. We have seen where that is likely to lead.

The Bush administration seems to suffer from a strange inhibition. If feels that it ought not to take the lead in offering economic assistance to Eastern Europe because it lacks the financial means to back up its promises. This attitude reflects a fundamental misconception. The United States is financially constrained today exactly because it has spent so much on defense. As a result, it enjoys a position of uncontested military leadership. If it is not ready to use that position, what was the point of running up a tremendous budget deficit in the process of attaining it? In other words, the United States has already paid its dues and can now draw on its accumulated credit; the rest of the world ought to put up the cash. It is willing to do so. The Germans are held back only by their desire not to be seen to be going too far on their own. That is why the French initiative to launch a European Investment Bank was so successful. Japan also wants to be a player in world politics, and it is up to the United States to provide the initiative. World leadership is ours for the asking, but if we fail to seize it, we shall lose it. Our military preparedness loses its value as the Soviet threat diminishes; and the economic and financial superiority of Japan is growing by the hour.

The choice confronting the United States can be formulated as follows: do we want to remain a superpower or do we want to be leaders of the free world? The choice has never been presented in these terms. On the contrary, we have come to believe that the two goals go together. They did indeed, as long as the free world was confronted by the "evil empire." But that is no longer the case. Nothing drives home the point better than to contrast world leadership with superpower status. If we insist on preserving our superpower status, we are no longer doing it in order to protect the free world but to satisfy our image of ourselves. If we want to retain our leadership role, we must help bring about a world that is no longer dominated by superpowers.

It so happens that the creation of a new world order would coincide with our narrow self-interest. The gap between the reality of our position and our image of ourselves has widened to the point where it has become unsustainable. The trouble is that we spend more than we earn, both as a country and as a government. The excess in spending almost exactly matches the increase in our military expenditures since President Ronald Reagan took office in 1981. As a result, our economic competitiveness has eroded and our financial condition has deteriorated to a point where the dollar is no longer qualified to serve as the reserve currency of the world.

The crisis is not acute, and we are only dimly aware of it because we have a willing partner, Japan, that is happy to produce more than it consumes and to lend us the excess. The partnership allows us to maintain our military power and allows Japan to increase its economic and financial dominance. Everybody gets what he wants, but in the long term the United States is bound to lose. Many empires have maintained their hegemony by exacting tributes from their vassals, but none have done so by borrowing from their allies. The problem could be resolved by downsizing our military commitments. The budget deficit could be not only reduced but eliminated, and we could recover our economic and financial strength.

What would happen to the world if we stopped standing guard over it? Until recently, virtually all local conflicts have been exploited, but also contained, by superpower rivalry. If the superpowers withdrew, the conflicts could rage out of control. Even at the height of their influence, there were many conflicts that the superpowers were unable to contain. If their power wanes, local wars may proliferate.

Superpower rivalry was a form of global organization. If we abandon it, some other form of organization must take its place. Since the United Nations and the Bretton Woods organizations have manifested their imperfections, we need to improve and strengthen the international institutional framework. Is the United States willing to accept an international authority that is not under its control? That is where our image of ourselves stands in the way of creating a new world order. To renounce superpower status would require a reshaping of our entire outlook on the world.

Our outlook is based on the doctrine of the survival of the fittest, which we extend both to the economy and to international relations. We recognize the debilitating effect of government intervention, and we extol the virtues of free enterprise. The doctrine of social Darwinism is especially appealing if you are the fittest. That is why it has become so intricately bound up with our superpower status. Like any other doctrine, it contains some inherent inconsistencies. To mention only the most obvious, superpower status implies government intervention on a very large scale—in other people's affairs as well as our own. One way to resolve the contradiction is to withdraw from international relations altogether—there has always been a strong isolationist streak in American politics—but withdrawal is not a viable option. The Soviet Union is on the verge of chaos, and Europe needs an American presence. We need to go a step further in revising our view of the world.

The doctrine of the survival of the fittest emphasizes the need to compete and to come out on top. But unrestrained competition is not sufficient to ensure the survival of the system. Civilized existence requires both competition and control. The Soviet Union discovered that control without competition does not work; we need to recognize that competition without control is equally unsatisfactory. That is true in the economy—stock markets can crash; freely floating exchange rates can disrupt the economy; unrestrained mergers, acquisitions, and leveraged buyouts can destabilize the corporate structure. It is true also in ecology, as we are beginning to discover after two centuries of unrestrained competition in exploiting natural resources. And it is equally true in international relations. The survival of the fittest is a nineteenth-century idea; a century of unprecedented growth has highlighted the problems of the system as a whole.

The question is, can the needs of the system take precedence over the needs of the participants? The issue does not arise when a system has no thinking participants. Only when there are people capable of formulating alternatives does a conscious choice present itself. At that point, the participants' views become an important element in shaping the system, and their attitude toward the system becomes a critical issue. Do they care about the system or only about their place within it? I shall argue in my theory of history that open society suffers from a potential weakness: the lack of allegiance to the concept of an open society. Now the problem presents itself in a practical form.

Historically, the United States has had a profound commitment to the ideal of an open society. It is enshrined in the constitution and has also imbued the conduct of foreign affairs. Its influence on foreign policy has not been wholly beneficial. Although it may have helped to keep the country out of foreign alliances until after World War II, there were some episodes that came suspiciously close to colonial conquests. Also, of course, the United States got involved in two world wars. At the end of both wars, the United States took the lead in trying to establish a world organization that would prevent world wars in the future. But in the first case the United States itself refused to become a member; in the second, the Soviet Union rendered the organization all but ineffective. The most glorious demonstration of the open society principle was the treatment of the defeated countries after World War II, the Marshall Plan in particular. At that time, the United States dominated the world economy to such an extent that there was practically no distinction between the needs of the system as a whole and the self-interest of the United States.

The United States has now lost its paramount position in the world economy, so the interests of the system as a whole and narrow self-interest are no longer identical. It is the Japanese who are the main beneficiaries. There is also a conflict between being a military superpower, which requires heavy spending on defense, and being a democracy that satisfies the electorate. The conflict has been resolved along the line of least resistance, through deficit financing. Deficit financing, in turn, has been an important element in our loss of economic hegemony.

A powerful military-industrial complex has come into existence and permeates our economic and political life. Its main drive is self-preservation and in this it is very successful. President Eisenhower warned us against it in his parting speech, but it has grown greatly in influence since then. It is the main base of our technology and an important feature of our self-image. It even has an ideology: social Darwinism and geopolitics. Unfortunately, there is no countervailing force, because deficit financing has obscured the costs. As the last two elections have demonstrated, the electorate simply does not recognize the budget deficit as a problem. Mondale lost because he made it an issue. Dukakis did not even try.

Open society as an ideal has been relegated to the status of all other ideals: a suitable dressing to cover actions that would be offensive to the public eye in their naked form. Anti-Communism and the defense of freedom are empty phrases to be used in presidential speeches. Policies are determined by cold calculations of self-interest. Since the various self-interests—national, institutional, and personal—are in conflict, their reconciliation is the art of politics. Those who practice it are professionals, those who are motivated by ideals that transcend self-interest are amateurs. Any suggestion of generosity or a larger point of view is treated with disdain; even the Marshall Plan has become a dirty word.

There is something fundamentally wrong in prevailing attitudes. The pursuit of self-interest is simply not sufficient to ensure the survival of the system. There has to be a commitment to the system as a whole that transcends other interests. Otherwise, a deficiency of purpose will cause open society to self-destruct. It is easy to be generous and to make sacrifices for the sake of the system when one is the system's main beneficiary; it is much less appealing to subordinate one's own interests to the greater good when the benefits accrue to others. And it is downright galling to do so when one has lost one's previously dominant position. That is the position the United States finds itself in, and that is why it is so painful to engage in any radical new thinking. It is much more tempting to hang on to the illusion of power.

Our attachment to superpower status is understandable, but it is nonetheless regrettable, because it prevents the resolution of a simmering crisis. The crisis will have to become more acute before it prompts any radical rethinking. In the meantime, a historic opportunity vis-à-vis the Soviet Union will be lost.

Yet the solution to our problems is close at hand. We no longer need to stand guard over the world. We can relinquish our burdens provided we are willing to abide by collective security arrangements. In the new dispensation the United States would no longer occupy the pre-eminent position it enjoyed at the end of World War II, but it would still be a world leader. More important, the United States would reaffirm its commitment to open society as a desirable form of social organization and in so doing would rediscover the purpose that led to its creation in the first place.

It is ironic that the leaders of the Soviet Union should demonstrate greater devotion to the ideal of an open society than our own administration, but it is not really surprising. Freedom has greater value when one is deprived of it. Moreover, people in the Soviet Union have been cut off from the Western world since Stalin's time and have preserved Western values as they used to be, while in the West values have changed: the distinction between what is right and what is expedient has become blurred. Thus the advocates of *glasnost* can now provide the West with the inspiration it has lost. The fact that Stalin's system has contributed to the degradation of Western values adds to the irony of the situation.

A note of caution is necessary. The gap between Gorbachev's vision and the reality in the Soviet Union is wide enough to sink the concept of open society. It will require the active and aggressive engagement of the Western world to bridge the gap, and even with the best will in the world, success is far from ensured. As we have seen, the best we can do is to slow down the process of disintegration so as to allow the infrastructure of an open society to develop. Gorbachev's failure would reinforce those who preach the gospel of social Darwinism and geopolitics.

Thus there are two ways to interpret the present situation, both of which are internally consistent, self-reinforcing, self-validating, and, of course, in conflict with each other. One of them stresses the survival of the fittest; the other advocates the merits of open society. Which of them will prevail depends primarily on the values that are applied. The outcome, in turn, will determine the shape of the world to come. We are truly at a critical decision point in history.

❏

In the wake of the Mideast conflict, a reassessment is in order. The Gulf War allowed the United States to resolve its crisis of national identity before the fact that a crisis existed had fully penetrated the national consciousness. It happened faster than one could have expected it. Saddam Hussein made it possible once again for the United States to be leader of the free world and superpower at the same time. President Bush rose to the occasion. He acted like a leader, ignored and overcame opposition both at home and abroad, mounted a brilliant military campaign, and won. It was fortunate for the world that the United States still enjoyed superpower status and was willing to deploy its military might against a serious threat to the world order. It was also fortunate for President Bush that the opportunity presented itself. It allowed him to put the awesome military machinery that the United States had built up against the Soviet Union to good use. No wonder that he acted with alacrity! He could demonstrate the superiority of American armaments; he could show the world that it needed the United States as a superpower; and he could give America a new sense of identity and pride.

Does this mean that the choice I posed is no longer valid? Did I present a false dichotomy in the first place? I do not think so. I believe the United States did have a choice, but the issue has been decided even before the alternatives have been clearly understood. The United States has chosen to remain a superpower while its erstwhile opponent has ceased to present a global challenge. That means that there is only one superpower left and the world will be dominated by the United States. It is unlikely, however, that the United States will fulfill its role as leader of the free world. I would not see this point so clearly had I not identified the alternatives before the choice was made.

The difference between a superpower and a leader of the free world is that the former pursues its self-interest as defined by geopolitical considerations, while the latter is guided by the interests of the system as a whole. The United States has acted as leader of the free world in the past—what better example could one ask for than the Marshall Plan?—but is unlikely to do so now. Prevailing attitudes are very different today.

The idea of creating a new world order based on international cooperation has been discredited. Gorbachev had a vision of the two superpowers forming a grand alliance that would preserve world peace while allowing the Soviet Union to re-enter the community of the free world with Western help. But that vision has dissolved like a dream and its authors can be dismissed as idle dreamers. Shevardnadze has resigned and the foreign ministry has lost influence to the military within the Soviet Union. The United Nations has been shown up to be a fragile instrument. Superpower cooperation lasted barely long enough to give the United States authorization for action. The war itself had to be conducted by the United States acting as superpower. Europe failed altogether to behave as a political unit. Great Britain and to a lesser extent France lined up behind the United States, but Europe as an entity had no coherent policy at all. It is obvious that without the leadership of the United States, the attempt to bring Saddam Hussein to task would have failed.

The idea that the United States could provide leadership only if it behaved as a superpower received strong endorsement. International cooperation did not really work; but the gadgets developed by the military did. This conclusion merely reinforced the set of beliefs President Bush started with. After all, he was not responsive to Gorbachev's plea for cooperation and aid, but he rose to the challenge posed by Saddam Hussein. Ironically, the Gulf crisis was the undoing of Shevardnadze and the end of new thinking in the Soviet Union, but that could not be helped. The new thinking was born of weakness and it was never viable; the world belongs to the strong.

It is hard to quarrel with this point of view, especially when it is victorious. Therefore it is likely to prevail. We are entering an era of American hegemony. But the flaws in the new world order are already visible. The discrepancy between the military power of the United States and its economic strength remains unresolved. Undoubtedly, the United States will derive some economic benefits from its military victory. The war itself proved to be good business, and there are lots of construction contracts to be had in the Middle East. But that is not enough to close the budget gap. A more permanent source of financing needs to be found if the United States is to continue acting as the world's policeman. In the good old days the strong could exact tribute from the weak; but those days are over. The attempt to impose war reparations on Germany after World War I had disastrous consequences; undoubtedly Iraq will be required to pay, but it may prove difficult to collect. In the past it was possible to obtain oil concessions, but to do so now would require a reversal of the trend toward self-determination. The main benefits of hegemony are to be reaped in trade. But the United States is not competitive enough and does not represent a large enough proportion of world trade any more. Similar considerations led Great Britain to withdraw from east of Suez after 1956.

Eventually the United States will be forced to engage in the kind of profound rethinking that ought to have occurred now. This may be fortunate for the world—a world order based on U.S. dominance is much better than no order at all—but it may prove unfortunate for the United States. It will continue losing competitiveness, and its economy will become increasingly dependent on its military position. When that position finally becomes unsustainable, it may be too late to rebuild the economy on a new basis, and world leadership is likely to pass into different hands. At that point the United States may be ready for new thinking—but only from a position of weakness.

□ PART TWO □

The Unfolding Crisis

□ 5 □

The Shatalin Plan

The story of my involvement in the Shatalin Plan starts at the beginning of July 1990, and the preceding chapters of this book (which in an earlier version formed part of *The Opening of the Soviet System*) give an account of my thinking at that time.

I had not been to Moscow for a few months. During the interval, the economic and political disintegration of the Soviet Union had continued apace. Boris Yeltsin had been elected President of the Supreme Soviet of the Russian Federation, and radical local governments had assumed power in the cities of Moscow, Leningrad, and Kiev. The conflict between the various governmental authorities compounded the paralysis at the decision-making center. The shops were empty, and shortages were appearing in certain basic commodities like cigarettes, which up to then had been available.

I got a fairly sharp insight into the chaos and confusion created by the conflict between central and local governments on the very day I arrived. A number of newly formed business enterprises had become associated with my foundation, seeking the protection of our very strong legal charter as well as the logistic support we could provide. The foundation staff had arranged for me to meet with a small group of these businessmen. I was very im-

99

pressed by what they had accomplished. One of them had set up a company that leased private aircraft owned by enterprises and ministries but rarely used. Another had organized the first auction of Soviet wine at Sotheby's in London. A third had gone into partnership with a Lebanese printer to print Islamic texts in the Soviet Union; and so on. They told me that under a recent decree they had to register their businesses with the Moscow City Council and, pending registration, their bank accounts were frozen. They were also worried that taxes paid to Moscow City or the Russian Federation might not be deductible from Union taxes. I raised these issues later in my conversations with Gavriil Popov, the Mayor of Moscow. He said that the granting of registration to a business would depend on what that business was willing to do for Moscow City. For instance, the aircraft leasing company could fly in some vegetables from Moldavia, he said. This sounded very much like one of the stories of military requisitioning my father used to tell me from the days of the Russian Revolution.

My discussion with Popov took place immediately after the meeting at the foundation on the evening of my first day in Moscow, as I was being received by Yeltsin at the headquarters building of the Russian Federation. Popov and his deputy, Sergei Stankevich, were there, as were the Mayor of Leningrad, Anatoly Sobchak, and Yeltsin's two economic advisers, Gennady Filchin and Mikhail Bocharov. The meeting had been arranged by Yuri Afanasyev, a leader of the democratic movement and a member of the board of my foundation. The hall in which I was received was impressive and Yeltsin had a charismatic presence, but—perhaps symbolic of the power of the Russian Republic—the building seemed empty.

Yeltsin wanted to enlist my support for the reform program of the Russian Federation, but I was reluctant to commit myself. "The Russian Federation cannot succeed on its own," I told him, "and even if you got my personal support, you would never be able to get any support from the Western powers, because

100

they will only deal with Gorbachev. There is only one way: you must form an alliance with Gorbachev." "That is impossible," he said. He pressed me to join his "innovation council" and provide Western expertise. I promised I would do so, but only after I had offered my assistance to Gorbachev and he had rejected it. That is how we parted. We adjourned to dinner with Filchin, Stankevich, and Afanasyev, with Nina Bouis acting as interpreter. We had a frank discussion, without any pretense about the precarious position of the radical "left," which they represented.

Later that night, I felt inspired to summarize my ideas in a short memorandum, which I intended to address to Western government leaders. Before doing so, I wanted to sound out the Soviet leadership. I called poor Nina, waking her in the early hours of the morning, and asked her to translate it into Russian. The next day, I sent a copy to Yeltsin with a request for written comments if possible. I also sent a copy to Stanislav S. Shatalin, who was resting in a sanatorium, and discussed the memorandum in person with Nikolai Y. Petrakov and Leonid A. Abalkin. Petrakov received me in the building of the Central Committee of the Communist Party. He was spending long hours with Gorbachev, educating him in economics, but he did not have even a secretary. He had to come down to the street himself to let us in. Abalkin received me in a more formal setting in the Kremlin.

The next day was July 4. I went to the reception at the American Ambassador's residence, Spaso House, and from there to the airport. At the reception, one of my closest Soviet friends told me that the Soviet military was beginning to pose a serious threat. General Makasov had attacked Gorbachev for losing the East European empire, and his position was supported by all the generals with the exception of the "Arbat district," where the Ministry of Defense and the command of the Moscow region were located.

To my surprise, I received a written reply from Yeltsin before leaving the country. Shatalin also returned my note with a brief but strong endorsement. Here are both my memorandum and Yeltsin's reply in their original wordings:

Memorandum to Boris Yeltsin

ON AID TO THE SOVIET UNION

1. The Soviet Union is in a process of disintegration heading towards a revolutionary climax. If events are allowed to take their course, they are likely to resemble the French Revolution: innovative fervor deteriorating into terror and chaos until order is restored by a military dictatorship dedicated to the pursuit of national glory. The analogy should not be pushed too far: instead of the guillotine, there will be pogroms and civil war, and the military regime that follows cannot pose a threat to the world similar to Napoleon; on the other hand, it will dispose over nuclear weapons.

2. It is in the interest of the world to prevent a decline into chaos. Contrary to the rules of behavior which apply in normal times, far-reaching intervention in the internal affairs of the Soviet Union is called for: only foreign assistance could alter the seemingly inexorable course of events. Again, contrary to expectations, the Soviet Union would welcome it warmly, provided it is well conceived and presented in the right way.

3. The controversy between conditional or unconditional aid is easily resolved. Intervention *must* be conditional to be effective and the Soviet leadership knows this; but the offer of unconditional and immediate aid may be a useful part of the package.

4. The only way in which the intervention can be made both effective and acceptable is by focusing it on the creation of a monetary system that would allow the transformation of the Soviet Union into a confederation of sovereign republics and, in the case of the Baltic countries, independent states. The transformation itself is an internal affair in which it would be inappropriate to interfere; but having a monetary system that would keep the economy integrated or, more exactly, provide a way for reconstituting a disintegrating economy would make the difference between success and

102

failure. The Soviet leadership recognizes that it cannot establish such a monetary system without assistance. What it needs is not just credit but the credibility that Western involvement would bring. If the G7 [countries represented at the Houston summit] indicated their willingness to help in establishing a monetary system for a reconstituted Soviet Union, their offer would be enthusiastically received and the seemingly inexorable decline into chaos could be reversed.

5. As the founder of the Soviet American Foundation Cultural Initiative, which has earned the trust of the Soviet Union's progressive elements, I am well equipped to prepare the basis for negotiations without preliminary conditions.

George Soros
The Soros Foundation—Soviet Union
July 3, 1990

Memorandum to George Soros

IN RESPONSE TO QUESTIONS IN YOUR LETTER DATED
JULY 3, 1990

1. The described finale in the Soviet Union is probable. The question is—for how long.

The situation has changed. Now Russia has a new leadership inclined to carry out radical changes.

Russia led by democrats and refusing services of all-Union departments can herself overcome the crisis and become a nucleus, a stabilizing factor, if her economy convalesces. Concluding treaties with other republic-states she can help in strengthening the Union on the basis of economic programmes.

2. Rather not "assistance," but participation through the concrete programmes of the Russian Federation, because the Union leadership has already proved that it will hardly resort to radical measures. (But it will accept assistance and it will be difficult to say how this assistance will be disposed of.)

3. Psychologically such "direct" assistance may once and for all damage "rating" of the President. Assistance should be given to the programmes and to the new people—that is the way out. Through Russia—for the whole country.

4. The new monetary system will not be accepted by the leadership of the country. There is no more credit or confidence among the people.

We propose to think over forms of intellectual cooperation within the Coordinating Council under the Presidium of the RSFSR Supreme Soviet.

"Revival of Russia"—that is the thing that can attract both "brain" and capital.

We are moving towards a confederation of states. The solution is to conclude direct treaties with Russia, because strong Russia (not only the Russians but all peoples in the republic) means strong Union.

5. I wish to believe, but hopes are not great.

The chance should be used.

Boris Yeltsin
July 4, 1990

After my return from the Soviet Union, I sent my memorandum, deleting the last paragraph, to my contacts in the various governments that were about to meet at the Houston Summit. I know for certain that Margaret Thatcher, Jacques Delors, and Gianni de Michelis read it; I am less sure about the U.S. leadership.

The Houston Summit decided to set up a number of study groups to assess the situation in the Soviet Union and to make recommendations for Western policy. There were five study groups in all. The first one had been set up by the European Community at its own summit meeting prior to Houston, and the others were commissioned in Houston largely to keep each other and the European mission in check, and to prevent any hasty decisions. The institutions involved were the International

104

Monetary Fund, the World Bank, the Organization for European Cooperation and Development, and the newly formed European Investment Bank. I was hoping that one or more of these institutions might enlist my assistance, but in vain. They were far too busy fighting for turf. The International Monetary Fund sought to emerge as the coordinator of the project and entrusted one of its senior officials, Alan Whittome, with the task. Not to be outdone, the World Bank also appointed a coordinator. So the coordinators had to coordinate each other. The European Commission, determined to get a jump on everyone else, sent a team to Moscow almost immediately.

After a number of contacts with the various institutions, I decided to fly to Moscow at the end of July. I realized that with so many missions descending on Moscow my chances as an outsider to play a significant role were rapidly diminishing. My timing could not have been better. There had been a breakthrough. Upon my arrival on July 29, I received a full briefing from a staff member of the foundation who had attended a meeting between Gorbachev and a small group of progressive economists. Gorbachev had started out with a review of the situation in China and warned that events could take a similar course in the Soviet Union unless the progressive forces pulled together. A reconciliation between Gorbachev and Yeltsin was in the making.

I repaired almost immediately to the gleaming and still largely empty building of the Russian Federation. I was received by the Russian Prime Minister, Ivan Silayev, who seemed to be cast in the same mold as Soviet Prime Minister Ryzhkov: a former engineer-manager from the military-industrial complex. But when he summoned his Deputy Prime Minister, Grigory Yavlinsky, and his Finance Minister, Boris Fyodorov, I discovered a new breed of men that I had not realized existed in the Soviet Union. They were much younger and, instead of the automatic speaking that Soviet officials usually resorted to, they spoke to the point. We found immediate rapport.

Next day I met with Alexander N. Yakovlev, Gorbachev's

105

chief political adviser. We had met several times before and established very good contact, but this time he was quite reserved. "I have begun to develop an allergic reaction to foreign advisers," he told me with his usual disarming frankness. "They waste my time. They keep on repeating the same record and we never get any farther." He suggested I go and see Stepan A. Sitaryan, Deputy Prime Minister in charge of foreign economic relations, but I said I felt that would be a waste of time. I was quite crestfallen when I left the meeting, but I found out later that it had served a useful purpose.

Then came my meeting with Nikolaiy Petrakov. At first, he was very evasive, but eventually he told me what was still a closely kept secret: Gorbachev and Yeltsin had agreed to cooperate and had commissioned a small group of like-minded progressive economists to develop a coherent program that both of them could endorse. That was what I had been hoping for. I offered to help in any way I could. He promised to check with Grigory A. Yavlinsky and get back to me. Eventually, through the good offices of Volodya Aksyonov, the director of the foundation, we set a date for the next afternoon.

Abalkin received me with open arms. He explained to me in detail the various reform programs that were currently in preparation. Apart from the 400-day program proposed by the Russian Federation, there was the Ryzhkov government plan, as well as an academic commission under the chairmanship of Abel Aganbegyan, whose job it was to consider all other plans put forward by all other parties. All these plans had to be coordinated and a single plan presented to the Supreme Soviet by the first of September. The group commissioned by Gorbachev and Yeltsin (later known as the Shatalin Group) was separate and additional. The prospect of five Western missions homing in on Moscow complicated matters even further. But Abalkin seemed to have a full grasp of the situation. He drew diagrams which clarified the relationships, and we discussed how a group of private Western advisers could facilitate his task. My under-

106

standing at the time was that Abalkin was going to participate in the Shatalin Group, and, indeed, he did so at the beginning.

On the morning of August 1 I had breakfast with Boris Fyodorov, the newly appointed Finance Minister of the Russian Republic, the first man I met in the Soviet Union who really understood how a monetary system is supposed to operate. When I met with Petrakov and Yavlinsky in the afternoon, they told me they were going into seclusion with the Shatalin Group immediately following our meeting. They had checked with their respective bosses (including Yakovlev) and would welcome a group of Western economists to discuss the plan as soon as the two leaders had signed off on it. That could happen by the end of August, they thought. We agreed that instead of lecturing the Soviets, as Western advisers are inclined to do, we would listen to what they had decided and help them make it operational. They left the composition of the Western group to me. We would set the date of the visit through Aksyonov. I was elated. What I had hoped for had finally happened. Everything I had done, including the book I had written, seemed to have been in preparation for this moment.

Later on, I was told the story behind the formation of the Shatalin Group. In the beginning of February 1990, when Yavlinsky was working as section head in the Abalkin commission, he prepared a radical program called "The Four Hundred Day Plan." Although it was rejected by the government, he published it under his own name in Vienna. Later on, one of his assistants showed it to Mikhail Bocharov, who had been commissioned by Yeltsin to formulate an economic program. Bocharov took the plan and adopted it as his own. When Yavlinsky found out about this, he confronted Yeltsin. He explained that the plan could not work for the Russian Republic because it had been designed for the Soviet Union. Yeltsin asked him to join his government and adapt the plan for the Russian Federation. Yavlinsky accepted. Then, at the beginning of July, he went to Petrakov and asked for a meeting with Gorbachev. He managed to convince Gorbachev that the only way out was to cooperate with Yeltsin and to create a new plan based on his "400-day" concept. Then he had to persuade Yeltsin to cooperate with Gorbachev for the same purpose. It took some doing. Yeltsin was vacationing by the Baltic Sea. They had a long and acrimonious discussion, but in the end Yeltsin agreed. And that was how the Shatalin Group came to be born.

Upon my return to New York, I started mobilizing a group of economists to take to the Soviet Union. Professor Jeffrey Sachs of Harvard University, with whom I had worked in Poland, was ready and eager to participate. He suggested a number of other participants: Romano Prodi from Italy, former head of IRI (the Italian holding company of state-owned enterprises); Guillermo de la Dehesa from Spain, who had been responsible for the Spanish privatization program at the Ministry of Finance; David Finch, retired official of the International Monetary Fund; and, of course, his own associate, David Lipton. I wanted to include a number of other macroeconomists so as to counterbalance Jeff, who at times could be overly persuasive: Stanley Fischer and Jacob Frenkel, heads of research of the World Bank and the IMF respectively; Larry Summers from Harvard; and Michael Bruno of the Central Bank of Israel. I added two leading experts on the Soviet economy, Ed Hewett of Brookings and Gur Ofer of Jerusalem University, both of whom had participated in my Open Sector project in 1988; along with Barry Bosworth of Brookings and Richard Cooper of Yale, both of whom had had practical government experience; and my old friend, Marton Tardos from Hungary. All those whom I called on were willing to volunteer their services, but unfortunately Jacob Frenkel was not allowed by his organization to participate, and Michael Bruno and Richard Cooper were not available. Even so, we formed a very impressive group.

We were all on tenterhooks waiting for word from Moscow. Aksyonov had difficulty maintaining contact with the Shatalin Group because it was in seclusion in a dacha outside Moscow.

Abalkin was pressing us to come and issued an official invitation, but we wanted to make sure that the Yeltsin side also wanted us. Finally, Yeltsin himself phoned Aksyonov and urged us to come at once. Then we moved very rapidly, so rapidly that the Soviet Consulate in Washington balked, insisting on its normal forty-eight-hour turnaround time. The Ambassador's personal assistant had to walk over to the Consulate to get visas issued.

We arrived in Moscow the day after Labor Day and found ourselves in a very awkward situation. I had thought that Abalkin was a member of the Shatalin team as well as working on the Ryzhkov program, but that was not the case. The Abalkin group was locked in deadly combat with the Shatalin Group, each ensconced in a different government rest house just outside Moscow: the Abalkin group at Pines and the Shatalin Group at Little Pines. The Abalkin group insisted that we should stay at Pines, while the Shatalin Group could not be reached. We managed to obtain a copy of the latest version of the Shatalin Plan, but that was all. To avoid becoming compromised, we decided to stay at a hotel in Moscow. The next day we visited Pines. Each of us was assigned to a room, although we were not planning to spend the night. They were not really prepared for us, but they were anxious for us to be there. We even got stuck in the elevator for half an hour. Then we had a long lunch. Eventually we had a meeting with a couple of second-grade officials. Both the program and the discussion contained the same empty generalities with which I was familiar from my experience with the Open Sector Task Force in 1988. The day was a washout.

The next day both Abalkin and Valentin S. Pavlov, the U.S.S.R. Minister of Finance, came to the foundation offices to meet with the group. They told us quite bluntly they needed a few kind words that Ryzhkov could quote to the Supreme Soviet next week when he presented his plan. They attacked the Shatalin Plan as irresponsible. I must admit, I have never heard either of them argue with greater conviction.

To understand their motivation, it is important to realize what was the main point of difference between the two plans. The Shatalin Plan sought to downgrade the existing central government bureaucracy and replace it with a new center of decision-making directly under the authority of the President. This would be accomplished by transferring economic powers to the republics and concurrently delegating some of those powers to an Inter-Republic Council functioning under the aegis of the President. The Council would have its own executive, which would determine the budget of the central government. It would impose a very tight budget indeed. For instance, it would suspend all investment programs and continue only those which could be economically justified; it would also cut military spending by 20 percent in the first year. By imposing budgetary discipline on the central authorities, it would gain for itself the popular support that was currently lacking.

By contrast, the Ryzhkov Plan sought to retain power in the hands of the central government. It proposed to start with an administrative price reform, which would bring administered prices closer to those that would prevail in a free market. This step would have been useful if it had been implemented three years before, but the government had failed to act; now it promised to do so under duress, but it was too late. Nobody had any confidence that it would be any more successful than it had been in the past.

This basic difference in approach determined the other points of difference in the two plans, particularly the sequence of the various measures. The Shatalin Plan proposed to start with the creation of an independent central bank along the lines of the Federal Reserve system, which would impose monetary discipline, and the creation of the Inter-Republic Council to impose fiscal discipline. It would also embark on a crash program of privatization, particularly in the fields of housing, land, small businesses, and road transportation, and would not touch consumer subsidies until the other measures had started to take

110

effect. The idea behind this sequence was that the population should not be asked to make sacrifices until it had seen evidence that the central government mechanism was being dismantled. By contrast, the Ryzhkov Plan would seek to achieve monetary stabilization first and embark on structural changes more gradu-ally.

Abalkin and Pavlov argued that the Shatalin Plan was unprofessional and irresponsible. They failed to take into account the political rationale behind it. And no wonder: the premise of the Shatalin Plan was that a new center of authority could gain popular support only by depriving the old center of its power and privileges. No bureaucracy can be expected to go to its own execution without offering some resistance.

After our debate with Pavlov and Abalkin, we still had no contact with the Shatalin Group. Only later did I find out that they were reluctant to meet with us because they were afraid we had been won over by Abalkin. The official excuse was that they were closeted with Gorbachev. Petrakov sent me a message that he might be able to see me, but not the whole group, on Saturday, after Gorbachev had left for Helsinki to meet with President Bush. There was nothing to do but to disband our advisory group. I felt bad about having dragged these distinguished economists halfway across the globe on a wild goose chase, but they showed no resentment. They had entered into the spirit of adventure and were ready to continue at a future date.

After most of the group had left, the three of us who remained (Ed Hewett, Gur Ofer, and I) were taken to Little Pines on Saturday, September 8. The atmosphere there was triumphant. Apparently, Gorbachev had come down in favor of the Shatalin Plan. Although he commissioned Abel Aganbegyan to reconcile the two programs, the Shatalin Plan was accepted as the basis for the compromise. The process of conciliation was taking place at Little Pines. Members of the Abalkin team were arriving one by one to be interviewed. Most of the Shatalin team was there. They were all in their thirties, with the exception of Professor

Yevgeny Yasin, who had been their mentor at the Economic Forecasting Institute. They belonged to the same new breed as Yavlinsky and Fyodorov. We did not discuss the substance of the plan in depth but focused on the practical steps to be taken. We planned a full-scale meeting in two weeks' time. It was only on my way to the airport that the idea occurred to me that it would be much more productive to take the Shatalin Group to Washington at the time of the World Bank meeting than to bring the Western economists to Moscow. I made the suggestion after I returned to London, and it was accepted with alacrity.

We had been the first to obtain a copy of the Shatalin Plan. We performed a rush job to have it translated into English. Although the plan contained some 650 pages, the translation was completed within a week. We made copies available to the various governments and international organizations and distributed it among the economists who were going to meet in Washington.

I had a few days to study the plan. While I was in complete agreement with the overall concept, I found it quite deficient in its particulars. It was really more like a life-size mockup of a plan than the plan itself. Its 650 pages were designed to impress the legislators and to prevent them from considering the plan in detail. If the plan had been adopted, it would have had to be designed at the same time as it was implemented. My suspicions were confirmed when I had a chance to discuss it with the authors.

I flew to Moscow to pick up the group and flew with them to Washington via New York with a very pleasant detour to Manhattan and Staten Island. On the flight I had a chance to get to know Yavlinsky and to learn the full background of the Shatalin Plan. I found in him a kindred soul. The reader can see for himself that the basic conception of the Shatalin Plan is the same as the one I have propounded quite independently in this book. Moreover, the way he dealt with both Yeltsin and Gorbachev reminded me of the stories my father had told me about the Russian Revolution. In revolutionary times, my father said, anybody with courage and imagination can assume command.

We arrived in Washington Friday night, September 21. The Supreme Soviet debated the economic reform program on the following Monday, and the reports received through the news media were very confusing indeed. Apparently no program was approved, but Gorbachev was given emergency powers and required to submit his own plan by October 15. Yavlinsky talked to Moscow by telephone, but the information he received did not make matters any clearer. He put a good face on it and carried on with our grueling schedule, but I could see he was under considerable strain.

It had been quite a feat to prepare the visit at such short notice. Barry Bosworth of Brookings acted as our host for the two-day session with the Western economic advisory group.* I enlisted the help of a friend of mine, Richard Medley, an old hand at organizing international economic conferences, to schedule appointments with all the major delegations attending the annual meeting. He did a superb job. The International Monetary Fund was not too happy with these arrangements. It had issued an official invitation to Prime Minister Ryzhkov to send observers, and the IMF did not relish the prospect of two rival delegations descending on Washington. In the end, however, it also came through, and the meeting with the IMF staff was one of the most productive. In addition to everything else, I also arranged for a legal review of the plan (which subsequently developed into a major legal project) and for meetings with a couple of management consulting firms to plan the reorganization of the Soviet oil industry. But the uncertainty about events in Moscow overshadowed all these activities.

---

* Janos Kornai, Richard Cooper, and Jacob Frenkel also attended.

After my return to London, I had a meeting with the Chef du Cabinet of Gianni de Michelis, the Italian Foreign Minister, who was acting President of the European Community, then flew to Brussels to meet with the task force of the European Commission. I proposed various ways in which the European Community could assist the Soviet Union. My best suggestion,* and one that could still be considered now, was to set up a special fund that would allow Western investors to convert ruble profits earned by supplying the domestic market. Western enterprises providing domestic distribution and financial services (retail and wholesale distribution, packaging, banking, insurance, etc.) would be given preference. This might be the most effective way to provide technical assistance for those segments of the Soviet economy most in need of it by mobilizing the Western private sector. The order of magnitude of this facility might be $5 billion over, say, five years. This should be sufficient to get Western managements interested.

From Brussels I flew to Moscow on October 5 just for a day to find out what was going on, but I did not learn much. The people around Abalkin felt very confident. They had tried to convince Gorbachev that he would become powerless within the Inter-Republic Council because he would be the only member without the backing of an actual republic. The argument was false, because Gorbachev, as head of the Inter-Republic Council, might have been able to regain the popularity he had lost. But they felt they had scored their point with Gorbachev. Yavlinsky, on the other hand, did not see the situation any more clearly than he had in Washington. He knew that Gorbachev had something up his sleeve, but he did not know what it was. They had talked a number of times on the telephone and were going to have a meeting on the following Monday. He agreed that the outlook was not promising. The likelihood was that Gorbachev

* Based on a paper by Gur Ofer.

would entrust the Ryzhkov government with putting the provisions of the Shatalin Plan into effect, thereby abandoning its key provision, namely the creation of a new center of power. If that happened, Yavlinsky said, he would resign. By doing so, he would avoid being compromised. The people in the Soviet Union were determined to move toward the market, he felt, and as long as there was any alternative left unexplored, they would continue to move in that direction. By dissociating himself from the present program, Yavlinsky would keep intact a more radical solution that people might turn to in the future. Only when the market solution had failed would people swing in the opposite direction. At that point, the situation would be ripe for a fundamentalist backlash or a military dictatorship.

I encouraged him in his resolve to resign. It would be to his benefit, I argued, not to be in a position where he could be blamed for what was about to happen. An inflationary explosion was more or less inevitable. If it occurred before a radical market reform was put into effect, the radical plan could not be blamed for it.* Yavlinsky agreed with me in principle but expressed his fear that the process of disintegration might become irreversible. For instance, when the republics made up the next year's budget, they would be likely to give in to popular pressures, creating enormous budget deficits at the republic level. The chance to balance the budget by cutting back severely on central government spending would then be lost forever. I tried out the same argument on Shatalin when I had dinner with him in Washington the following week, claiming that a delay in adopting a radical program might be beneficial. His answer was more succinct. "Use it in your oration at my funeral," he said.

My worst suspicions were confirmed. The central bureaucracy executed a classic defensive maneuver: it co-opted the plan that

---

* The authors of the Shatalin Plan made this point in an article entitled "Why the 500 Day Program Cannot Be Realized Today," *Komsomolskaya Pravda*, November 4, 1990.

threatened its existence and by so doing ensured that it would fail. Exactly how the bureaucracy prevailed is still shrouded in mystery, but the outcome is clear: the chance to reverse the trend toward disintegration has been lost. The Shatalin Plan sought to introduce a discontinuity into the process by creating a new center of power which would gain public support by doing battle with the much-hated old center. It was a brilliant conception not widely understood either inside the Soviet Union or outside. Unfortunately it was well enough understood by the bureaucracy, which managed to defuse it.

The Shatalin Plan was probably the last chance to create a new center of power whose authority would extend over the entire territory of the Soviet Union. The mistrust of central authority is so pervasive that even the Shatalin Plan would have had great difficulty in obtaining popular endorsement although it explicitly envisaged associate status for those republics that did not want to remain full members of the Union. There is now a widespread rejection of all central power. It may be possible to gather popular support for a local or national authority but not for one that seeks to govern the entire Soviet Union; and it would be easier for such an authority to be located in Kiev or Leningrad than in Moscow.

The Soviet Union can be held together only by force and it is highly doubtful whether the required force can be mobilized at present. Only after the process of disintegration has gone much further is such a force likely to emerge.

It boggles the mind to imagine how the disintegration of the Soviet Union may unfold. Russia has passed through periods of chaos and anarchy before, most recently during the Russian Revolution. But the nature of the system that was collapsing was quite different. Russia was not far removed from a subsistence economy, but in the Soviet Union not even the villages can sustain themselves because Stalin has deliberately destroyed their ability to do so. They are dependent on tractor stations and centralized grain storage facilities. Never in history has there been such a fully integrated and centralized system as the one Stalin has brought into existence. As it disintegrates, large numbers of people may literally starve or freeze to death. The presence of atomic weapons and nuclear power stations adds to the uncertainties. We may be facing one of the major cataclysms of modern history.

□6□

The Outlook for
Eastern Europe

I gave a blow-by-blow account of my involvement with the Shatalin Plan because it is perhaps the most important thing I have
done in my life, even if it failed. I shall now take a more detached
view as I survey developments in what has become Central Europe. My personal efforts do not deserve such detailed reporting,
because they did not make much impact.

Before the 1990 spring elections in Hungary, I participated
in a "blue ribbon commission" that sought to lay down the
basic principles to be followed by the first democratically elected
government. Unfortunately, it did not produce much more than
pious words. Separately, my foundation commissioned a so-called
Hundred-Day Program from a group of Hungarian economists.
Although two members of the study group subsequently joined
the new government, few of its recommendations were actually
implemented. The main thrust of the program was to impose
market discipline on the state sector by pushing failing enterprises
into bankruptcy, but very little was done in the first hundred
days.

My own efforts were directed at the twin problems of debt

and privatization. I was looking for ways to link the two issues, because I felt that, since they represented items on opposite sides of the balance sheet, they might be easier to tackle together than separately. Specifically, the sale of state enterprises to foreign interests might be politically more palatable if it were connected with a debt reduction scheme; conversely, a debt reduction scheme might be more acceptable to the creditors if it were associated with the large-scale introduction of foreign equity capital. The subject was highly sensitive; any public mention of debt reduction schemes could have undermined the already tenuous credit standing of the country. The discussion was meant to be purely exploratory and strictly confidential, with representatives of the two main parties participating. As it happened, some public statements were made by the Free Democrats and some details of the confidential discussions were leaked to the press by the Hungarian Democratic Forum. I backed off immediately, but I returned to the theme at a later date, as I shall recount at the end of this chapter.

The Bulgarian economy was falling off a cliff when I visited there in October 1990. Cars were lined up at gas stations, abandoned by their drivers until the stations reopened. Electric power was cut off for part of the day. Because the country could not pay its debt, hard currency imports came to a standstill and spare parts became unavailable. Most of industry was rendered uneconomic by the collapse of the Soviet market and the rise in the cost of energy. Nearly a million people would have to be moved back into agriculture, but even then the question would remain: where to sell the produce? Living standards would have to fall by 25 percent even if an orderly transition was to be engineered. But how can a transition be orderly with that kind of dislocation, especially when the government does not have the necessary political backing? The political problem is the same as in the Soviet Union: the *nomenklatura* is unwilling to release its hold on the levers of power. However, the situation has not yet deteriorated as far as in the Soviet Union.

119

The structural problems confronting Czechoslovakia are similar, but the political situation is significantly better. Hungary is the country in the best position to absorb the shocks it has received. It has been very successful in redirecting its exports from the Soviet Union to the West, and its industry has already been paying more or less world market prices for energy. These are the benefits of a long-drawn-out reform process; the accumulated debt represents the negative aspect. The Polish economy has also become more responsive to market stimuli. The trouble is that living standards have already fallen so far that any further fall may shatter the so far remarkably positive attitude of the population.

How the West responds to the needs of Central and Eastern Europe will determine the future not only of the region but of Europe itself, and ultimately of the world. So far, Europe has been able to live up to its role as the ideal to which the people of Central Europe can aspire. The countries of Europe, acting both jointly and severally, have maintained a remarkably constructive attitude toward their struggling Eastern neighbors. Their actions have not been very effective, but the goodwill has been there. West Germany led the field, driven partly by economic motives and partly by the desire for reunification, but also, to a significant extent, by a belief in the values of an open society. The other Continental countries did not want to be left behind, and the European Commission in Brussels felt a true sense of mission. Great Britain was the most reluctant to get too deeply involved, mainly because of Margaret Thatcher's reservations about Europe, but she has been forced out of power.

Nevertheless, there is now a danger that the positive bias prevailing in Europe will be reversed. One of its main forces, the drive for German reunification, is spent, and the costs of integrating East into West Germany exceed all expectations. At the same time, the cost of keeping Central Europe afloat has risen by the same order of magnitude and for much the same reasons. The collapse of the Soviet market, the rise in the price of oil, and the blockade of Iraq will cost the East European countries something in the range of $10 billion to $20 billion in 1991. That is a shock they will not be able to absorb. Will the West come to their aid when its own situation is also deteriorating?

If Europe ceases to be as welcoming and accommodating as it was during the heady days of the revolution, the change in attitude is likely to aggravate the political situation in Central Europe. As I said earlier, the newly liberated countries face a choice between integrating into Europe and moving back into the past. All the political developments of the last few months have confirmed this view.

In Hungary the struggle between a European orientation and a return to the past is clearly visible. The governing coalition parties unite some of the best and some of the worst elements of the prewar Horthy regime, but within the government the better, pro-European element prevails. The Prime Minister, Jozsef Antal, regards his father, who was a liberal official of the Horthy regime and who protected Jews and Polish refugees, as his role model. He is a Christian Democrat in the German sense of the word "Christian"—not in the Hungarian, in which it usually means non-Jewish. The German connection was very important both in helping his party, the Hungarian Democratic Forum, to victory and afterward in excluding the extreme nationalist wing from the government. The Hungarian Democratic Forum had originally been formed by a group of populist writers with the tacit support of Imre Pozsgai, a reform communist leader who failed in his attempt to become President of Hungary. Since they had been excluded from power, these writers became quite shrill in the expression of their chauvinistic and anti-Semitic views, but they have been rebuffed by public opinion. All this is very healthy, provided the deterioration in economic conditions and the mistreatment of Hungarian minorities in neighboring countries does not cause a reversal in public opinion. The attitude

121

of the public during the gasoline riots of late October 1990 was very encouraging from this point of view: the government tried to use patriotic platitudes, but people said, "What has that got to do with the price of gasoline?"

Poland is following in the footsteps of Hungary. The presidential elections have divided Solidarity along lines somewhat similar lines to those dividing the anticommunist opposition in Hungary. In Poland the split was provoked by my friends who are believers in an open society, such as Adam Michnik. They raised the specter of nationalism, while in truth the election revolved around personalities. Insofar as there was a political issue, it was the fate of the communist *nomenklatura*. The public declared, "A plague on both your houses," and voted in large numbers for a nebulous character who appeared out of nowhere, descended by helicopter, and made impossible promises. What could be a better demonstration of public disaffection?

Nevertheless, I am optimistic about Poland—more so than most of my Polish friends. The electoral success of Stanislaw Tyminski is a salutary reminder to both wings of Solidarity that they do not have a monopoly on political power. The election of Lech Walesa as president has created a dynamic situation which is likely to move the country forward. Largely as a result of Western pressure he retained Leszek Balcerowicz as Minister of Economics while setting up a shadow cabinet in the presidential palace. He is posing a credible threat that he may change course if the pain of the present policy becomes unbearable. Consequently both Balcerowic and the new Prime Minister, Jan Krzysztoj Bielecki, will have to do their best to make their policy succeed, and the West will have to exert itself to keep the pain bearable. These dynamics have already produced a favorable settlement of Poland's debt with the Paris Club.

By contrast, the political evolution of Czechoslovakia has taken a turn for the worse. The prime minister of Slovakia, Vladimir Meciav, has emerged as a nationalist demagogue. He is a former

122

reform-Communist who was nominated as Prime Minister by VPM, the party of former dissidents which had no competent candidate of its own. He tried to take over the party and turned against it when he failed. Now he has the support of the former Communist nomenclature. As the only nonintellectual political figure, he has attained incredible popularity within a very short period of time. He was personally vulnerable and did not last long as prime minister, but the political direction he represents will not go away. It offers a simple solution to those who are baffled by the complexity of an open society. Vaclav Havel is in a very difficult situation. He has no simple solutions. For instance, he is opposed to arms sales and does not want to authorize the sale of tanks to Syria and Iran. But the factories are in Slovakia and have no other orders. What is to be done?

At my last meeting with Marian Calfa, the Czechoslovak Prime Minister, he complained about the Polish debt settlement. What is the West going to do for Czechoslovakia? The countries of Central Europe are competing with each other for connections with the West. The spirit of cooperation, which was so strong during the resistance and the revolution, is fading fast. Remember the Czech–Polish Solidarity meeting in Wroclaw (co-sponsored by my foundations), which was a precursor of the gentle revolution in Prague? President Havel does remember; but his influence is waning. The newly elected leader of the Civic Forum, Vaclav Klaus, in his capacity as economics minister, keeps the Czech–Polish borders closed in order to prevent Poles from buying up subsidized Czech goods.

Will the West start competing in its connections with Central Europe? In economic matters, competition is both desirable and unavoidable; but if it comes to dominate political and cultural relations, the chance of integrating these countries into Europe will be lost.

The effect on Europe would be profound. Instead of an open system, the European Community may become a closed one.

123

The borders may have to be literally closed to keep out a flood of refugees from the East. Markets may have to be protected from the products of cheap labor, and Fortress Europe may become a reality. Within the fortress, tremendous tensions are bound to arise. Germany is too big to be accommodated by a community which is only a rump of Europe. The other countries may gang up on Germany, or the community may come to be dominated by Germany. There will be a temptation to revive the alliances of the interwar period; Poland in particular would be a willing partner because the antagonism between Germans and Poles is already very strong. The possibilities are too numerous to be considered. One thing is certain: the concept of Europe as an open society is undergoing a severe test. It will survive only if people in the West are willing to make greater efforts and sacrifices than they have shown a taste for up to now.

❏

Following the settlement of the Polish debt, I reverted to the problem of the debt in Hungary.* Hungary has come a long way in developing a market-oriented economy. Although the bulk of industry is still state-owned, even state-owned enterprises have learned to respond to market signals. The private sector is growing by leaps and bounds, and foreign enterprises find the environment congenial to doing business. The economy gave proof of its flexibility last year: exports to the Soviet Union were cut by 24 percent while exports to hard currency countries rose by 18 percent, yielding an overall surplus in the balance of trade of $1 billion. This performance exceeded the most optimistic expectations.

The government is following a responsible if uninspired eco-

* The following comments appeared in my article "An EC Gift for the Hungarian Economy," *The Wall Street Journal Europe*, April 4, 1991.

nomic policy. Tough decisions had to be taken in order to reduce the budget deficit for 1991 to about $1 billion—a figure acceptable to the IMF. The international monetary institutions in turn are extending about $2 billion in credit, which should be sufficient to enable Hungary to absorb the economic shocks resulting from the dissolution of Comecon and the collapse of the Soviet economy.

Nevertheless, the country is on the verge of economic and political breakdown. The standard of living, which has been falling for several years, is taking another severe drubbing as a result of the elimination of subsidies. Come next fall, many people will find that their bills for housing, heating and electricity will jump by as much as 150 percent. Some will be simply unable to pay. A few hundred people may be dispossessed with impunity, but if ten thousand people fail to pay, a serious economic and political problem may arise. The inflation rate is hovering between 35 and 40 percent.

There is a danger that it may accelerate if the budget deficit exceeds the target. In the worst case there could be social unrest. An unfortunate precedent was created in October 1990 when a sudden jump in gasoline prices precipitated a nationwide rebellion that forced a partial recision of the price hike.

The main source of difficulties is the heavy burden of debt that Hungary is carrying: $22 billion for a population of ten million makes Hungary one of the most highly indebted countries in the world. The debt is the legacy of the preceding reform communist governments, but—in contrast to Poland and Bulgaria, which have defaulted—Hungary is still paying in full. It is the only country in the world with such a heavy debt-load to remain current on its obligations. The effect is felt primarily in inflation and in declining living standards, because the export earnings that are used to pay the interest are not available to satisfy domestic demand. At the same time the export surplus is not sufficient to service the debt, so the total amount outstanding is still growing faster than the economy. That means there is no relief in sight.

Lenders are of course aware of Hungary's predicament and are disinclined to increase their exposure. The incremental lending is coming mainly from international monetary institutions, and it is only with the greatest difficulty that the maturing debt can be rolled over.

Paradoxically, Hungary finds itself heavily penalized for trying to live up to its obligations. Not only does it have to bear the full cost of the debt, but it cannot even raise the issue of relief, because to do so would undermine its already shaky credit standing. Doing so would also interfere with its efforts to attract equity capital, even though the debt problem has become a serious disincentive for foreign investors. The Japanese, who hold the second largest stake in Hungary's debt, are particularly leery of also taking equity stakes.

What is to be done? Hungary needs debt relief just as much as Poland did, even though it cannot ask for it. Indeed, the problem is more acute because the effect is felt in the present—whereas, in the case of Poland, debt relief was needed to clarify the future. But it would be a serious error to blot Hungary's unblemished record by penalising the creditors. Relief must take a different form.

I propose that the European Community, with the help of Japan and other interested parties, should guarantee a long-term loan of 10 billion ecus for Hungary and make a gift of the interest on that loan for the first three years. This course of action would immediately re-establish Hungary's credit standing and provide a much-needed breathing space for the Hungarian economy. It would enable Hungary to bring inflation under control both by allowing the budget to be balanced—the interest forgiveness is roughly equal to the budget deficit—and by providing a powerful incentive to abide by the IMF agreement. The gift of the interest would of course be subject to Hungary's fulfilling the conditions of its IMF program.

It is true that the current commercial creditors of Hungary would also benefit from the EC's generosity because the quality of their loans would improve, but that fact should not be held against the scheme. Commercial banks will be required to take substantial write-offs both in Poland and in Bulgaria. They will be in a better position to do so if they receive some benefit in Hungary.

The proposal should be seen in the context of an overall settlement for the region. Each country needs some support from the West because the already difficult problems of transition have been compounded by the collapse of the Soviet economy, but each country needs a different kind of support. In the case of Czechoslovakia, the main need is for structural adjustment.

The proposed scheme would have a tremendous impact on Hungary. It would open the prospect of a better future ahead. Yet the cost to the European Community would be surprisingly small. The gift of interest would merely replace loans whose chances of repayment cannot be rated high. The cost of the guarantee on the long-term loan can be offset against Hungary's prospect of joining the European Community. If Hungary defaulted, it would lose the chance of joining, and the European Community would probably come out ahead on the bargain.

Eastern Europe is poised on a knife's edge. It would require only a modicum of imagination and political will to swing the balance in favor of success.

□ 7 □

The Foundation Network

My policy in my own foundations has been guided by the considerations I outlined in the previous chapters. My original objective has been attained: the communist system is well and truly dead. My new objective is the establishment of an open society in its stead. That will be much harder to accomplish. Construction is always more laborious than destruction and much less fun. The task far exceeds my own capacity; fortunately, I am not alone in pursuing it. Helping Eastern Europe has become a major industry. I must concentrate the resources of my foundations where we enjoy a comparative advantage.

Most of the efforts that go into the making of an open society do so by indirection: the profit motive and cultural and political pursuits can all contribute to the diversity that is a precondition of an open society. My foundations are almost unique in treating open society as their primary goal. I have now established a network of such foundations, which span the entire region. Each foundation is defining its own character depending on the character of the people associated with it and the particular needs of the country in which it is operating, but they all share a common goal. Herein lies our comparative advantage, which we can exploit.

We support East–West contacts, but there are now many other organizations doing so. Every Western country devotes some resources to the cause, and the European Community has quite a large program for it under the acronym PHARE. But contacts among the member countries of the erstwhile Soviet empire have practically no sponsors other than my foundations. Moreover, most East–West programs are country-by-country, while we try to organize them on a multilateral basis. Along these lines, we try to pick particular spots where we can make a difference. This is a very different approach from the one we followed in trying to break the monopoly of communist dogma. Then, we were practically throwing our money around, like a traditional peasant sowing seeds. Now we are focusing our efforts.

Two major projects stand out. One is the Central European University. The idea was first mooted in May 1988, when we held a weekend meeting in Dubrovnik in connection with our first Central European seminar series. At that time I rejected it in no uncertain terms. "I am interested not in starting institutions but in infusing existing institutions with content," I declared. After the fall of the Berlin Wall, I changed my mind. A revolution needs new institutions to sustain the ideas that motivated it, I argued with myself. I overcame my aversion toward institutions and yielded to the clamor for a Central European University. I reconciled my decision with my principles by announcing that my support is for a limited duration: $5 million a year for five years. After that, the institution will have to stand on its own feet or fold.

Everybody wanted it, but everybody had a different conception of what "it" stood for. We had a number of inconclusive discussions, and I was ready to abandon the project, but it would not die. We now have a commitment from the Czech government of a modern building in Prague with live-in facilities for 250 students and a less well defined offer from the Hungarian government. We have the sponsorship of President Havel, President Goncz of Hungary, and the majority leader of the Polish Sejm,

129

Bronislaw Geremek. We have found an academic planner, Ladislav Cerych, who designed the Tempus program for the European Community, and he is setting up an academic planning board. In the meantime, practical work has started on the first two modules: a graduate school of social studies and a graduate center for ecology. The latter is moving particularly fast, and the first class will start in the summer of 1991. I want to combine the practical education of East and Central European experts with the creation of a center for evolutionary systems theory. The juxtaposition of practical and theoretical studies should benefit both. I have been able to mobilize some of the leading intellects in the field, and I see a chance for establishing a world-class institution.

The other major project is the creation of an international network for the placement of East and Central European candidates as trainees in Western firms. The core of the system is a databank open to all applicants, along with a computerized search protocol that allows Western firms to locate suitable candidates.

We organized the first get-together of foundation staff in Karlovy Vary (Carlsbad), outside Prague, on September 27–30, 1990. About eighty-five attended. I was shocked by the large number, and in my closing remarks I managed to shock them, too:

I don't like foundations. I think foundations corrupt the impulse that led to their formation. That is so because foundations become institutions and institutions take on a life of their own. A lot of people feel good when they have created an institution, but I feel bad. There is only one thing that can excuse the crime: if the foundations do something really worthwhile. Otherwise they have no business existing.

In the financial markets I have made a career out of taking advantage of institutions, of doing better than institutions, because the financial markets are dominated by institutions and the institutions always respond to the past and not to the future. That gave me a chance to make the fortune which I am giving away through my foundations. So I am quite serious in what I am saying about my opposition to institutions.

And I am very good at killing foundations. Before I started the

Open Society Fund I got involved in a very small local project in New York to help renovate Central Park, which is a beautiful park and was in terrible shape. We formed a small organization, the Central Park Community Fund. There was another organization—the Central Park Conservancy—which turned out to be more successful. We were on the verge of attacking what the other foundation was doing because it wasn't us doing it. Fortunately at that point I killed the foundation, and I am more proud of that than I am of having created it.

But then I relented. "Don't worry, I said. "I am not about to kill our foundations, because they are doing something really worthwhile. There is a powerful idea behind them which justifies their existence. The idea is not as simple as it was at the beginning when it could be summed up in two words: civil society. It can still be summed up in two words: open society, but it is not so simple, because open society is a complex system, much more complex than the oppressive totalitarian state to which civil society was opposed." Then I went on to explain my concept of open society. Finally, I gave an account of the network of foundations, which has also become a very complex structure since it is based on the principle of self-organization.

Each foundation has its own profile, which is very much what I wanted, because it is meant to serve the needs of the society in which it functions and not my need of having a very clear and neat picture of what the foundations are doing. So I am very pleased that the foundations are different in character because they draw on the energies of the people involved in them.

Each of you has your own picture of your own foundation. I shall give you my picture. I shall use the Hungarian foundation as a reference point because it was the first and in many ways the most successful. That foundation has already gone through three phases. In the first phase it was an institution of civil society, but that phase is now over. Then came a short period when civil society was successful and we enjoyed the fruits of victory. We had a moral authority far exceeding our financial resources because the government had no legitimacy

131

and no authority. It was ready to do practically anything we asked. We could write our own ticket and we tried to do so. For instance, we embarked on a rather ambitious program to reform the teaching of humanities in the universities. But this period lasted only for a very short time, until the elections, because now there is a legitimate government whose outlook is somewhat different from mine. I am accused of being in cahoots with the opposition, and although we have been careful not to support the Free Democrats or the Young Democrats as political parties, I do not deny that I have a greater affinity with them than I do with the government. Once again, there is a distance between me and the government, and I think that is a very healthy development. We have now entered phase three, which I would describe as institution building for open society. In this context, open society does not end at the borders of Hungary, nor are the institutions we are trying to build confined to Hungary.

There is another model that has emerged, the Polish model, which is quite different from the Hungarian. After some false starts it has managed to tap into energies that are passionately committed to the concept of an open society, but the way the people involved in the foundation perceive their task is quite different from my concept. They do not see the foundation as a grant-giving organization open to all and trying to support other people, but rather as being the people with energy themselves. In other words, they run an institute rather than a grant-giving organization. It is a perfectly legitimate conception, but I would prefer to see a two-tier structure, with a grant-giving organiza-tion at the top and an institute underneath.

Taking the three phases of the Hungarian foundation and the Polish model, I can place the various foundations. Romania, for instance, is at stage one of the Hungarian foundation because in Romania civil society still needs to be established. We are having a difficult start because the government is less than helpful. There is also a danger that the foundation will follow the Polish model because our association with the Group for Social Dialogue is too close. But I am very much in support of the endeavor because I feel that the need is great and the task is one which we have already proven we can do. Bulgaria belongs to stage two of the Hungarian foundation because we are dealing with a reform communist government which is very receptive to our efforts, and the foundation is off to a flying start. Czechoslovakia is somewhat different because the foundation has been in existence for

132

ten years, but operating outside the country and underground. Even though it supported a civil society, actually there was not that much civil society inside Czechoslovakia, so the foundation could not establish itself in public consciousness as it did in Hungary. Nevertheless, it has great legitimacy because it was practically the only manifestation of civil society during the years of repression, and in that sense it belongs to stage two of the Hungarian foundation. But it has not yet deserved the credentials it has, and it faces a tremendous challenge to justify its existence.

I have also offered to set up a small foundation in Yugoslavia to operate on a federal level and overcome the tendency to have a quota based on nationality for everything. I have reached an agreement with the government, but the people who are supposed to run the foundation have not moved, and I am not going to remind them. If they do not care, I can certainly spend the money elsewhere. So there is no foundation in Yugoslavia. *

Then we come to the Soviet Union, where the process of disintegration is not yet complete, yet the need for constructive activities is very pressing. That makes the task of the foundation very difficult. We have tried to establish ourselves as an institution of civil society, but we could not possibly succeed in the way we have in Hungary because of the sheer size of the country. I am spending about as much money in the Soviet Union as I am spending in Hungary, but the country is twenty times larger, so we cannot make much of an impact. Within the circumstances I think we did a pretty good job, but our main role has to be on the constructive side. I have been an avid supporter of the Shatalin Plan, and I have tried to create the model of a confederation in our foundation network. We have established independent foundations in the Ukraine, Estonia, and Lithuania, with others to follow. Within the Cultural Initiative Foundation there is now a commission for economic initiative, which is gathering momentum. There is also a commission for legal culture, which has gained considerable stature lately.

Then I described the Central European University and the East West Management Institute, which I could envision as

---

* The Yugoslav foundation was officially inaugurated on June 17, 1991.

permanent institutions, while the national foundations may eventually fade into history—because I do not think that the support of civil society is an activity that needs to continue once the oppressive, dogmatic system has been properly destroyed and an open society has taken root. This gives a fairly complete picture of where the foundations stood at the time of the Karlovy Vary meeting.

Since that time the activities of the foundation network have grown by leaps and bounds. I have given priority to Romania and the Ukraine. In Romania the devastation wrought by the Ceaucescu regime is so complete that there is hardly any basis left for the construction of an open society. It is difficult to find people with a clean past, and those who qualify lack any aptitude or experience in practical matters. The influence of the Securitate has been so pervasive that people are mistrustful to the point of being paranoid. The fact that I am Hungarian has made the foundation a suitable target for an extreme nationalist organization called Vatra Romanesca. The government has followed a policy of "malign neglect." In these circumstances the foundation was foundering until I engaged a young Romanian expatriate, Sandra Pralong, to help put it on its feet. She has worked wonders. She cut through the atmosphere of suspicion by simply ignoring it. She advertised for staff and engaged four young women and a young man who are full of energy and good will. She organized competitions for places on our foreign travel programs and published the results, so that we are now operating in the full glare of publicity. By these means she prepared the ground, and when we were ready we held a grand opening, at which we announced that we want not only to help build an open society but also to be the prototype of an open society. After the festivities in Bucharest we flew to Iasi, a university town on the border of the Soviet Union. Uncharacteristically, I chartered a private plane because that was the only way to get around. It was minus 18 degrees and a snowstorm was raging when we arrived; one-third of the town was without heat, because the Soviets had cut the supply of natural gas—our hotel had heat but practically no light. Nevertheless, we found an enthusiastic group of people waiting for us, and we launched a local branch. Then we flew to Cluj in Transylvania, where the accommodations were more comfortable but the atmosphere less stimulating. I have a very good feeling about the work of the Romanian foundation. The main problem is the lack of communications. We cannot get through by telephone or fax, and sometimes weeks go by without contact. It is difficult to maintain momentum.

The Bulgarian foundation has produced excellent results without any help from the outside. It has grown into a clearinghouse for Western assistance, and the scope of its activities far exceeds the financial support I provide. To a lesser extent the same is true of the Stefan Batory foundation in Poland. The Charta 77 foundation is functioning less smoothly, but is receiving a large endowment from the Czech government in recognition of its past services.

It is the Hungarian foundation, the most successful one in the past, that is having the greatest difficulties at present. We have lost most of our leverage. In the past we could turn the weaknesses of the communist system to our advantage and have a large impact with relatively small amounts of money. By giving small grants to people working in state institutions we enabled them to do what they wanted and not what the state wanted. And by making dollars available against repayment in Hungarian currency we could subvert the institutions themselves. For instance, our program of providing photocopying machines was a glorious success. But those days are over. The state is no longer the enemy and, what is worse, the state is exceedingly poor. Apart from the matching funds we receive, we must rely on our own resources. Our capacity has shrunk even though I spend more money. Neither the staff nor the public fully appreciates the extent of the transformation. As the country gets poorer, the demands made on the foundation increase, and there is no

135

way we can satisfy them. It is not just the lack of money but even more the lack of controls that obliges us to change our method of operation. In the past we could simply trust the people who received our grants. But conditions have changed. Everyone is out for himself. We are no longer the only foundation in existence and the normal rules that govern the relationship between grant giver and grant recipient have begun to apply. We have been slow to adjust and therefore probably easy to take advantage of. As we fail to satisfy the demand, the attitude toward the foundation begins to change. Once it starts, the process is liable to become self-reinforcing. We are in a crisis, but we are reluctant to face it. We must change, but any changes we make will be for the worse, because our past has been so satisfactory.

Interestingly, the solution is to confine our activities on specific programs and cease functioning as a grant-giving organization open to all comers. We announced the end of the open application system in May 1991. In the future we shall have four kinds of activities: those we have decided to continue out of the present activities of the foundation (e.g. travel grants and support to certain cultural organizations that could not survive otherwise); Western know-how programs (e.g. media workshops and other forms of training); East-East programs (e.g. publishing articles and books from other East European countries); and the successor foundations (e.g. Central European University). This means that we are moving toward the format adopted by the Stefan Batory Foundation much against my desires. Having started later, they may have been ahead of the Hungarians in this respect—only I did not recognize it.

The Cultural Initiative Foundation in Moscow is also going through a difficult period. The official attitude toward the foundation has changed for the worse since my involvement in the Shatalin Plan. When Valentin S. Pavlov came to the foundation to meet with the group of economic advisors whom I brought to Moscow, he openly told the staff that he would withdraw

136

the tax-exempt status of the foundation unless the economists gave him the endorsement he wanted. Subsequently he followed up on his threat. Now he is Prime Minister. In April 1991 the foundation was attacked in the hard-line newspaper *Sovietskaia Russiya* for engaging in subversive activities. Our internal organization leaves much to be desired. The foundation is not as open to the public as I would like it to be. The attempt to build a network of businesses associated with the foundation turned chaotic, and we had to engage a business consultant to try and sort it out. We acted in the nick of time to avoid a serious embarrassment. But we have an eminent and committed board, and I am determined to continue supporting the foundation as long as possible. We may have to batten down the hatches and reduce the scope of our activities, but we shall refuse to compromise our principles. What these principles are I have made clear in this book and elsewhere, and if they are unacceptable, the authorities will undoubtedly make our life difficult.

The foundations in the republics are functioning much more effectively than the Cultural Initiative Foundation itself. In Lithuania the committee continued to select candidates even while the Parliament building was under siege. I am particularly keen on the Ukrainian Renaissance Foundation.

If a new center of organization, which can command the allegiance of the people, is to emerge, it has a better chance to do so outside Moscow, for the simple reason that it would be geographically distinguishable from the old center. That is what makes the Ukraine a more promising base for building a new center than the center itself. Moscow is, of course, the natural center of a new Russia, but it may be more difficult to bring a new Russia into existence than a new Ukraine exactly because of the pervasive mistrust of the old center.

Not that the creation of a new Ukraine would be easy! As a country, it does not have any more cohesion than Russia; indeed, it has less. The eastern part has a large Russian population, and the western part, which used to be part of Poland before

137

World War II, has a much more vivid memory of what it is like outside the Soviet Union than does the rest of the country. The Crimea has no more reason to belong to the Ukraine than to Russia, and Odessa has an ambience all its own. Only if it adopts a loose confederate structure does the Ukraine have any chance of becoming a viable unit. Fortunately, the present leadership of Rukh, the nationalist movement, recognizes this fact, and that makes it attractive in my eyes. There are some good people involved in the Ukrainian Renaissance Foundation, as my enterprise there is called. I am ready to back them even if their chances of success are slim.

I have now come under attack in several countries: in Hungary from Hungarian nationalists; in Romania from the Vatra Romanesca; in Slovakia from the communist party newspaper *Pravda*; in the Soviet Union by the organ of the hard-liners, *Sovietskaia Russiya*. If I had any concern that my foundations have a mission to fulfill, these attacks have removed it. I had begun to feel some doubts as to whether all my activity was justified, whether the idea of an open society might be too abstract and detached and lacking in commitment to anything or anybody in particular. Now, however, I have been reminded that there is something even more unsound in the idea of a closed society, because it allows its adherents to reject and suppress anyone who does not belong. As long as the threat of a closed society remains so acute, the concept of open society remains a goal worth fighting for. I had foreseen a conflict between nationalism and freedom, but it is one thing to anticipate it in theory and quite another to experience it in the real world. The issue has arisen sooner, more pervasively, and more virulently than I had expected. I am ready to stand up and be counted.

□ 8 □

A Personal Account

My involvement in Eastern Europe has wrought a profound transformation in my own life. I have developed a public persona. It was strange to see it grow and take on a separate existence. People know me without my knowing them, and their picture of me, although related to what I have done, is different from what I am. The relationship between me and my persona is very complex. It resembles the relationship between thinking and reality, with the difference that my persona exists only in other people's thinking and not in what may be called objective reality. There is the same reflexive interaction between me and my persona as in any other historical process, and the same basic rule applies: I must maintain a measure of separation between me and my persona if I want to keep the process from getting too far from equilibrium. Of course, the separation is more a normative rule introduced by me than a fact observable in reality. What I do shapes my persona even if the two of them do not correspond, and my persona influences my own thinking—it is that influence which has wrought such a profound transformation in my life.

I have lived with a double personality practically all my life. It started at age fourteen in Hungary, when I assumed a false

139

identity in order to escape persecution as a Jew. It continued in England, where I was a refugee and had to work in various menial jobs in order to maintain myself and had to pretend I was not very different from the people around me in order to get by. I developed the duality into a fine art when I worked as a traveling salesman selling fancy goods at the seaside; I learned not to mix up my personal feelings with business. I remember making a sale to a small shopkeeper whose shop was cluttered with unsold merchandise. He needs more goods like a hole in the head, I thought to myself, but I could not allow that to influence my selling effort, otherwise I would have been no good as a salesman.

The duality continued when I came to America, until I moved from what is called the "sell side" in the securities business to the "buy side." Then my ego was really put on the line, and this turned out to be a very painful experience. For one thing, my ego suffered an incredible battering whenever I made the wrong move in the market. For another, I did not really want to identify myself with money-making to the extent that was necessary in order to be successful. I had to deny my own success in order to maintain the discipline that was responsible for that success. Eventually, in 1980, when I could no longer deny my success, I had a kind of identity crisis. "What is the point of undergoing all this pain and tension if I cannot enjoy my success?" I asked myself. "I must start enjoying the fruits of my labor even if it means destroying the goose that lays the golden egg." A battle ensued between me and the investment fund I was managing. I won and the fund lost—26 percent in 1981 to be exact. That was the only year my fund lost money. My investors were not too happy. About a third of them withdrew their investment, and I could not blame them. But I did emerge a happier man.

That was also the time when I started the Open Society Fund, the seed of the present network of foundations. I made a resolution from the very beginning not to let my ego get mixed up with the activities of the foundation. The argument was very much the same as the one I used when I was selling fancy goods at the seaside. The foundation was meant to do some real good in the real world. If I allowed my personal interests to interfere, it would lose its effectiveness and become a self-serving sham. When I was helping dissidents, it was their existence that was on the line; it was their cause that was at stake. Compared to their commitment, my ego was dwarfed to the point of insignificance.

This attitude was indispensable to our success when we started operating inside Hungary. When I concluded a contract with the Hungarian government in 1984, its representatives thought they were dealing with a well-meaning rich expatriate who wanted to have a foundation in order to gratify his ego. They agreed to practically all my conditions, thinking that once I had set up the foundation, they could control it. But they had a surprise waiting for them. When they failed to meet my conditions, I threatened to quit, and I meant it. They had to give in more than once. It was those victories that established the reputation of the foundation. Then again, the fact that I did not seek personal recognition or publicity allowed me to expect the same from those who were associated with the foundation, either as organizers or as recipients. We were lucky that the media, which were under the control of the Agitprop Department of the party, maintained a discreet silence about our activities. People found out about our existence through our practical deeds, a welcome change from all the official activities, which were carried on with the full blast of propaganda.

When I set up foundations in other countries, I had to be very cautious in my public utterances. The various countries were at various stages of development, and what would have been acceptable in one country might have raised hackles in another. This consideration ceased to be valid after I wound up my foundation in China. Since then, I have felt free to say whatever I think. But there were other advantages in keeping my ego in the background. It allowed my foundations to cooperate

141

with others without too many conflicts over who would claim credit. Since our method of operation is to exploit and reinforce the energy of others, this has been a key factor in our continuing success. It sets us apart from other foundations whose main motivation seems to be to fight for turf and recognition.

Unfortunately, the difference between us and other foundations is not as great as I would like. Gone are the happy days when we were forced to build our image the roundabout way, by delivering on the substance. We can, and do, seek publicity. The result is that we are better known and find it easier to get things done, but we do not necessarily do them as well as we used to. Even if we did, they would not be as highly appreciated as in the good old days of a closed society, when we were the only game in town. Interestingly, in no other country have we been able to establish such a clean reputation as in Hungary. Moreover, it is only a question of time before the image of the foundation changes in Hungary too.

I must confess I am not very comfortable with the change, although I recognize its inevitability. The fact that I have become a public personality makes it difficult for me to demand selfless devotion from others. It is true that I try to keep a distance between my ego and my foundations in my own mind, but the fact remains that my public personality feeds off the foundations. Why should others starve? We must abandon the spirit of volunteerism that characterized the foundations in their heyday and replace it by professionalism. That is the main reason why I feel that the foundations cannot continue in their present form indefinitely and need to be replaced by a different set of institutions—like the Central European University—which are to be run along professional lines. Still, I should like to preserve the spirit that imbues the foundations as long as possible; I am even trying to infuse it into the Central European University, at least during its formative stages. When that spirit is gone I shall have little in common with the institutions I have helped bring into existence; but presumably I shall be gone, too.

❑

In the course of the revolution, my own role has expanded far beyond my foundations. As the reader has seen, I have become what I like to call a stateless statesman. I enjoy the role; I identify myself fully with what I am doing. Still, I feel I must maintain a separation between myself and my persona. Without it, both I and my persona would be endangered. I feel this more strongly than I can explain rationally, but I shall try to support my deeply felt conviction with rational arguments.

I hold my persona in high regard, from both a subjective and an objective point of view. Objectively, I am working for the common good of mankind and of the particular societies in which I am active. I do so without ulterior motives. Moreover, I am effective in what I am doing. Although my grand schemes seem to fail by a hair's breadth (I include the Shatalin Plan among them, even though it was not my invention), many of the smaller initiatives I have backed have been successfully realized. My image is that of a man who gets things done, and on the whole it is justified. On the subjective level, I am proud of what I have done. In some ways I find more gratification in the grand schemes that I have tried unsuccessfully to bring about than in the smaller ones that have succeeded. Although I remain a champion of losing causes, how much closer I have come to realizing them than when I first started!

Often I feel frustrated. My frustration started at the time of the Polish economic reform, when I felt I could have done more than I was allowed to do. And it continued to build up in Hungary in the spring of 1990, where my efforts to find a solution to the debt problem were effectively double-crossed. But my frustration was released by the role I was able to play in the Shatalin Plan, even though it was not successful.

A separation between me and my persona is indispensable for this state of affairs. Without it, my persona would become less attractive, because it would be more self-serving. As it is,

143

the fact that my self is not in need of my persona is a source of profound satisfaction. It allows me to feel, and to express, my pride in my persona and to cope with the frustrations I have felt. And now comes the crucial consideration: my involvement in the revolutionary process, including the writing of this book, has made me a happy man; yet, the probable outcome of the process arouses the most profound anxiety in me. The dividing line I have introduced between myself and my persona allows me to reconcile the two feelings.

◻ PART THREE ◻

A Theoretical Framework

□ 9 □

Philosophical Foundations

I must start at the beginning, with an old philosophical problem that seems to lie at the root of many other problems. What is the relationship between thinking and reality? This is a very roundabout way of approaching the subject of contemporary developments in the Soviet bloc; but the answer I shall give informs not only my own views and actions but also the actual course of events and the way they are interpreted. Most important, it illuminates the choice that confronts the world.

I realize that my approach is not going to be popular and I may lose the bulk of my readers even before I get started. Philosophical questions are not fashionable nowadays. Contemporary Western civilization is addicted to positive results, and philosophy seems incapable of producing any. Philosophical questions do not have final answers or, more exactly, every purported answer seems to raise new questions. Moreover, most avenues of inquiry have been fully explored so that there seems to be little new left that is worth saying. Indeed, starting with Wittgenstein, English language philosophy has been more interested in analyzing the difficulties of philosophical discussion than in discussing the philosophical questions themselves.

The fact that philosophical questions are incapable of final resolution does not make them any less important. On the contrary, the positions we take, however inadequate, have a profound influence on the kind of society we live in and the kind of lives we live. For instance, the predilection of contemporary Western civilization to leave philosophical questions alone and to pursue "positive" results is itself a philosophical position, although we may not be aware of it because of our lack of interest in philosophy.

The communist system is, of course, based on very explicit philosophical foundations, and the flaws in its dogma are directly responsible for its collapse. People in Eastern Europe do not shy away from philosophical questions; on the contrary, they take a passionate interest in them. Philosophy and literature, especially poetry, really matter. Since I come from Eastern Europe myself, I have found this attitude very congenial.

I recognize that philosophical discussions can be very unproductive. It is only too easy to get bogged down in a never ending argument in which one abstraction begets another. There can be only one excuse for starting at the beginning: I must have something pertinent and significant to say. I believe I do, and I shall say it as simply and directly as I can. Even so, I must ask the reader's indulgence. The subject is very complex. Indeed, that is the gist of my contention: reality is best understood as a complex system, and the participants' thinking is a major source of its complexity.

THINKING VERSUS REALITY

The relationship between thinking and reality has been, in one form or another, at the center of philosophical discourse ever since people became aware of themselves as thinking beings. But, since philosophical discourse is conducted in abstract terms, thinking and reality came to be considered separate categories, and much of the discussion revolved around the relationship between them. Is reality to be defined by our thinking (*cogito ergo sum*), or is our thinking to be defined by reference to reality— that is, a thought is true if and only if it corresponds to reality?

Discussing the relationship between thinking and reality has proved to be very fertile. It has allowed the formulation of basic concepts like truth and knowledge and has provided the foundations of scientific method. As I shall argue later, the distinction between thinking and reality lies at the heart of open society and the critical mode of thinking. But, beyond a certain point, the separation of thinking and reality into independent categories ran into difficulties. The problem was first identified by Epimenides the Cretan when he posed the paradox of the liar. Cretans always lie, he said, bringing into conflict what he said and what he was. The paradox of the liar was treated as an intellectual curiosity for a very long time—until Bertrand Russell made it a centerpiece of his philosophy. Statements must be kept rigorously apart from their subject matter, he insisted, to establish whether they are true or false. He developed a logical method, the theory of types, to accomplish this task.

Logical Positivism

The school of logical positivism carried Lord Russell's argument a step further and proclaimed that statements that cannot be classified as true or false are meaningless. It was a dogma that exalted scientific knowledge as the sole form of understanding worthy of the name and outlawed philosophical discourse. Those who have understood my argument, said Wittgenstein in the conclusion of his *Tractatus Logico Philosophicus*, must realize that everything I have said in the book is meaningless. It seemed like the end of the road for philosophy, and, indeed, it was the culminating point of the attempt to separate thinking and reality.

Soon thereafter, even natural science encountered the boundaries beyond which observations could not be kept apart from their subject matter. Natural science managed to penetrate the barrier, first with Einstein's theory of relativity, then with Heisenberg's uncertainty principle, and more recently with the theory of complex systems, also known as chaos theory. But philosophy has never recovered from the shock of logical positivism. It seems to have disintegrated into particular pursuits. It has continued with the analysis of statements which, under the inspiration of the later Wittgenstein, broadened into an analysis of language. Other schools with which I am less familiar have recognized the ineluctable connection between thinking and being, but they do not seem to offer any great new insights.

Yet exactly what the logical positivists regarded as the end of the road holds the promise of a new beginning. The insight I want to offer here is that the separation between thinking and reality has been overdone. Thinking is part of reality. Instead of separate categories, we have to deal with a relationship between a part and the whole. This puts matters into quite a different perspective from the one with which we are familiar from philosophy.

How can we understand the whole—that is, reality—when the means at our disposal—thinking—is a constituent part of the whole? That is the new way in which the age-old question presents itself, and the failure of logical positivism provides a useful starting point in formulating an answer.

The answer is that whenever our thinking forms part of the subject matter our understanding is bound to be flawed. The participants' imperfect understanding, in turn, becomes part of the situation in which they participate. That is the insight I bring to our understanding of the communist system and its disintegration.

The logical positivists have done their best to banish the participants' imperfect understanding from their universe of discourse. They insisted on perfect knowledge. Propositions had to be true

150

or false; those which could not be classified as one or the other were declared to be meaningless. Their endeavor was not without positive results. There are many propositions in logic, mathematics, and natural science that can meet the criterion established by logical positivism. These propositions qualify as knowledge; moreover, they set a standard by which other propositions can also be judged.

Where logical positivists went too far was in declaring meaningless those propositions which did not meet their standard. People cannot exist by knowledge alone. Their thinking has to deal with situations in which they participate. These situations resemble the one described by Epimenides the Cretan, because what is true depends on what the participants decide. It follows that their decisions cannot be based on knowledge; yet they are meaningful in a way that mere knowledge is not: they actually change the course of events.

The Inherent Imperfection of Human Understanding

It can be seen that logical positivism is fatally flawed: it fails to recognize the role of thinking in shaping reality. But the fallacy can be turned to advantage. Using the criterion established by logical positivism we can assert that the participants' understanding of the situation in which they participate is inherently imperfect. Knowledge is confined to those areas where propositions can be kept separate from the subject matter to which they refer. There are many subjects that can meet this requirement, but there are many others that cannot, and the situation of a thinking participant is certainly one of them. Using knowledge as the yardstick, our understanding of reality is inherently imperfect. This proposition holds good not only for reality as a whole but also for all those aspects of reality in which thinking beings participate. These aspects are too significant to be ignored. We may eschew any consideration of reality as a whole, but we cannot escape the consequences of our imperfect understanding as participants in the events we think about. Whether we accept it, ignore it, or deny it, imperfect understanding is the human condition.

This is as simple and direct a statement of my insight as I am capable of. I want to emphasize, however, that it is not the conclusion of my quest but rather its point of departure. Philosophy, as we know it, has taken either reason or reality as its starting point in trying to understand the relationship between the two and has become bogged down in a never ending debate in trying to establish the primacy of one or the other. Unfortunately, when thinking is part of what one is thinking about, the relationship is a circular one: thinking seeks to formulate a view that corresponds to reality, but it also changes the reality it seeks to comprehend. That is why the participant's understanding of the situation in which he or she participates is inherently imperfect. By taking imperfect understanding as the starting point, we can leave the interminable debate behind us: we can formulate a view of the world in which neither thinking nor reality has primacy but both are interconnected in a circular fashion. Philosophy itself is not much use in formulating such a view, because as long as thinking and reality are treated as separate categories the trap of circular reasoning cannot be avoided; but help is available from a different quarter: the burgeoning science of complex systems.

THE CONCEPT OF REFLEXIVITY

I have been trying to describe the two-way connection between thinking and reality using the categories of philosophical discourse most of my adult life, but time and again I got caught in the web of circular reasoning. I even gave a name to the circular relationship I was trying to describe: reflexivity. Reflexivity bears considerable resemblance to self-reference, a term in logic which is useful in analyzing the paradox of the liar. But reflexivity cannot be described in purely logical terms, because it is not purely a logical phenomenon. On one level it describes a mental process; on the other, it is a process that occurs in reality. I call the mental process the cognitive function and the process that affects reality the participating function. It is clear that the two functions connect thinking and reality in opposite directions: in the cognitive function reality is supposed to be a given and thinking refers to it; in the participating function thinking is supposed to be the constant and reality the dependent variable. But the simultaneous operation of the two functions renders the distinction between thinking and reality illusory: what is supposed to be a purely mental process is also part of reality.

Objective Versus Subjective

I have tried to overcome the difficulty by distinguishing between the objective and subjective aspects of reality. The objective aspect is the way things really are, and the subjective aspect is the way the participants perceive them. According to this scheme, every situation has only one objective aspect but as many subjective aspects as there are participants.

At first sight, such a scheme is appealing, but on further consideration it merely defers the difficulty it is designed to resolve. The trouble is that the objective aspect defies definition. Why this should be so becomes clear when we realize that every subjective aspect must also have its own objective aspect since the participants' thinking is part of the situation. In other words, the objective aspect presents the same problem as reality did in the first place, and if we pursue the scheme to its logical conclusion we face an infinite regression.

I remained bogged down in this infinite regression in one

153

form or another for many years until I abandoned the attempt to formulate the concept of reflexivity in purely philosophical terms. In the meantime I started using the concept experimentally, first as a participant in the financial markets and later as a participant in the demise of the Soviet system. I succeeded as a practitioner where I failed as a theoretician. Eventually, my practical success gave me the courage, and the reputation, to try my hand again at a theoretical formulation of my ideas. The result was *The Alchemy of Finance*, published in 1987, which impressed academics with my financial achievements and confounded financial experts with the obscurity of my philosophy.

The device I employed in the book was to narrow the discussion from reality to "events." It allowed me to distinguish between events and the participants' view of events without encountering the problem of infinite regression. It involved doing some violence to reality—clearly, people think about many things besides the events in which they participate. What is more important, their situation consists of more than a simple succession of events. But that was a small price to pay for escaping the trap of circular reasoning, which had held me captive for more than a quarter of a century. By substituting "events" for reality, I succeeded in turning reflexivity into an operative concept. Using financial markets as a laboratory, I was able to demonstrate its usefulness. That was quite an accomplishment, especially in an age when there is such a strong bias in favor of operative concepts and positive results. I published the book with a great sense of relief, even though it did not fully satisfy me.

Indeterminacy

The paradox of the liar, properly formulated, is logically indeterminate: it is true if it is false and false if it is true. I wanted to express a similar indeterminacy in the situation of the thinking participant. That was the idea I was not able to formulate properly. I recognized that the indeterminacy could not be stated in purely logical terms, because one side of the reflexive relationship involved a sequence of events and the other a sequence of thoughts. Still, I would have liked to prove it with a greater degree of logical rigor than I was capable of. All I could do was to produce a twin feedback mechanism in which the participants' views affected the course of events and events affected the participants' views. The indeterminacy had to be introduced in the form of an assumption: I postulated a divergence between the participants' views and the situation to which they related. I contended that the postulate was more realistic than the alternative, namely the assumption of perfect knowledge, and I had plenty of evidence on my side. Since the assumption of perfect knowledge had served as the foundation of economic theory, my argument had far-reaching implications. Nevertheless, as a statement of the relationship between thinking and reality, it was less than satisfactory.

I built a strong case in favor of imperfect understanding but failed to clinch it. It remained possible to argue that the participants' view of events is fully determined by a combination of their psychological makeup and previous events. The argument is tenuous—it hangs on the belief that the universe we live in is fully determinate and things must happen of necessity—but, at the time I wrote *The Alchemy of Finance*, I was unable to refute it.

COMPLEX SYSTEMS

That is where the theory of complex systems has come to my aid. Chaos theory, as it is popularly known, is only on the verge of attaining respectability in scientific circles. I have seen the head of the Institute of Advanced Studies at Princeton cringe when I mentioned the word. The theory has brought into question some of the basic tenets of scientific method, notably the predictability of complex natural phenomena.

Until the emergence of chaos theory, natural science pursued an analytical approach: it sought to isolate phenomena and discover general rules that could be used to explain and predict them in a timelessly valid, reversible fashion. That means that the same rules can be used for both explanation and prediction, and the fact that the rules are timelessly valid allows them to be tested. As Karl Popper has shown, scientific laws cannot be validated; but testing allows them to be falsified, and scientific laws that have survived testing enjoy an authority that would be otherwise impossible to attain.

Chaos theory tends to undermine this authority. It deals with complex phenomena whose course cannot be determined by timelessly valid laws. They follow an irreversible path in which even slight variances become magnified with the passage of time. Experiments cannot be repeated, and the outcome cannot be predicted. No wonder the scientific establishment feels threatened! The fact remains that chaos theory has been able to shed light on many phenomena, such as the weather, that have previously proved impervious to scientific treatment, and it has made the idea of an indeterminate universe, where events follow a unique, irreversible path, more acceptable.

I believe there is an element of indeterminancy in human affairs that is not present in chaotic natural phenomena like the weather. As Mark Twain said, everybody talks about the weather but nobody does anything about it. Not so in human affairs. What people think influences what happens. Yet what happens does not determine what people think and vice versa. That makes the course of events indeterminate in a more profound sense than in the case of natural phenomena. This point may be easier to accept now that chaos theory has provided a method for studying difficult-to-determine phenomena like the weather.

The Recursive Loop

The theory of complex systems is closely bound up with the development of computers. The exponential growth in computing power has enabled scientists to take a synthetic rather than an analytical approach and to study phenomena that previously defied description. But the connection goes much deeper: it involves the mode of thinking with which the subject is approached. Computer logic works differently from deductive logic. The differences are too broad to be summarized here; I want to focus on one particular point.

Scientific method is grounded in the rules of deductive logic, which requires the rigid separation of statements and their subject matter. Computers are built differently: the distinction between messages and their content is not given *a priori* but is introduced by the messages themselves. That means that they must refer to themselves in some way or another in order to make sense. In practice, computer algorithms take the form of recursive loops and find expression in an iterative process.

The iterative process is peculiar to computers; the human mind employs a variety of shortcuts, which may be lumped together under the collective name of intuition, that computers have a hard time imitating. But the recursive loop cannot be confined to computers; the inherent lack of separation between message and content must apply to the human mind with just as much force as to the computer. Thus, computers have an important lesson to teach us about human thought: there must be a recursive loop in our thinking somewhere, even if we are not aware of it. The loop may take the form of beliefs or postulates. In the case of scientific method, it finds expression in the instruction to ignore recursive loops and accept only statements relating to facts.

The growth of computing power allowed the iterative process to be applied in science, in the form of model building and scenario construction. Iteration implied the use of recursive loops, but at first scientists were unaware of this implication and continued to base their models on theories that ignored recursive connections. Only gradually did the practical experience with model building begin to influence the shape of the theories on which the models were based, and the process is far from complete. Indeed, there is a whole new world view in the making.

I had been aware of the implications of recursive loops when I wrote *The Alchemy of Finance*. I had read Douglas Hofstdter's *Gödel, Escher, Bach: an Eternal Braid*, which was a celebration of recursive relations in all their various manifestations; previously, I had read Gregory Bateson's *Steps to an Ecology of Mind* and had been greatly inspired by both books. Bateson was present at the creation of cybernetics and applied its precepts to many different areas, from alcoholism to schizophrenia to urbanization and the genetic code. Bateson's book, in particular, was instrumental in moving me out of the quicksand into which the concept of self-reference had led me. But I had little or no awareness of the theory of complex systems at that time; my attention was drawn to it by readers of my book. Interestingly, the first person to mention to me the name of Ilya Prigogine—whose book, *Order out of Chaos*, written in partnership with Isabelle Stengers, * is the best introduction for laymen like me—was Hu Weiling, a Chinese scholar who was also instrumental in establishing the Fund for the Reform and Opening of China. Professor Stuart Umpleby of George Washington University and Robert Crosby of the Washington Evolutionary Systems Society also had a hand in my education, introducing me to Peter Allen of the Cranfield Institute of Technology, among others. Peter Allen familiarized

---

* Ilya Prigogine and Isabelle Stengers, *Order out of Chaos: Man's New Dialogue with Nature*, New Science Library (Boulder, Colo.: Shambhala, 1984).

me with practical applications of the theory of complex systems. That is what has prompted me to try again to confront the problem I sidestepped in *The Alchemy of Finance*. Here it goes.

THINKING AS A COMPLEX SYSTEM

We can envision a situation which has thinking participants as a complex system whose complexity is compounded by the participants' thinking. Thinking introduces additional layers or levels of complexity into the system. Participants form their views and take their decisions on one level; the results of their behavior register on another. Those results are, in turn, reflected at a later point in time at the level at which decisions are taken, setting up a feedback loop. Let us call the level at which decisions are made the subjective level, and the level at which the results of the participants' behavior are felt the objective one. Assuming that all decisions are made at the same level, which is already a great simplification, there are as many subjective levels as there are participants. Speaking of just one objective level involves a similar simplification, but it merely serves to strengthen the argument. So far, the framework is the same as I used before.

What is then the relationship between the various levels? Thinking involves forming a picture or building a model of reality at the subjective level. Since the system itself, called reality, contains all levels, we can establish a general rule about these pictures or models which is valid whether the models recognize it or not: the models cannot adequately reproduce reality.

This proposition can be proved using the method developed by Kurt Gödel. My mathematics are not strong enough to do it formally, so I shall do it in words. Gödel numbers denote the laws of mathematics. By combining the laws with the universe to which they relate, Gödel has been able to prove not only

159

that the number of laws is infinite but also that it exceeds the number of laws that can be known, because there are laws about laws about laws *ad infinitum*, and what is to be known expands in step with our knowledge. The same line of reasoning can be applied to reality. To reproduce reality adequately, every model must contain a model of every relevant model—and there are as many models as there are participants. The more levels the models recognize the more levels there are to be recognized— and if the models fail to recognize them, as they must sooner or later, they no longer reproduce reality. Q.E.D.*

Since the models do not correspond to reality, yet serve as the basis for decisions, they play a role in shaping the course of events. Models and events are tied together in a two-way feedback loop: events influence the models (cognitive function) and the models influence events (participating function). The two-way feedback can never produce an identity between the models and reality, because reality is a moving target, moved by the two-way feedback system called reflexivity. The framework is the same as the one I used in *The Alchemy of Finance*, with the difference that I am now able to provide the proof that had eluded me there: thinking and reality cannot correspond.

The Gödel technique and the concept of complex systems do more than just prove a point which I was willing to take for granted anyhow. It opens up a new way of looking at the relation- ship between thinking and reality. Reality is no longer given. It is formed in the same process as the participants' thinking: the more complex the thinking, the more complex reality be- comes. But thinking can never quite catch up with reality: reality is always richer than our comprehension. Thinking interacts with events, but thinking also interacts with other people's think-

---

* It has been pointed out to me by William Newton-Smith that my interpretation of Gödel numbers differs from Gödel's own. Apparently, Gödel envisaged a Platonic universe in which Gödel numbers existed before he discovered them; whereas I think that Gödel numbers were invented by him, thereby enlarging the universe in which he was operating. I think my interpretation makes more sense. It certainly makes Gödel's theorem intuitively easier to accept.

ing and there are events that people do not think about at all. Reality has the power to surprise, and thinking has the power to create. These are features of an interactive and open system called reality.

When we speak of reality we tend to think of the outside world. Yet the comments I have just made apply to the thinking participant with perhaps even greater force than to the outside world. There is a divergence between people as they really are and as they picture themselves, and there is a two-way, reflexive connection between image and reality which is even stronger than in the outside world, because it does not require the mediation of an outside event for thinking to affect its subject matter. If the Gödel method is turned inward, the concept of self can become a complex system whose complexity rivals that of the outside world. A self-centered person's thinking may easily take such an inward direction, endangering his or her contact with the outside world. I know whereof I speak. Interestingly, the complete denial of self, transcendental meditation, may lead to the same result.

The picture of reality that emerges here is quite different from the one we are familiar with. Western philosophical and scientific tradition has led us to envisage two planes, one called reality and the other called knowledge, which lie parallel to each other and, like good Euclidean parallels, touch each other only in infinity. In the new Gödelian universe, neither reality nor our understanding can be envisaged as a flat surface. They both impinge on each other and, where they do so, open up new dimensions each of which has the potential of extending into infinity.

This way of thinking about reality and thinking about thinking strikes me with the force of a revelation. It may not have the same effect on others because, for one thing, the technique has already been established and used in a number of similar arguments; for another, the argument itself is so abstract that its import may not be readily apparent. Yet I consider it of

161

paramount importance exactly because of its level of abstraction.

The Participant's Bias

The point is that the participants' understanding of the situation in which they participate is inherently flawed or biased, and the fallibility of the participants' thinking plays a crucial role in shaping the course of events. There is an indeterminate relationship between thinking and reality in which the participants' views are not determined by reality and reality is, of course, not determined by the participants' thinking.

Strange as it may seem, the point is far from generally accepted. On the contrary, most scientific theories about human affairs deliberately exclude the participants' imperfect understanding from consideration. Classical economic theory, for instance, postulated perfect knowledge; and Marxist doctrine, firmly rooted in the nineteenth century, sought to predict the future course of history on the basis of strictly objective considerations. As I have shown in *The Alchemy of Finance*, the social sciences have gone through incredible contortions in order to eliminate the imperfect understanding of the participants from their subject matter.

Why this strange reluctance to accept a fact of life? Part of the answer must be that the kind of situation I am depicting is extremely complex and very hard to deal with. The human mind is not sufficiently sophisticated to cope with a universe constructed on the principle of infinite regressions and recursive loops. How many people really understand Gödel numbers, myself included? It has taken a long time for Gödel numbers to be discovered, and this is perhaps the first occasion that an attempt has been made to apply them to the human condition. And what a feeble attempt it is!

But this can be only part of the answer. If it were the whole

162

answer, then one could reasonably expect the inherent indeterminacy of human affairs to become generally recognized as soon as the argument of this chapter is properly digested and widely disseminated—assuming, of course, that it will not be falsified in the process. Clearly, that is too much to hope for. The historical evidence indicates that there have been many occasions in the past when the fallibility of human thought was widely recognized and served as an organizing principle of society; but those occasions were followed by others in which a particular set of ideas was accepted as the incontrovertible truth and no dissent was tolerated. Why should history be different in the future?

There is a powerful influence militating against the general acceptance of one's own fallibility. Fallibility implies uncertainty, and in our role as participants we cannot possibly accept the uncertainty which we may recognize in the role of observers. To be a participant means taking decisions; and decisions require a commitment to a particular point of view. We cannot dispense with a set of values even if we recognize that they distort and misinterpret reality.

The fallibility of the participants' thinking that I have enunciated here must be understood in this context. It is not only a theory about the human condition; it also serves as the basis of a value system that may allow us to deal with the complexities of the human condition better than any other principle. I certainly believe so and I have relied on it even before I could prove it. But even if my proof withstands critical examination, it does not follow that it must be generally accepted. Other people may find other value systems more gratifying. Mine has the drawback that it forces one to accept uncertainty. Others may offer the comfort of absolute certainty, although, if my argument is correct, they have the disadvantage of distorting reality. Since we are not dealing with logicians but with participants, there is a genuine choice involved. The choice of principles may vary among participants and from one historical period to the other.

This argument clears the ground for erecting a theoretical

framework based on two opposite simplifying principles. The principle I have developed here is the basis of a critical mode of thinking and an open society; its denial gives rise to a dogmatic mode of thinking and a closed society. The two principles will be explored in depth in Chapter 11. But first I must use the philosophical foundations I have established here to develop a theory of history that can shed light on the rise and fall of the Soviet system.

▫10▫

A Reflexive Theory of History

In order to understand the rise and fall of the Soviet system, or any other historical development, we need a frame of reference. But there is no adequate theory of history into which the course of events readily fits. We have been repeatedly surprised by what has happened.

I believe that the concept of reflexivity I have introduced in the previous chapter can be developed into a theory of history. The theory can help to explain the course of events as it unfolds and to identify the choices as they arise, but it cannot predict the future. The best it can do is indicate the line of least resistance. By the standards of natural science, it does not qualify as a scientific theory, because it cannot provide unequivocal predictions and determinate explanations. But that is as it should be, because the concept of reflexivity implies that history is not determinate. To produce a deterministic theory of history would do violence to its subject matter; but an indeterministic one also encounters difficulties. The most serious is: how can it be tested?

I have relied on my theory of history both in my financial dealings and in my dealings in communist countries. I cannot say that I was never surprised; but I can say that I was better prepared for what happened than most people. My theory is not complete. It does not even seek to be comprehensive. Nevertheless, it has enabled me to anticipate developments and to make sense of them after they have happened. Without belittling the methodological problems involved in testing, I contend that any theory that can throw light on such disparate subjects as the behavior of financial markets and the fate of the Soviet system is worthy of some consideration.

I shall try to state my theory as simply as possible. It starts with the two interrelated propositions I established in the previous chapter. One is that the participants' thinking plays an important part in determining the course of events; the other is that participants always operate with a bias. Their views do not correspond to the situation in the same way in which a scientist's observations are supposed to correspond to the phenomena he is observing. That is so because they are participants and not detached observers. Their thinking affects the situation to which it refers. The participants' bias can take many forms. Perhaps the simplest example is the attitude of a married couple toward each other at the time of their wedding and at the time of their divorce. In financial markets, either a bullish or a bearish bias tends to predominate. But biases can be much more specific. Geopolitics or the belief in the survival of the fittest are biased ideas, as I tried to show in Chapter 4, but the communist attitude toward capital is even more biased, as I explained in Chapter 2.

BIAS AS A FACTOR IN HISTORY

It is no exaggeration to say that *all* ideas are biased, including those which are demonstrably valid. The fact that their validity can be demonstrated tends to enhance their importance so that they are employed, either directly or metaphorically, far outside the sphere of their validity. For instance, most of our demonstrably valid ideas come from natural science; as a consequence, natural science enjoys an exaggerated reputation, and its method is extended beyond the limits of its competence. Both Marx and Freud sought to gain acceptance for their theories by claiming scientific status. In order to do so they couched them in a deterministic form, which rendered them false. As I argued in *The Alchemy of Finance*, social science is a false metaphor.

I shall make no attempt here to define the participants' bias, because it would land me in insuperable philosophical difficulties. I would also have to define what the situation would be if it were not distorted by the participants' bias—a logical impossibility. I can sidestep the issue by simply asserting that there is a distortion involved. What is important is that the distortion not only occurs in the participants' minds but also affects the situation in which they participate.

The absence of bias can be described as a condition of static equilibrium, in which the participants' perceptions correspond to the actual state of affairs. It is an ideal condition which may be postulated but cannot prevail in history, because it would contradict our twin starting propositions. As I explained in the previous chapter, there is a two-way interaction between the participants' view of the world and the actual state of affairs. On the one hand, their view influences events; I call this the participating function. On the other hand, events influence their view; I call this the cognitive function. The two functions work in opposite directions, so that perception and reality are connected by a two-way feedback loop, which I call reflexivity. This gives rise to an irreversible historical process in which neither the situation nor the participants' views remain unaffected.

THE BOOM–BUST PATTERN

To understand reflexivity, let us postulate a prevailing bias and a prevailing trend. Doing so sidesteps the problem of identifying them but allows us to explore the theoretical possibilities. One possibility is that the prevailing bias and the prevailing trend are mutually self-reinforcing, so that the trend develops further than it would have done in the absence of the bias. When that happens, the bias is also strengthened by the fact that it is validated by what is happening in the real world. The divergence between perception and reality gets wider, the longer the self-reinforcing process continues. But it cannot go on forever. Eventually, the distortion in perceptions must become apparent and when it does, the trend—which had become increasingly dependent on the bias—is also subject to correction, causing a reversal in both trend and bias that also becomes mutually self-reinforcing. The reversal tends to be faster and more spectacular than the original process. I call this the boom–bust pattern. It can be observed both in history and in financial markets. In history it leads to revolutions, as in Eastern Europe in 1989, and in financial markets it leads to crashes, as in 1929 or 1987. But that is not the only pattern that can be identified. It is also possible that the prevailing bias and the prevailing trend are initially self-correcting, so that the boom–bust process does not even get started. Alternatively, the bias may be corrected at an early stage. This self-correcting process accounts for stability in society and in financial markets. It is less dramatic but more frequent.

Two Kinds of Interaction

Can we make any worthwhile generalizations about the reflexive interaction between thinking and reality? I believe we can. To start with, if we define a correspondence between theory and reality as equilibrium, we can rule out a condition of static equilibrium for the reasons I have already stated. Two possibilities remain.

The first is a near-equilibrium situation in which the participants learn from experience. They act on the basis of biased views, but there is a critical process at work that tends to correct the bias before it can influence the course of events sufficiently to reinforce the bias. Perfect knowledge remains unattainable, but there is at least a tendency toward correspondence. The participating function ensures that the real world, as experienced by the participants, is constantly changing, but there is a learning mechanism that prevents the participants' bias from getting too far out of line with real events. That is what I call dynamic equilibrium. This state of affairs is characteristic of an open society such as the modern Western World. In such a society critical thought is cultivated. We may call this the "normal" relationship between thinking and reality, because we are familiar with it from everyday experience and it also fits in well with our concept of an equilibrium situation. A theoretical equilibrium need not prevail in the real world as long as there is a tendency toward it.

But we can also encounter conditions in which the participants' views are quite far removed from the way things really are and the two show no tendency to approximate each other. Such conditions are difficult to envisage in theory because they seem to contradict our conception of equilibrium, but we have dealt with them in practice throughout this book. As I have noted, in its heyday the Stalinist system managed to impose a totally distorted view of the word, and now that it is collapsing, the pace of events has accelerated to a point where it exceeds most people's imagination. There is no tendency toward equilibrium either in the rise or in the fall of the Soviet system.

The Concept of Equilibrium

The idea of equilibrium needs to be re-examined, and we shall discover a large element of bias in it. It is closely associated with the concept of knowledge, permanence, and perfection, and it has a strongly positive connotation. The equilibrium, if it exists, is determined by timelessly valid laws which are reversible in the sense that they can be used both to explain and to predict events. Reversibility renders testing easier. Hence the greatest accomplishments of natural science consist in discovering equilibrium in nature. Nothing quite equals the Newtonian system in that respect. Significantly, the Newtonian system functions totally independently of the observer. As soon as the observer becomes a participant, the equilibrium is disturbed. The disturbance occurs at the margin of natural sciences—Heisenberg's uncertainty principle in quantum physics is the classic example—but it goes to the very heart of the so-called social sciences. The participants' bias renders a static equilibrium unattainable; nevertheless, the most "scientific" of the social sciences, economic theory, has struggled long and hard to attain it. It postulated perfect knowledge, and when that became untenable, perfect information in order to determine the theoretical equilibrium. But the postulate is worse than useless for understanding history, because it eliminates what we have recognized as a crucial factor, namely the participant's bias.

By contrast, if we admit the existence of far-from-equilibrium situations where there is not even a tendency toward equilibrium, a whole new approach to the study of historical processes opens up before us. The divergence between thinking and reality assumes central importance, and the participants' bias emerges as a key to understanding history. But to follow up this approach we have to re-evaluate some of our most cherished ideas, notably those which connect scientific method to the concept of equilibrium. I have in mind the model of science first established by my spiritual mentor, Karl Popper, which held that scientific theories are timelessly valid and capable of being falsified—but not verified—by testing. Explanations and predictions based on such theories are logically reversible.

COMPLEX SYSTEMS THEORY

Fortunately natural science has also begun to come to grips with phenomena that are not determined by timelessly valid laws. A whole new body of science, variously called evolutionary or complex systems theory or chaos theory, has sprung up to study irreversible processes. It offers a context and a vocabulary in terms of which the lack of correspondence between perception and reality can be considered. I have in mind particularly the concept of "far-from-equilibrium conditions" introduced by Ilya Prigogine. In far-from-equilibrium conditions the tendency toward equilibrium ceases to prevail.

Natural science carries a lot of weight, exactly because it has been able to produce timelessly valid laws which fit the Popper mold. The social sciences have not been able to equal the natural sciences in this respect, but the habit of trying to imitate the natural sciences has become well established. Therefore, the study of irreversible processes in natural science bodes well for the study of history.

The new approach in natural science cannot be applied to the human sphere too slavishly. Let us recall that our concern is with the relationship between thinking and reality. This means that thoughts as well as events form part of our subject matter. Natural science, by contrast, is concerned exclusively with events, and scientific method consists of keeping events meticulously apart from the statements that refer to them. It can be seen that the pursuit of scientific method in human affairs encounters problems from which the natural sciences are largely exempt. I shall not explore these problems here.* Suffice it to say that the slavish imitation of natural science is not likely to prove any more productive than it did in the past. As I have shown in the previous chapter, the presence of thinking participants adds an element of complexity that is missing in natural phenomena.

STATIC VERSUS DYNAMIC DISEQUILIBRIUM

The novelty in our approach to history is the discovery that under certain circumstances there is no tendency for perception

* I have discussed these matters in *The Alchemy of Finance*.

and reality to approximate each other. We need to explore what these circumstances are.

We may distinguish between two kinds of far-from-equilibrium conditions. At one extreme, participants operate with a fixed bias as, for instance, in a religious community. This is easy to reconcile with static conditions in the real world, but it creates increasing tensions and difficulties when the real world is changing, because the gap between beliefs and facts tend to get too wide. Such static disequilibrium is characteristic of what I call closed society and is found in societies where critical thought is discouraged, such as Egypt under the pharaohs or the Soviet Union under Stalin.

The other possibility is that the interaction between the participants' bias and prevailing conditions intensifies to a point where the participants' views cannot keep up with changes in the real world, and social conditions undergo a revolutionary transformation. This is a possibility that has been rarely considered. It did not figure in the framework I had originally constructed during the 1950s under the influence of my mentor, Karl Popper. But it is inherent in the concept of reflexivity, and its relevance to the current state of affairs in Eastern Europe hardly needs to be pointed out. And of course it fits in well with chaos theory. There are many cases in the natural phenomena studied by chaos theory where a lot happens in a short period of time and little happens over long periods—the history of the universe itself is the prime example.

We may therefore identify three forms that the reflexive interaction between thinking and reality may take: dynamic near-equilibrium, i.e. open society; static far-from-equilibrium, i.e. closed society; and dynamic far-from-equilibrium, i.e. revolution or the boom–bust sequence familiar in financial markets. These three cases may be compared with the three states in which water can be found in nature: liquid, solid, and gaseous. The analogy may be far-fetched, but it is certainly striking. To make it meaningful, we need to identify a demarcation line which

172

separates near-equilibrium from far-from-equilibrium conditions. It need not be as precise and quantitative as the one that separates water and ice, but it must provide an observable distinction; otherwise the whole framework becomes a mere flight of the imagination.

A Criterion of Demarcation

I suggest, as a first approximation, the following criterion: do people recognize a distinction between their own thinking and reality? In a near-equilibrium state, they do; but in far-from equilibrium conditions the distinction becomes blurred. In a closed society, such as Stalin's Soviet Union, the prevailing order takes on a fixed character, and it is difficult to distinguish between the subjective and the objective. In a revolution, almost anything is possible, and the perception of reality ceases to act as a constraining influence on the participants' imagination. I shall try to make this criterion more precise in Chapter 12.

It is easy to see why the criterion is relevant. When people are aware that there is a reality apart from their own thinking, they will exert themselves not to allow their thinking to stray too far. It is much more difficult to determine the conditions in which the separation of thinking and reality will be recognized and respected. The trouble arises because thinking and reality are not, in fact, separate, and to treat them as if they were involves some bias or distortion of the true state of affairs. It is a bias that is deeply ingrained in Western intellectual tradition, but, having established the concept of reflexivity, we must now recognize it as a bias. How can we then use it as demarcation line between near-equilibrium and far-from-equilibrium conditions? The problem is not as insoluble as it may appear because it is part of the concept of reflexivity that a bias can validate itself. Still, the question remains, under what circumstances does the bias prevail? When does a self-correcting mechanism

173

come into play, and when is a boom–bust process set into motion?

There are two demarcation lines to be drawn: one for the static disequilibrium that is characteristic of a closed society and one for the dynamic disequilibrium that typifies revolutions. It is best to deal with them separately. Distinguishing between open and closed society presents less of a problem than separating the near-equilibrium conditions of an open society from the unstable conditions of a boom–bust process. I shall deal with the first issue in Chapter 11 and with the second in Chapter 12. This procedure will have the advantage of letting me present my ideas in more or less the same sequence in which they evolved. The framework of open and closed society dates back to the 1950s; the boom–bust process is a more recent addition. By introducing the framework as I originally envisaged it, I shall make clear the need for a new framework, which also includes the boom–bust process.

A word of caution is in order. I started developing the original framework in my student days. Although I have revised it thoroughly, it differs in style from the rest of the book. Perhaps the most important difference is that it was not written with the collapse of the Soviet system in mind. On the contrary, at the time I wrote it, in the late 1950s, it was more likely that the open societies of the West would succumb to totalitarian pressures than that the closed society of the Soviet empire would spring open. I did not make any attempt to change the perspective—after all, a theoretical framework is supposed to be timelessly valid.

□ 11 □

Open and Closed Societies

In this chapter I shall present the framework of open and closed societies as I originally conceived it—that is to say, as a choice that confronts humanity at the present moment in history.

The constructs, being reflexive, have two aspects. One depicts the way people think, and the other, the way things really are. The two aspects interact in a reflexive fashion: the mode of thinking influences the actual state of affairs, and vice versa, without ever reaching a correspondence between the two.

I must point out a flaw in the construction of the models, as distinct from the distortions in the situations they depict. They are theoretical constructs and not historical ones, but the situations they describe are not timeless but evolutionary. There is a process of learning (and forgetting) involved, and it is not adequately dealt with. The solution I chose was to distinguish between changelessness in its original form (organic society and the traditional mode of thinking) and changelessness imposed later on in the evolutionary process (closed society and the dogmatic mode of thinking). Since then I have found a better solution, which I shall present in the next chapter.

Change is an abstraction. It does not exist by itself but is always combined with a substance that is changing or is subject to change. Of course, the substance in question is also an abstrac-

175

tion, without independent existence. The only thing that really exists is substance-cum-change, which is separated into substance and change by the human mind in its quest to introduce some sense into a confusing universe. Here we are concerned not with changes as they occur in reality, but with change as a concept.

The important point about change as a concept is that it requires abstract thinking. Awareness of change is associated with a mode of thinking characterized by the use of abstractions; lack of awareness reflects the lack of abstractions. We can construct two distinct modes of thinking along these lines.

In the absence of change the mind has to deal only with one set of circumstances: that which exists at the present time. What has gone before and what will come in the future is identical with what exists now. Past, present, and future form a unity, and the whole range of possibilities is reduced to one concrete case: things are as they are because they could not be any other way. This principle tremendously simplifies the task of thinking; the mind needs to operate only with concrete information, and all the complications arising out of the use of abstractions can be avoided. I shall call this the traditional mode of thinking.

Now let us consider a changing world. Man must learn to think of things not only as they are but also as they have been and as they could be. There is then not only the present to consider but an infinite range of possibilities. How can they be reduced to manageable proportions? Only by introducing generalizations, dichotomies, and other abstractions. Once it comes to generalizations, the more general they are, the more they simplify matters. The world is best conceived as a general equation in which the present is represented by one particular set of constants. Change the constants and the same equation will apply to all past and future situations. Working with general equations of this kind, one must be prepared to accept any set of constants that conforms to them. In other words, everything is to be considered possible, unless it has proved to be impossible. I shall call this the critical mode of thinking.

The traditional and the critical modes of thinking are based on two diametrically opposed principles, yet each presents an internally consistent view of reality. How is that possible? Only by presenting a distorted view. But the distortion need not be as great as it would be if it applied to the identical set of circumstances, because, in accordance with the theory of reflexivity, the circumstances are bound to be influenced by the prevailing mode of thinking. The traditional mode of thinking is associated with what I shall call organic society, the critical mode with "open" society. This provides the starting point for the theoretical models I seek to establish.

THE TRADITIONAL MODE OF THINKING

Things are as they have always been—therefore they could not be any other way. This may be taken as the central tenet of the traditional mode of thinking. Its logic is less than perfect; indeed, it contains the built-in flaw we expect to find in our models. The fact that its central tenet is neither true nor logical reveals an important feature of the traditional mode of thinking: it is neither so critical nor so logical as we have learned to be. It does not need to be. Logic and other forms of argument are useful only when one has to choose between alternatives.

Changeless society is characterized by the absence of alternatives. There is only one set of circumstances the human mind has to deal with: the way things are. While alternatives can be imagined, they appear like fairy tales, because the path that would lead to them is missing.

In such circumstances, the proper attitude is to accept things as they seem to be. The scope for speculation and criticism is limited: the primary task of thinking is not to argue but to come to terms with a given situation—a task that can be performed without any but the most pedestrian kind of generalizations.

177

This saves people a great deal of trouble. At the same time, it deprives them of the more elaborate tools of thinking. Their view of the world is bound to be primitive and distorted.

Both the advantages and the drawbacks become apparent when we consider the problems of epistemology. The relationship of thoughts to reality does not arise as a problem. There is no world of ideas separate from the world of facts. Even more important, there seems to be nothing subjective or personal about thinking; it is firmly rooted in the tradition handed down by generations. Its validity is beyond question. Prevailing ideas are accepted as reality itself, or, to be more precise, the distinction between ideas and reality is simply not drawn.

This may be demonstrated by looking at the way language is used. Naming something is like attaching a label to it.* When we think in concrete terms, there is always a "thing" to which a name corresponds, and we can use the name and the thing interchangeably: thinking and reality are co-extensive. Only if we think in abstract terms do we begin giving names to things that do not exist independently of our naming them. We may be under the impression that we are still attaching labels to "things," yet these "things" have come into existence through our labeling them; the labels are attached to something that was created in our mind. This is the point at which thinking and reality become separated.

By confining itself to concrete terms, the traditional mode of thinking avoids the separation. But it has to pay heavily for this supreme simplicity. If no distinction is made between thinking and reality, how can one distinguish between true and false? The only statement that can be rejected is one that does not conform to the prevailing tradition. Traditional views must be accepted automatically because there is no criterion for rejecting them. The way things appear is the way things are: the traditional mode of thinking cannot probe any deeper. It cannot establish

* Ludwig Wittgenstein, *Philosophical Investigations*, I.15.

causal relationships between various occurrences, because these could prove to be either true or false; if they were false there would be a reality apart from our thinking, and the very foundations of the traditional mode of thinking would be undermined. Yet if thinking and reality are to be regarded as identical, an explanation must be provided for everything. The existence of a question without an answer would destroy the unity of thinking and reality just as surely as would the existence of a right and a wrong answer.

Fortunately it is possible to explain the world without recourse to causal laws. Everything behaves according to its nature. Since there is no distinction between natural and supernatural, all questions can be put to rest by endowing objects with a spirit whose influence explains any occurrence whatsoever and eliminates the possibility of internal contradictions. Most objects will seem to be under the command of such a force, because in the absence of causal laws most behavior has an arbitrary quality about it.

When the distinction between thoughts and reality is missing, an explanation carries the same conviction whether it is based on observation or on irrational belief. The spirit of a tree enjoys the same kind of existence as its body, provided we believe in it. Nor do we have any reason to doubt our beliefs: our forefathers believed in the same thing. In this way the traditional mode of thinking with its simple epistemology may easily lead to beliefs that are completely divorced from reality.

To believe in spirits and their magic is equivalent to accepting our surroundings as being beyond our control. This attitude is profoundly appropriate to a changeless society. Since people are powerless to change the world in which they live, their task is to acquiesce in their fate. By humbly accepting the authority of the spirits who rule the world, they may propitiate them; but to probe into the secrets of the universe will not do any good at all. Even if people did discover the causes of certain phenomena, the knowledge would bring no practical advantages unless they believed that they could change the conditions of their existence, which is unthinkable. The only motive for inquiry that remains is idle curiosity; and whatever inclination they may have to indulge in it, the danger of angering the spirits will effectively discourage it. Thus the search for causal explanations is likely to be absent from people's thoughts.

In a changeless society social conditions are indistinguishable from natural phenomena. They are determined by tradition, and it is just as much beyond the power of people to change them as it is to change the rest of their surroundings. The distinction between social and natural laws is one that the traditional mode of thinking is incapable of recognizing. Hence the same attitude of humble submissiveness is required toward society as toward nature.

We have seen that the traditional mode of thinking fails to distinguish between thoughts and reality, truth and falsehood, social and natural laws. If we searched further, other omissions could be found. For instance, the traditional mode of thinking is very vague on the question of time: past, present, and future tend to melt into each other. Such categories are indispensable to us. Judging the traditional mode of thinking from our vantage point, we find it quite inadequate. It is not so, however, in the conditions in which it prevails. In a society that lives by oral tradition, for instance, it can fulfill its function perfectly: it contains all necessary concrete information while avoiding unnecessary complications. It represents the simplest possible way of dealing with the simplest possible world. Its main weakness is not its lack of subtlety but the fact that the concrete information it contains is inferior to that which can be attained by a different approach. This is obvious to us, blessed as we are with superior knowledge. It need not disturb those who have no knowledge other than tradition, but it does make the whole structure extremely vulnerable to outside influences. A rival system of thought can destroy the monopolistic position of existing beliefs and force them to be subjected to critical examination. This would mean the end of the traditional mode of thinking and the beginning of the critical mode.

Take the case of medicine. The tribal medicine man has a completely false picture of the workings of the human body. Long experience has taught him the usefulness of certain treatments, but he is liable to do the right things for the wrong reasons. Nevertheless he is regarded with awe by the tribe; his failures are attributed to the work of evil spirits with whom he is on familiar terms but for whose actions he is not responsible. Only when modern medical science comes into direct competition with primitive medicine does the superiority of correct therapies over mistaken ones become manifest. However grudgingly and suspiciously, the tribe is eventually forced to accept the white man's medicine because it works better.

The traditional mode of thinking may also come up against difficulties of its own making. As we have seen, at least part of the prevailing body of beliefs is bound to be false. Even in a simple and unchanging society, some unusual events occur that must be accounted for. The new explanation may contradict the established one, and the struggle between them might tear apart the wonderfully simple structure of the traditional world. Yet the traditional mode of thinking need not break down every time there is a change in the conditions of existence. Tradition is extremely flexible as long as it is not threatened by alternatives. It encompasses all prevailing explanations by definition. As soon as a new explanation prevails, it automatically becomes the traditional one and, with the distinction between past and present blurred, it will seem to have prevailed since timeless times. In this way, even a changing world may appear to be changeless within fairly wide limits. For instance, the primitive tribes of New Guinea have been able to accommodate themselves to the advent of civilization by adopting the cargo cult.

Traditional beliefs may be able to retain their supremacy even in competition with modern ideas, especially if they are supported by the requisite amount of coercion. Under these circumstances,

181

however, the mode of thinking can no longer be regarded as traditional. It is not the same to declare the principle that things must be as they have always been as to believe in it implicitly. In order to uphold such a principle, one view must be declared correct and all others eliminated. Tradition may serve as the touchstone of what is eligible and what is not, but it can no longer be what it was for the traditional mode of thinking, the sole source of knowledge. To distinguish the pseudo-traditional from the original, I refer to it as the "dogmatic mode of thinking." I shall discuss it separately.

ORGANIC SOCIETY

As we have seen, the traditional mode of thinking does not recognize the distinction between social and natural laws: the social framework is considered just as unalterable as the rest of man's environment. Hence the starting point in a changeless society is always the social Whole and not the individuals who constitute it. While society fully determines the existence of its members, the members have no say in determining the nature of the society in which they live. That has been fixed for them by tradition. This does not mean that there is a conflict of interest between the individual and the Whole in which the individual must always lose out. In a changeless society the individual as such does not exist at all; moreover, the social Whole is not an abstract idea that stands in contrast to the idea of the individual but a concrete unity that embraces all members. The dichotomy between the social Whole and the individual, like so many others, is the result of our habit of using abstract terms. In order to understand the unity that characterizes a changeless society, we must discard some of our ingrained habits of thought, especially our concept of the individual.

The individual is an abstract concept and as such has no place in a changeless society. Society has members, each of whom is capable of thinking and feeling; but, instead of being fundamentally similar, they are fundamentally different according to their station in life.

Just as the individual as an abstraction has no existence, so the social Whole exists not as an abstraction but as a concrete fact. The unity of a changeless society is comparable to the unity of an organism. Members of a changeless society are like organs of a living body. They cannot live outside society, and within it there is only one position available to them: that which they occupy. The functions they fulfill determine their rights and duties. A peasant differs from a priest as greatly as the stomach from the brain. It is true that people have the ability to think and feel, but as their position in society is fixed, the net effect is not very different from what it would be if they had no consciousness at all.

The term "organic society" applies only to a society in which the analogy would never be thought of, and it becomes false the moment it is used. The fact that Menenius Agrippa found it necessary to propose it indicates that the established order was in trouble.

The unity of an organic society is anathema to another kind of unity, that of mankind. Since the traditional mode of thinking employs no abstract concepts, every relationship is concrete and particular. The fundamental similarity of one man to another and the inalienable rights of man are ideas of another age. The mere fact of being human has no rights attached to it: a slave is no different from another chattel in the eyes of the law. Privileges belong more to a position than to a person. For instance, in a feudal society the land is more important than the landlord; the latter derives his privileges only by virtue of the land he holds.

Rights and titles may be hereditary, but this does not turn them into private property. We may be inclined to consider private property as something very concrete; actually it is the opposite. To separate a relationship into rights and duties is already an abstraction; in its concrete form it implies both. The concept of private property goes even further; it implies absolute possession without any obligations. As such, it is diametrically opposed to the principle of organic society, in which every possession carries corresponding obligations. Indeed, private ownership of productive assets cannot be reconciled with organic society, because it would permit the accumulation of capital and introduce a potent source of change. Common ownership, by contrast, ensures that the property will be left unimproved, because every time a person invests his time and energy he bears all the costs but derives only a small part of the benefits. No wonder that the enclosure of common lands marks the beginning of modern agriculture. *

Nor does organic society recognize justice as an abstract principle. Justice exists only as a collection of concrete rights and obligations. Nevertheless, the administration of law involves a certain kind of generalization. Except in a society that is so changeless as to be dead, each case differs in some detail from the previous one, and it is necessary to adapt the precedent in order to make it applicable. Without abstract principles to guide him, it depends upon the judge how he performs this task. There is at least a chance that the new decision will be in conflict with the precedent. Fortunately this need not cause any difficulties since the new ruling itself immediately becomes a precedent that can guide later decisions.

What emerges from such a process is common law, as opposed to legislative statutes. It is based on the unspoken assumption that the decisions of the past continue to apply indefinitely. The assumption is strictly speaking false, but it is so useful that it may continue to prevail long after society has ceased to be

---

* Roman Frydman and Andrzej Rapaczynski, *Markets and Institutions in Large Scale Privatizations* (New York: New York University, C. V. Starr Center, 1990).

organic. The effective administration of justice requires that the rules be known in advance. In view of man's imperfect knowledge, legislation cannot foresee all contingencies, and precedents are necessary to supplement the statutes. Common law can function side by side with statute law because, in spite of the underlying assumption of changelessness, it can imperceptibly adjust itself to changing circumstances. By the same token organic society could not survive the codification of its laws, because it would lose its flexibility. Once laws are codified the appearance of changelessness cannot be maintained and organic society disintegrates. Fortunately, the need to codify laws, draw up contracts, or record tradition in any permanent way is not very pressing as long as tradition is not threatened by alternatives.

The unity of organic society means that its members have no choice but to belong to it. It goes even further. It implies that they have no desire but to belong to it, for their interests and those of society are the same: they identify themselves with society. Unity is not a principle proclaimed by the authorities but a fact accepted by all participants. No great sacrifice is involved. One's place in society may be onerous or undignified, but it is the only one available; without it, one has no place in the world.

Nevertheless, there are bound to be people who do not abide by the prevailing mode of thinking. How society deals with such people is the supreme test of its adaptability. Repression is bound to be counterproductive because it provokes conflict and may encourage the evolution of alternative ways of thinking. Tolerance mixed with disbelief is probably the most effective answer. Craziness and madness in all its variety can be particularly useful in dealing with people who think differently, and primitive societies are noted for their tolerance of the mentally afflicted.

It is only when traditional ties are sufficiently loosened to enable people to change their relative positions within society by their own efforts that they come to dissociate their own interests from those of the Whole. When this happens, the unity of organic society falls apart, and everyone seeks to pursue his self-interest. Traditional relationships may be preserved in such circumstances, too, but only by coercion. That is no longer a truly organic society but one that is kept artificially changeless, like the Soviet system. The distinction is the same as that between the traditional and dogmatic modes of thinking, and to emphasize it I shall refer to this state of affairs as Closed Society.

THE CRITICAL MODE OF THINKING

Abstractions

As long as people believe that the world is changeless, they can rest happily with the conviction that their view of the world is the only conceivable one. Tradition, however far removed from reality, provides guidance, and thinking need never move beyond the consideration of concrete situations.

In a changing world, however, the present does not slavishly repeat the past. Instead of a course fixed by tradition, people are confronted by an infinite range of possibilities. To introduce some order into an otherwise confusing universe they are obliged to resort to simplifications, generalizations, abstractions, causal laws, and all kinds of other mental aids.

Thought processes not only help to solve problems; they create their own. Abstractions open reality to different interpretations. Since they are only aspects of reality, one interpretation does not exclude all others: every situation has as many aspects as the mind discovers in it. If this feature of abstract thinking were fully understood, abstractions would create fewer problems. People would realize that they are dealing with a simplified image of the situation and not the situation itself. But even if everyone were fully versed in the intricacies of modern linguistic philosophy, the problems would not disappear, because abstractions play a dual role. In relation to the things they describe they represent aspects of reality without having a concrete existence themselves. For instance, the law of gravity does not make apples fall to the ground but merely explains the forces that do. In relation to the people who employ them, however, abstractions are very much a part of reality: by influencing attitudes and actions they have a major impact on events. For instance, the discovery of the law of gravity changed people's behavior. Insofar as people think about their own situation, both roles come into play simultaneously, and the situation becomes reflexive. Instead of a clear-cut separation between thoughts and reality, the infinite variety of a changing world is compounded by the infinite variety of interpretations that abstract thinking can produce.

Abstract thinking tends to create categories which contrast opposite aspects of the real world against each other. Time and Space; Society and the Individual; Material and Ideal are typical dichotomies of this kind. Needless to say, the models I am constructing here also belong to the collection. These categories are no more real than the abstractions that gave rise to them. That is to say, they represent a simplification or distortion of reality in the first place but, through their influence on people's thinking, may also introduce divisions and conflicts into the real world. They contribute to making reality more complex and abstractions more necessary. In this way the process of abstraction feeds on itself: the complexities of a changing world are, to a large extent, of man's own making.

In view of the complications, why do people employ abstract concepts at all? The answer is that they avoid them as much as possible. As long as the world can be regarded as changeless, they use no abstractions at all. Even when abstractions become indispensable, they prefer to treat them as part of reality rather than as the product of their own thinking. Only bitter experience will teach them to distinguish between their own thoughts and reality. The tendency to neglect the complications connected

187

with the use of abstractions must be regarded as a weakness of the critical mode of thinking, because abstractions are indispensable to it, and the less they are understood, the greater confusion they create.

Despite their drawbacks, abstractions serve us well. It is true that they create new problems, but the mind responds to these with renewed efforts until thinking reaches degrees of intricacy and refinement that would be unimaginable in the traditional mode. A changing world does not lend itself to the kind of certainty that would be readily available if society were changeless, but in its less than perfect way thinking can provide much valuable knowledge. Abstractions generate an infinite variety of views; as long as a fairly effective method is available for choosing between them, the critical mode should be able to come much closer to reality than the traditional mode, which has only one interpretation at its disposal.

The Critical Process

Choosing between alternatives may then be regarded as the key function of the critical mode of thinking. How is this task performed?

First, since there is a divergence between thinking and reality, one set of explanations will fit a given situation better than another. All outcomes are not equally favorable; all explanations are not equally valid. Reality provides an inducement to choose and a criterion by which the choice may be judged. Second, since our understanding of reality is imperfect, the criterion by which choices may be judged is not fully within our grasp. As a result, people will not necessarily make the correct choice and, even if they do, not everybody will accept it as such. Moreover, the correct choice represents merely the better of the available alternatives, not the best of all possible solutions. New ideas and interpretations may emerge at any time. These are also bound to be flawed and may have to be discarded when the flaws become apparent. There is no final answer, only the possibility of a gradual approximation to it. It follows that the choice between alternatives involves a continuous process of critical examination rather than the mechanical application of fixed rules.

It is to emphasize these points that I speak of "the critical mode of thinking." The expression should not be taken to suggest that in a changing world everyone maintains an open mind. People may still commit themselves unreservedly to a particular view; but they cannot do so without at least being aware of alternatives. The traditional mode of thinking accepts explanations uncritically, but, in a changing society, no one can say "this is how things are, therefore they cannot be any other way." People must support their views with arguments. Otherwise they will convince no one but themselves, and to believe unconditionally in an idea rejected by everyone else is a form of madness. Even those who believe they have the final answer must take into account possible objections and defend themselves against criticism.

The critical mode of thinking is more than an attitude: it is a prevailing condition. It denotes a situation in which there are a large number of divergent interpretations; their proponents seek to gain acceptance for the ideas in which they believe. If the traditional mode of thinking represents an intellectual monopoly, the critical mode can be described as intellectual competition. This competition prevails regardless of the attitude of particular individuals or schools of thought. Some of the competing ideas are tentative and invite criticism; others are dogmatic and defy opposition. One could expect all thinking to embody a critical attitude only if people were completely rational—a contradiction of our basic premise.

Critical Attitude

It can be argued that a critical attitude is more appropriate to the circumstances of a changing world than a dogmatic one.

189

Tentative opinions are not necessarily correct, and dogmatic ones need not be completely false. But a dogmatic approach can only lose some of its persuasive force when conflicting views are available: criticism is a danger, not a help. By contrast, a critical attitude can and does benefit from the criticism offered; the view held will be modified until no further valid objection can be raised. Whatever emerges from this rigorous treatment is likely to fulfill its purpose more effectively than the original proposition.

Criticism is basically unpleasant and hard to take. It will be accepted, if at all, only because it is effective. It follows that people's attitude greatly depends on how well the critical process functions; conversely, the functioning of the critical process depends on people's attitude. This circular, reflexive relationship is responsible for giving the critical mode of thinking its dynamic character, as opposed to the static permanence of the traditional mode.

What makes the critical process effective? To answer this question, we must recall the demarcation line between near-equilibrium and far-from-equilibrium conditions introduced in the previous chapter. If there is a clear separation between thinking and reality, people have a reliable criterion for recognizing and correcting bias before it becomes too influential. But when the participating function is actively at work, bias and trend become hard to disentangle. Thus, the effectiveness of the critical process varies according to the subject matter and purpose of thinking. But even in those areas where the separation is not given by nature, it can be introduced by thinking.

Scientific Method

The critical process functions most effectively in natural science. Scientific method has been able to develop its own rules and conventions on which all participants are tacitly agreed. These rules recognize that no individual, however gifted and honest, is capable of perfect understanding; theories must be submitted to critical examination by the scientific community. Whatever emerges from this interpersonal process will have reached a degree of objectivity of which no individual thinker would be capable.

Scientists adopt a thoroughly critical attitude not because they are more rational or tolerant than ordinary human beings but because scientific criticism is less easily disregarded than other forms: their attitude is more a result of the critical process than a cause of it. The effectiveness of scientific criticism is the result of a combination of factors. On the one hand, nature provides easily available and reliable criteria by which the validity of theories can be judged; on the other hand, there is a strong inducement to recognize and abide by these criteria: nature operates independently of our wishes, and we cannot utilize it to our benefit without first understanding how it works. Scientific knowledge not only serves to establish the truth; it also helps us in the business of living. People might have continued to live quite happily believing that the Earth was flat, despite Galileo's experiments. What rendered his arguments irresistible was the gold and silver found in America. The practical results were not foreseen: indeed, they would not have been achieved if scientific research had been confined to purely practical objectives. Yet they provided the supreme proof for scientific method: only because there is a reality, and because man's knowledge of it is imperfect, was it possible for science to uncover certain facets of reality whose existence people had not even imagined.

Outside the realm of natural phenomena the critical process is less effective. In metaphysics, philosophy, and religion the criteria are missing; in social science the inducement to abide by them is not so strong. Nature operates independently of our wishes; society, however, can be influenced by the theories that relate to it. In natural science theories must be true to be effective; not so in the social sciences. There is a shortcut: people can be swayed by theories. The urge to abide by the conventions of science is less compelling, and the interpersonal process suffers as a result. Theories seeking to change society may take on a scientific guise in order to exploit the reputation science has gained without abiding by its conventions. The critical process offers little protection, because the agreement on purpose is not as genuine as in the case of natural science. There are two criteria by which theories can be judged—truth and effectiveness—and they no longer coincide.

The remedy proposed by most champions of scientific method is to enforce the rules developed by natural science with redoubled vigor. Karl Popper has proposed the doctrine of the unity of science: the same methods and criteria apply in the study of both natural and social phenomena. As I have argued in *The Alchemy of Finance*, I consider the doctrine misguided. There is a fundamental difference between the two pursuits: the subject matter of the social sciences is reflexive in character, and reflexivity destroys the separation between statement and fact which has made the critical process so effective in the natural sciences. The very expression "social science" is a false metaphor; it would seem more appropriate to describe the study of social phenomena as alchemy, because the phenomena can be molded to the will of the experimenter in a way that natural substances cannot. Calling the social sciences alchemy would preserve the critical process better than the doctrine of the unity of science. It would acknowledge that the criteria of truth and effectiveness do not coincide, and it would prevent social theories from exploiting the reputation of natural science. It would open avenues of investigation that are currently blocked: differences in the subject matter would justify differences in approach. The social sciences have suffered immeasurably from trying to imitate the natural sciences too slavishly.

Democracy

Having abandoned the convention of objectivity, how are social theories to be judged? The artificial distinction between scientific

192

theories, which purport to describe society as it is, and political ones, which seek to decide how it should be, disappears, leaving ample room for differences of opinion. The various views divide into two broad classes: one contains those that propose a fixed formula; the other makes the organization of society dependent on the decisions of its members. As we are not dealing with scientific theories, there is no objective way of deciding which approach is correct. It can be shown, however, that the latter represents a critical attitude, while the former does not.

Definitive social schemes assume that society is subject to laws other than those enacted by its members; moreover, they claim to know what those laws are. This makes them impervious to any positive contributions from the critical process. On the contrary, they must actively seek to suppress alternative views because they can command universal acceptance only by forbidding criticism and preventing new ideas from emerging—in short, by destroying the critical mode of thinking and arresting change. If, by contrast, people are allowed to decide questions of social organization for themselves, solutions need not be final: they can be reversed by the same process by which they were reached. Everyone is at liberty to express his or her views, and, if the critical process is working effectively, the view that eventually prevails may come close to representing the best interests of the participants. This is the principle of democracy.

For democracy to function properly, certain conditions must be met. They may be compared to those which have made scientific method so successful: in the first place there must be a criterion by which conflicting ideas can be judged, and in the second there must be a general willingness to abide by that criterion. The first prerequisite is provided by the majority vote as defined by the constitution, and the second by a belief in democracy as a way of life. A variety of opinions is not enough to create democracy; if separate factions adopt opposing dogmas the result is not democracy but civil war. People must believe

193

in democracy as an ideal: they must consider it more important that decisions be reached by constitutional means than to see their view prevail. This condition will be satisfied only if democracy does in fact produce a better social organization than a dictatorship would.

There is a circular relationship here: democracy can serve as an ideal only if it is effective, and it can be effective only if it is generally accepted as an ideal. This relationship has to evolve through a reflexive process in which the achievements of democracy reinforce democracy as an ideal and *vice versa*. Democracy cannot be imposed by edict.

The similarity with science is striking. The convention of objectivity and the effectiveness of scientific method are also mutually dependent on one another. Science relies on its discoveries to break the vicious circle: they speak more eloquently in its favor than any argument. Democracy, too, requires positive accomplishments to ensure its existence: an expanding economy, intellectual and spiritual stimulation, a political system that satisfies man's aspirations better than rival forms of government.

Democracy is capable of such achievements. It gives free rein to what may be called the positive aspect of imperfect knowledge, namely creativity. There is no way of knowing what that will produce; the unforeseen results may provide the best justification for democracy, just as they do for science. But progress is not assured. The positive contributions can come only from the participants. The results of their thinking cannot be predicted; they may or may not continue to make democracy a success. Belief in democracy as an ideal is a necessary but not a sufficient condition of its existence. This makes democracy as an ideal very tricky indeed. It cannot be enforced by eliminating rival views; its success cannot be guaranteed even by gaining universal acceptance for the ideal. Democracy simply cannot be assured, because it remains conditional on the creative energies of those who participate in it. Yet it must be regarded as an ideal if it is to prevail. Those who believe in it must put their faith in the positive aspect of imperfect knowledge and hope that it will produce the desired results.

The Quest for Certainty

Democracy as an ideal leaves something to be desired. It does not provide a definite program, a clear-cut goal, except in those cases where people have been deprived of it. Once people are free to pursue alternative goals, they are confronted by the necessity of deciding what their goals are. And that is where a critical attitude is less than totally satisfactory. It is generally assumed that people will seek to maximize their material well-being. That is true as far as it goes, but it does not go far enough. People have aspirations beyond material well-being. These may surface only after the material needs have been satisfied; but often they take precedence over narrow self-interest. One such aspiration is the creative urge. It is likely that material wealth is being pursued in modern Western society long after material needs have been filled exactly because the pursuit gratifies the creative urge. In other societies, wealth has ranked much lower in the hierarchy of values and the creative urge has found other means of expression. For instance, people in Eastern Europe care much more about poetry and philosophy than do people in the West.

There is another set of aspirations that the critical attitude is singularly ill-equipped to satisfy: the quest for certainty. Natural science can produce firm conclusions because it has an objective criterion at its disposal. Social science is on far shakier grounds, because reflexivity interferes with objectivity; when it comes to creating a dependable value system, a critical attitude is not much use at all. It is very difficult to base a value system on the individual. For one thing, individuals are subject to the ultimate in uncertainty, death. For another, they are part of the situation they have to cope with. Truly independent thought is an illusion. External influences, be it family, peer group, or merely the spirit of the age, are much more potent than one would care to admit. Yet we need an independent set of values if the perils of disequilibrium are to be avoided.

The traditional mode of thinking meets the quest for certainty much more effectively than the critical mode. It draws no distinction between belief and reality: religion, or its primitive equivalent, animism, embraces the entire sphere of thought and commands unquestioning allegiance. No wonder people hanker after the lost paradise of primeval bliss! Dogmatic ideologies promise to satisfy that craving. The trouble is that they can do so only if they eliminate conflicting beliefs. This makes them almost as dangerous to democracy as the existence of alternative explanations is to the traditional mode of thinking.

The success of the critical mode of thinking in other areas may help to minimize the importance attached to dogmatic beliefs. There is an area of vital interest, namely, the material conditions of life, where positive improvement is possible. The mind tends to concentrate its efforts where they can produce results, neglecting questions of a less promising nature. That is why business takes precedence over poetry in Western society. As long as material progress can be maintained—and continues to be enjoyed—the influence of dogma can be contained.

OPEN SOCIETY

Perfect Competition

A perfectly changeable society seems difficult to imagine. Surely, society must have a permanent structure and institutions that ensure its stability. Otherwise, how could it support the intricate relationships of a civilization? Yet not only can the perfectly changeable society be postulated, but it has already been extensively studied in the theory of perfect competition. Perfect competition provides economic units with alternative situations that are only marginally inferior to the one they actually occupy. Should there be the slightest change in circumstances, they are ready to move; in the meantime their dependence on present relationships is kept at a minimum. The result is a perfectly changeable society that may not be changing at all.

I am in fundamental disagreement with the theory of perfect competition, but I shall use it as my starting point, because it is relevant to the concept of a perfectly changeable society. By showing how I differ from the approach taken by classical economics, I can throw more light on the concept than if I tried to approach it independently. My basic objection to the theory of perfect competition is that it produces a static equilibrium, while I maintain that a static equilibrium is a theoretical impossibility.

Perfect competition is described by economic theory in the following way: a large number of individuals, each with his or her own scale of values, is faced with a large number of alternatives among which they can freely choose. If each man chooses rationally he will end up with the alternative most to his liking. Classical theory then goes on to argue that, owing to the large number of alternatives, the choice of one individual does not interfere with the alternatives available to others, so that perfect competition leads to an arrangement that would maximize everyone's welfare.

The argument itself will be dealt with later; let us first consider the assumptions. The theory assumes that there is a large number of units, each with perfect knowledge and mobility. Each unit has its own scale of preferences and is faced with a given scale of opportunities. Even a cursory examination shows that these assumptions are completely unrealistic. The lack of perfect knowledge is one of the starting points of this study, and of scientific method in general. Perfect mobility would negate fixed assets and specialized skills, both of which are indispensable to the

197

capitalistic mode of production. The reason economists have tolerated such unacceptable assumptions for so long is that doing so produced results that were considered desirable in more ways than one. First, it established economics as a science comparable in status with physics. The resemblance between the static equilibrium of perfect competition and Newtonian thermodynamics is no coincidence. Second, it proved the point that perfect competition maximizes welfare.

In reality, conditions approximate those of perfect competition only when new ideas, new products, new methods, and new preferences keep people and capital on the move. Mobility is not perfect: it is not without cost to move. But people are on the move nevertheless, attracted by better opportunities or dislocated by changing circumstances, and once they start moving they tend toward the more attractive opportunities. They do not have perfect knowledge but, being on the move, are aware of a larger number of alternatives than if they occupied the same position all their lives. They will object to other people taking their places, but, with so many opportunities coming up, their attachment to the existing situation is less strenuous, and they will be less able to align support from others who are actually or potentially in the same situation. As people move more often, they develop a certain facility in adjusting, which reduces the importance of any specialized skills they may have acquired. What we may call "effective mobility" replaces the unreal concept of perfect mobility, and the critical mode of thinking takes the place of perfect knowledge. The result is not perfect competition as defined in economics but a condition I shall call "effective competition." What sets it apart from perfect competition is that values and opportunities, far from being fixed, are constantly changing.

Should equilibrium ever be reached, the conditions of effective competition would cease to apply. Every unit would occupy a specific position, which would be less easily available to others for the simple reason that he would fight to defend it. Having developed special skills, moving would involve him in a loss. He would resist any encroachment. If necessary, he would rather take a cut in remuneration than make a move, especially as he would then have to fight someone else's vested interest. In view of his entrenched position and the sacrifices he would be willing to make to defend it, an outsider would find it difficult to compete. Instead of almost unlimited opportunities, each unit would then be more or less tied to the existing arrangement. And, not being endowed with perfect knowledge, they might not even realize the opportunities they are missing. A far cry from perfect competition!

Instability

The differences with the classical analysis of perfect competition are worth pursuing. To some extent I have already done so in *The Alchemy of Finance*, but I did not present my argument as strongly there as I could have. I did not insist that there is a flaw in the very foundations of economic theory: it assumes that the demand and supply curves are independently given, and that is not necessarily the case. The shape of the demand curve may be altered by advertising or, even worse, may be influenced by price movements. That happens particularly in financial markets, where trend-following speculation is rampant. People are buying futures contracts not because they want to own the underlying commodity but because they want to make a profit on them. The same may be true of stocks, bonds, currencies, real estate, or even art. The prospects for profit depend not on the intrinsic value of the underlying objects but on the intentions of other people to buy and sell as expressed by the movement in prices.

According to economic theory, prices are determined by demand and supply. What happens to prices when the demand and supply curves are themselves influenced by price movements? The answer is that they are not determined at all. The situation is unstable, and in an unstable situation trend-following specula-tion is often the best strategy. Moreover, the more people adopt it, the more rewarding it becomes, because the trend in prices acts as an ever more important factor in determining the trend in prices. Price movements feed on themselves until prices be-come totally unrelated to intrinsic values. Eventually, the trend becomes unsustainable and a crash ensues. The history of finan-cial markets is littered with such boom and bust sequences. This is far-from-equilibrium territory where the distinction be-tween fundamentals and valuations is blurred, and instability reigns.

Clearly the contention that independently given supply and demand curves determine prices is not based on fact. On closer examination, it turns out to be a partially self-validating illusion, because its widespread acceptance can be helpful in fostering stability. Once it is recognized as an illusion, the task of maintain-ing stability in financial markets can get awfully complicated.

It can be seen that instability is an endemic problem in a market economy. Instead of equilibrium, the free play of market forces produces a never ending process of change in which excesses of one kind yield to those of another. Under certain conditions, particularly where credit is involved, the disequilibrium may become cumulative until a breaking point is reached.

This conclusion opens a Pandora's box. Classical analysis is based entirely on self-interest; but if the pursuit of self-interest does *not* lead to a stable system, the question arises whether individual self-interest is sufficient to ensure the survival of the system. The answer is a resounding "no." The stability of finan-cial markets can be preserved only by some form of regulation. And once we make stability a policy objective, other worthy causes follow. Surely, in conditions of stability, competition must also be preserved. Public policy aimed at preserving sta-bility and competition and who knows what else is at logger-heads with the principle of *laissez-faire*. One of them must be wrong.

The nineteenth century can be invoked as an age in which *laissez-faire* was the generally accepted and actually prevailing economic order in a large part of the world. Clearly, it was not characterized by the equilibrium claimed by economic theory. It was a period of rapid economic advance during which new methods of production were invented, new forms of economic organization were evolving, and the frontiers of economic activity were expanding in every direction. The old framework of economic controls had broken down; progress was so rapid that there was no time for planning it; developments were so novel that there was no known method of controlling them. The mechanism of the state was quite inadequate for taking on additional tasks; it was hardly in a position to maintain law and order in the swollen cities and on the expanding frontiers.

As soon as the rate of growth slowed down, the mechanisms of state regulation began to catch up with the requirements made on it. Statistics were collected, taxes were gathered, and some of the more blatant anomalies and abuses of free competition were corrected. As new countries embarked on a course of industrialization, they had the example of others before them. For the first time the state was in a position to exercise effective control over industrial development, and people were given a real choice between *laissez-faire* and planning. As it happened, this marked the end of the golden age of *laissez-faire:* protectionism came first, and other forms of state control followed later.

By the beginning of the twentieth century the state was in a position to set the rules by which the game was played. And when the instability of the financial markets led to a general breakdown of the banking system, causing the Great Depression of the 1930s, the state was ready to step into the breach.

The principle of *laissez-faire* has enjoyed a strong revival in recent years. President Reagan invoked the magic of the marketplace, and Margaret Thatcher encouraged the survival of the fittest. Again, we are living in a period of rapid change, innovation, and instability. But the principle of *laissez-faire* just as flawed as it was in the nineteenth century.

The fact is that every social system, every human construct is flawed, and discovering the drawbacks of one arrangement ought not to be used to justify its opposite. Doing so is a common fault. One of the major lessons to be learned from recent experience is that narrow self-interest does not provide an adequate set of values for dealing with the policy issues confronting us today. We need to invoke broader values that relate to the survival of the system and not merely to the prosperity of the individual participant. This is a point to which I shall return when I consider the question of values.

Freedom

Effective competition does not produce equilibrium, but it does maximize the freedom of the individual by reducing his dependence on existing relationships. Freedom is generally regarded as a right or a series of rights—freedom of speech, of movement, of worship—enforced by law or the Constitution. This is too narrow a view. I prefer to give the word a wider meaning. I regard freedom as the availability of alternatives. If the alternatives to one's current situation are greatly inferior, or if moving involves great effort and sacrifice, people remain dependent on existing arrangements and are exposed to all kinds of restraints, insults, and exploitation. If they have alternatives at their disposal that are only marginally inferior, they are free from these pressures. Should pressure be applied, they merely move on. Freedom is then a function of people's ability to detach themselves from their existing positions. When the alternatives are only marginally inferior, freedom is maximized.

This is very different from the way people usually look at freedom, but then freedom is generally regarded as an ideal and not as a fact. As an ideal, freedom is generally associated with sacrifice. As a fact, it consists of being able to do what one wants without having to make sacrifices for it.

People who believe in freedom as an ideal may fight for it passionately, but they do not necessarily understand it. Since it serves them as an ideal, they tend to regard it as an unmitigated blessing. As a matter of fact, freedom is not devoid of undesirable aspects. When the sacrifices have borne fruit and freedom is accomplished, this may become more apparent than it was when freedom was only an ideal. The aura of heroism is dispelled, the solidarity based on a common ideal dissipated. What is left is a multitude of individuals, each pursuing his own self-interest as he perceives it. It may or may not coincide with the public interest. This is freedom as it is to be found in an open society, and it may seem disappointing to those who have fought for it.

Private Property

Freedom, as defined here, extends not only to human beings but to all other means of production. Land and capital can also be "free" in the sense that they are not tied to particular uses but are provided with marginally graduated alternatives. This is a prerequisite of the institution of private property.

Factors of production are always employed in conjunction with other factors, so that any change in the employment of one must have an influence on the others. As a consequence, wealth is never truly private; it impinges on the interests of others. Effective competition reduces the dependence of one factor upon another, and under the unreal assumptions of perfect competition the dependence disappears altogether. This relieves the owners of any responsibility toward other participants and provides a theoretical justification for regarding private property as a fundamental right.

It can be seen that the concept of private property needs the theory of perfect competition to justify it. In the absence of the

203

unreal assumptions of perfect mobility and perfect knowledge, property carries with it not only rights but also obligations toward the community.

Effective competition also favors private ownership, but in a more qualified manner. The social consequences of individual decisions are diffuse, and adverse effects are cushioned by the ability of the affected factors to turn to alternatives. The social obligations associated with wealth are correspondingly vague and generalized, and there is much to be said for property being privately owned and managed, especially as the alternative of public ownership has worse drawbacks. But, in contrast to classical analysis, private ownership rights cannot be regarded as absolute, because competition is not perfect.

Social Contract

When freedom is a fact, the character of society is determined entirely by the decisions of its members. Just as in an organic society the position of the members could be understood only in relation to the Whole, now the Whole is meaningless by itself and can be understood only in terms of the individuals' decisions. It is to underscore this contrast that I use the term "open society." A society of this kind is likely to be open also in the more usual sense that people are able to enter and leave at will, but that is incidental to my meaning.

In a civilized society people are involved in many relationships and associations. While in organic society these are determined by tradition, in open society they are shaped by the decisions of the individuals concerned: they are regulated by written and unwritten contract. Contractual ties take the place of traditional ones.

Traditional relationships are closed in the sense that their terms and conditions are beyond the control of the interested parties. For instance, the inheritance of land is predetermined;

so is the relationship between serf and landlord. Relationships are closed also in the sense that they apply only to those who are directly involved and do not concern anyone else. Contractual relationships are open in the sense that the terms are negotiated by the interested parties and can be altered by mutual agreement. They are also open in the sense that the contracting parties can be replaced by others. Contracts are often publicly known, and flagrant discrepancies between arrangements covering similar situations are corrected by competition.

In a sense, the difference between traditional and contractual relationships corresponds to that between concrete and abstract thought. While a traditional relationship applies only to those who are directly involved, the terms of a contract may be considered to have universal validity.

If relationships are determined by the participants, then membership in the various institutions that constitute civilized society ought also to be the subject of a contract. It is this line of reasoning that has led to the concept of a social contract. As originally expounded by Rousseau, the concept has neither theoretical nor historical validity. To define society in terms of a contract freely entered into by completely independent individuals would be misleading; and to attribute the historical genesis of civilized society to such a contract would be an anachronism. Nevertheless, Rousseau's concept pinpoints the essence of open society as clearly as Menenius Agrippa's allegory defined organic society.

Open society may be regarded as a theoretical model in which all relations are contractual in character. The existence of institutions with compulsory or limited membership does not interfere with this interpretation. Individual freedom is assured as long as there are several different institutions of roughly equal standing open to each individual so that he can choose which one to belong to. This holds true even if some of those institutions, such as the state, carry compulsory powers, and others, such as social clubs, limit their membership. The state cannot oppress individuals, because they can contract out by emigrating; social clubs cannot ostracize them, because they can contract in elsewhere.

Open society does not ensure equal opportunities to all. On the contrary, if a capitalistic mode of production is coupled with private property, there are bound to be great inequalities which, left to themselves, tend to increase rather than diminish. Open society is not necessarily classless; in fact, it is difficult—although not impossible—to imagine it as such. How can the existence of classes be reconciled with the idea of open society? The answer is simple. In open society classes are merely generalizations about social strata. Given the high level of social mobility, there can be no class consciousness of the kind Marx spoke about. His concept applies only to a closed society, and I shall discuss it more fully under that heading.

Brave New World

Let me try to carry the concept of an open society to its logical conclusion and describe what a perfectly changeable society would look like. Alternatives would be available in all aspects of existence: in personal relations, opinions and ideas, productive processes and materials, social and economic organization, and so on. In these circumstances, the individual would occupy a paramount position. Members of an organic society possess no independence at all; in a less than perfectly changeable society, established values and relationships still circumscribe people's behavior; but in a perfectly open society none of the existing ties are final, and people's relation to nation, family, and their fellows depends entirely on their own decisions. Looking at the reverse side of the coin, this means that the permanence of social relationships has disappeared; the organic structure of society has disintegrated to the point where its atoms, the individuals, float around without any roots.

How the individual chooses among the alternatives available to him or her is the subject matter of economics. Economic analysis therefore provides a convenient starting point. All that is necessary is to extend it. In a world in which every action is a matter of choice, economic behavior characterizes all fields of activity. That does not necessarily mean that people pay more attention to the possession of goods than to spiritual, artistic, or moral values, but merely that all values can be reduced to monetary terms. This renders the principles of the market mechanism relevant to such far-ranging areas as art, politics, social life, sex, and religion. Not everything that has value is subject to buying and selling, because there are some values that are purely personal and therefore cannot be exchanged (e.g. maternal love), others that lose their value in the process of exchange (e.g. reputation), and still others that it would be physically impossible or illegal to trade (e.g. the weather or political appointments). Still, in a perfectly changeable society the scope of the market mechanism would be extended to its utmost limit. Even where the operation of market forces is regulated by legislation, legislation itself would be the result of a process of haggling akin to economic behavior.

Choices arise that would not even have been imagined in an earlier age. Euthanasia, genetic engineering, and brainwashing become practical possibilities. The most complex human functions, such as thinking, may be broken down into their elements and artificially reproduced. Everything appears possible until it has been proved impossible.

Perhaps the most striking characteristic of a perfectly changeable society is the decline in personal relationships. What makes a relationship personal is that it is tied to a specific person. Friends, neighbors, husbands and wives would become, if not interchangeable, at least readily replaceable by only marginally inferior (or superior) substitutes; they would be subject to choice under competitive conditions. Parents and children would presumably remain fixed, but the ties that connect them may become less influential. Personal contact may altogether decline in importance as more efficient means of communication reduce the need for physical presence.

The picture that emerges is less than pleasing. As an accomplished fact, open society may prove to be far less desirable than it seems to those who regard it as an ideal. To put things in perspective, it should be remembered that any social system becomes absurd and intolerable if it is carried to its logical conclusion, be it More's *Utopia*, Defoe's imaginary countries, Huxley's *Brave New World*, or Orwell's *1984*.

The Question of Values

The great boon of open society, and the accomplishment that qualifies it to serve as an ideal, is the freedom of the individual. The most obvious attraction of freedom is a negative one: the absence of restraint. But freedom has a positive aspect, too, which is even more important. It allows people to learn to think for themselves, to decide what they want and to translate their dreams into reality. They can explore the limits of their capabilities and reach intellectual, organizational, artistic, and practical achievements that otherwise they might not have even suspected were attainable. That can be an intensely exciting and satisfying experience.

On the debit side, the paramount position enjoyed by individuals imposes a burden on them that at times may become unbearable. Where can they find the values they need to make all the choices that confront them? Economic analysis takes both values and opportunities as given. We have seen that the assumption is diametrically opposed to the principle of a perfectly changeable society. It is a contradiction in terms to expect an unattached individual to operate with a fixed set of values. Values are just as much a matter of choice as everything else. The choice may be conscious and the result of much heart-searching

208

and reflection; it is more likely to be impulsive or based on family background, advice, advertising, or some other external influence. When values are changeable, changing them is bound to be an important part of business activities. Individuals have to choose their values under great external pressures.

If it were only a matter of consumption there would be no great difficulty. When it comes to deciding which brand of cigarette to choose, the sensation of pleasure may provide adequate guidance—although even that is doubtful in light of the amounts spent on cigarette advertising. But a society cannot be built on the pleasure principle alone. Life includes pain, risks, dangers, and ultimately the prospect of death. If pleasure were the only standard, capital could not be accumulated, and many of the associations and institutions that go to make up society could not survive, nor could many of the discoveries, artistic and technical creations that form a civilization, be accomplished.

Deficiency of Purpose

When we go outside those choices that provide immediate satisfaction we find that open society suffers from what may be termed a "deficiency of purpose." By this I do not mean that no purpose can be found, but merely that it has to be sought and found by each individual for and in themselves.

It is this obligation that creates the burden I referred to. People may try to identify themselves with a larger purpose by joining a group or devoting themselves to an ideal. But voluntary associations do not have the same reassuringly inevitable quality as organic society. One does not belong as a matter of course but as a result of conscious choice, and it is difficult to commit oneself wholeheartedly to one particular group when there are so many to choose from. Even if one does, the group is not committed in return: there is constant danger of being rejected or left out.

The same applies to ideals. Religious and social ideals have to compete with each other so that they lack that inevitability that would enable people to accept them unreservedly. Allegiance to an ideal becomes as much a matter of choice as allegiance to a group. The individual remains separate; his adherence does not signify identity but a conscious decision. The consciousness of this act stands between the individual and the ideal adopted.

The need to find a purpose for and in themselves places individuals in a quandary. The individual is the weakest among all the units that go to make up society and has a shorter life span than most of the institutions that depend on him. On their own, individuals provide a very uncertain foundation on which to base a system of values sufficient to sustain a structure that will outlast them and which must represent a greater value in their eyes than their own life and welfare. Yet such a value system is needed to sustain open society.

The inadequacy of the individual as a source of values may find expression in different ways. Loneliness or feelings of inferiority, guilt, and futility may be directly related to a deficiency in purpose. Such psychic disturbances are exacerbated by people's tendency to hold themselves personally responsible for these feelings instead of putting their personal difficulties into a social context. Psychoanalysis is no help in this regard: whatever its therapeutic value, its excessive preoccupation with the individual tends to aggravate the problems it seeks to cure.

The problems of the individual become greater the more wealth and power he or she possesses. Someone who can hardly make ends meet cannot afford to stop and ask about the purpose of life. But what I have called the "positive aspect of imperfect knowledge" can be relied on to make open society affluent, so that the quandary is likely to present itself in full force. A point may be reached where even the pleasure principle is endangered: people may not be able to derive enough satisfaction from the results of their labor to justify the effort that goes into reaching them. The creation of wealth may provide its own justification as a form of creative activity; it is when it comes to the enjoyment of the fruits that signs of congestion tend to appear.

Those who are unable to find a purpose in themselves may be driven to a dogma that provides the individual with a ready-made set of values and a secure place in the universe. One way to remove the deficiency of purpose is to abandon open society. If freedom becomes an unbearable burden, closed society may appear as the salvation.

THE DOGMATIC MODE OF THINKING

We have seen that the critical mode of thinking puts the burden of deciding what is right or wrong, true or untrue, squarely on the individual. Given the individual's imperfect understanding, there are a number of vital questions—notably those that concern the individual's relation to the universe and his place in society—to which he or she cannot provide a final answer. Uncertainty is hard to bear, and the human mind is likely to go to great lengths to escape from it.

There is such an escape: the dogmatic mode of thinking. It consists in establishing as paramount a body of doctrine that is believed to originate from a source other than the individual. The source may be tradition or an ideology that has succeeded in gaining supremacy in competition with other ideologies. In either case, it is declared as the supreme arbiter over conflicting views. Those who conform are accepted, and those who are in conflict are rejected. There is no need to weigh alternatives: every choice is ready made. No question is left unanswered. The fearful specter of uncertainty is removed.

The dogmatic mode of thinking has much in common with the traditional mode. By postulating an authority that is the source of all knowledge, it attempts to retain or recreate the wonderful simplicity of a world in which the prevailing view is

211

not subject to doubt or questioning. But it is exactly the lack of simplicity that differentiates it from the traditional mode. In the traditional mode, changelessness is a universally accepted fact; in the dogmatic mode, it is a postulate. Instead of a single universally accepted view, there are many possible interpretations but only one that is in accord with the postulate. The others must be rejected. What makes matters complicated is that the dogmatic mode cannot admit that it is making a postulate, because that would undermine the unquestionable authority that it seeks to establish. To overcome this difficulty, incredible mental contortions may be necessary. Try as it may, the dogmatic mode of thinking cannot recreate the conditions of simplicity which characterized the traditional mode. The essential point of difference is this: a genuinely changeless world can have no history. Once there is an awareness of conflicts past and present, precepts lose their inevitable character. This means that the traditional mode of thinking is restricted to the earliest stages of man's development. Only if people could forget their earlier history would a return to the traditional mode be possible.

A direct transition from the critical to the traditional mode can thus be ruled out altogether. If a dogmatic mode of thinking prevailed for an indefinite period, history might fade out gradually, but at the present juncture this does not deserve to be regarded as a practical possibility. The choice is only between the critical and the dogmatic modes.

In effect, the dogmatic mode of thinking extends the assumption of changelessness (which permits perfect knowledge) to a world that is no longer perfectly changeless. This is no easy task. In view of man's imperfect understanding, no explanation can be fully in accord with reality. As long as observation has any bearing on what is regarded as incontrovertible truth, some discrepancies are bound to arise. The only really effective solution is to remove truth from the realm of observation and reserve it for a higher level of consciousness in which it can rule undisturbed by conflicting evidence.

The dogmatic mode of thinking therefore tends to resort to

a superhuman authority such as God or History, which reveals itself to mankind in one way or another. The revelation is the only and ultimate source of truth. While men, with their imperfect intellect, argue endlessly about the applications and implications of the doctrine, the doctrine itself continues to shine in its august purity. While observation records a constant flow of changes, the rule of the superhuman power remains undisturbed. This device maintains the illusion of a well-defined permanent world order in the face of much evidence that would otherwise discredit it. The illusion is reinforced by the fact that the dogmatic mode of thinking, if successful, tends to keep social conditions unchanging. Yet even at its most successful, the dogmatic mode does not possess the simplicity that was the redeeming feature of the traditional mode.

The traditional mode of thinking dealt entirely with concrete situations. The dogmatic mode relies on a doctrine that is applicable to all conceivable conditions. Its tenets are abstractions which exist beyond, and often in spite of, direct observation. The use of abstractions brings with it all the complications from which the traditional mode was exempt. Far from being simple, the dogmatic mode of thinking can become even more complex than the critical mode. This is hardly surprising. To maintain the assumption of changelessness in conditions that are not fully appropriate, without admitting that an assumption has been made, is a distortion of reality. One must go through complicated contortions to achieve a semblance of credibility, and must pay heavy penalties in terms of mental effort and strain. Indeed, it would be difficult to believe that the human mind is capable of such self-deception if history did not provide actual examples. It appears that the mind is an instrument that can resolve any self-generated contradiction by creating new contradictions somewhere else. This tendency is given free rein in the dogmatic mode of thinking, because, as we have seen, its tenets are exposed to minimum contact with observable phenomena.

With all efforts devoted to resolving internal contradictions,

213

the dogmatic mode of thinking offers little scope for improving the available body of knowledge. It cannot admit direct observation as evidence because in case of a conflict the authority of dogma would be undermined. It must confine itself to applying the doctrine. This leads to arguments about the meaning of words, especially those of the original revelation—sophistic, talmudic, theological, ideological discussions, which tend to create new problems for every one they resolve. Since thinking has little or no contact with reality, speculation tends to become more convoluted and unreal the further it proceeds. How many angels can dance on the head of a needle?

What the actual contents of a doctrine are depends on historical circumstances and cannot be made the subject of generalizations. Tradition may provide part of the material, but in order to do so it must undergo a radical transformation. The dogmatic mode of thinking requires universally applicable statements, while tradition was originally couched in concrete terms. It must now be generalized in order to make it relevant to a wider range of events than it was destined for. How this can be accomplished is clearly demonstrated by the growth of languages. One of the ways in which a language adjusts itself to changing circumstances is by using in a figurative sense words that originally had only a concrete connotation. The figurative meaning retains only one characteristic aspect of the concrete case and may then be applied to other concrete cases which share that characteristic. The same method is used by preachers who take as their text a piece of narrative from the Bible.

A doctrine may also incorporate ideas originating in an open society. Every philosophical and religious theory offering a comprehensive explanation for the problems of existence has the makings of a doctrine; all it needs is unconditional acceptance and universal enforcement. The originator of a comprehensive philosophy may not have intended to put forth a doctrine that is to be unconditionally accepted and universally enforced, but personal inclinations have little influence on the development

214

of ideas. Once a theory becomes the sole source of knowledge, it assumes certain characteristics which prevail irrespective of its original intention.

Since the critical mode of thinking is more powerful than the traditional mode, ideologies developed by critical thinking are more likely to serve as the basis of dogma than tradition itself. Once established, they may take on a traditional appearance. If language is flexible enough to permit the figurative use of concrete statements, it can also lend itself to the reverse process, and abstract ideas can be personified. The Old Testament God is a case in point, and Frazer's *Golden Bough* offers many other examples. We may find in practice that what we call tradition incorporates many products of critical thinking translated into concrete terms.

The primary requirement of dogma is to be all-embracing. It must provide a yardstick by which every thought and action can be measured. If one could not evaluate everything in its light, one would have to cast around for other methods of distinguishing between right and wrong; such a search would destroy the dogmatic mode of thinking. Even if the validity of the dogma were not attacked directly, the mere fact that the application of other criteria can have divergent results would tend to undermine its authority. If a doctrine is to fulfill its function as the fountain of all knowledge, its supremacy must be asserted in every field. It may not be necessary to refer to it all the time: the land can be cultivated, pictures painted, wars fought, rockets launched, each in its own fashion. But whenever an idea or action comes into conflict with a doctrine, the doctrine must be given precedence. In this way, ever larger areas of human activity may come under its control.

The other main characteristic of dogma is its rigidity. The traditional mode of thinking is extremely flexible. As tradition is timeless, any alteration is immediately accepted not only in the present but as something that has existed since time immemorial. Not so the dogmatic mode. Its doctrines provide a yardstick

215

by which thoughts and actions are to be judged. Hence they must be permanently fixed, and no amount of transgression can justify a change. If there is a departure from the norm, it must be corrected at once. The dogma itself must remain inviolate.

In the light of our inherently imperfect understanding, it is clear that new developments may clash with established doctrines or create internal contradictions in unforeseen ways. Any change represents a potential threat. To minimize the danger, the dogmatic mode of thinking tends to inhibit new departures both in thinking and in action. It does so not only by eliminating unregulated change from its own view of the universe but also by actively suppressing unregulated thoughts and actions. How far it will go in this direction depends on the extent to which it is attacked.

In contrast with the traditional mode of thinking, the dogmatic mode is inseparably linked with some form of compulsion. Compulsion is necessary to ensure the supremacy of dogma over actual and potential alternatives. Every doctrine is liable to raise questions that do not resolve themselves by mere contemplation; in the absence of an authority that defines the doctrine and defends its purity, the unity of the dogmatic view is bound to break up into conflicting interpretations. The most effective way to deal with this problem is to charge a human authority with interpreting the will of the superhuman power from which the validity of doctrines is derived. Its interpretations may evolve with time and, if the authority operates efficiently, prevailing doctrines can keep pace with changes occurring in reality to a considerable extent. But no innovation not sanctioned by the authority can be tolerated, and the authority must have sufficient power to eliminate conflicting views.

There may be circumstances in which the authority need have little recourse to force. As long as the prevailing dogma fulfills its function of providing an all-embracing explanation, people will tend to accept it without question. After all, the dogma enjoys monopoly: while there may be various views available on particular issues, when it comes to reality as a whole

216

there is only one view in existence. People are brought up under its aegis and are trained to think in its terms: it is more natural for them to accept than to question it.

Yet when internal contradictions develop into ever more unrealistic debates, or when new events occur that do not fit in with established explanations, people may begin to question the foundations. When this happens, the dogmatic mode of thinking can be sustained only by force. The use of force is bound to have a profound influence on the evolution of ideas. Thinking no longer develops along its own lines but becomes intricately interwoven with power politics. Particular thoughts are associated with particular interests, and the victory of an interpretation depends more on the relative political strength of its proponents than on the validity of the arguments marshaled in its support. The human mind becomes a battlefield of political forces, and, conversely, doctrines become weapons in the hands of warring factions.

The supremacy of a doctrine can thus be prolonged by means that have little to do with the validity of arguments. The greater the coercion employed to maintain a dogma in force, the less likely it is to satisfy the needs of the human mind. When finally the hegemony of a dogma is broken, people are likely to feel that they have been liberated from terrible oppression. Wide new vistas are opened, and the abundance of opportunities engenders hope, enthusiasm, and tremendous intellectual activity.

It can be seen that the dogmatic mode of thinking fails to recreate any of the qualities that made the traditional mode so attractive. It turns out to be convoluted, rigid, and oppressive. True, it eliminates the uncertainties that plague the critical mode, but only at the cost of creating conditions that the human mind would find intolerable if it were aware of any alternatives. Just as a doctrine based on a superhuman authority may provide an avenue of escape from the shortcomings of the critical mode, the critical mode itself may appear as the salvation to those who suffer from the oppression of a dogma.

CLOSED SOCIETY

Organic society presents some very attractive features to the observer: a concrete social unity, an unquestioned belonging, an identification of each member with the collective. Members of an organic society would hardly consider this an advantage, ignorant as they are that the relationship could be any different; only those who are aware of a conflict between the individual and the social Whole in their own society are likely to regard organic unity as a desirable goal. In other words, the attractions of organic society are best appreciated when the conditions required for its existence no longer prevail.

It is hardly surprising that throughout history mankind should have shown a yearning to return to its original state of innocence and bliss. The expulsion from the Garden of Eden is a recurrent theme. But innocence, once lost, cannot be regained—except perhaps by forgetting every experience. In any attempt to recreate artificially the conditions of an organic society, it is precisely the unquestioning and unquestionable identification of all members with the society to which they belong that is the most difficult to achieve. In order to re-establish organic unity it is necessary to proclaim the supremacy of the collective. The result, however, will differ from organic society in one vital respect: individual interests, instead of being identical with those of the collective, become subordinated to them.

The distinction between personal and public interest raises a disturbing question as to what the public interest really is. The common interest must be defined, interpreted, and, if necessary, enforced over conflicting personal interests. This task is best performed by a living ruler, because he or she can adjust his or her policies to the circumstances. If it is entrusted to an institution, it is likely to be performed in a cumbersome, inflexible, and ultimately ineffective manner. The institution will seek to prevent changes, but in the long run it cannot succeed.

However the common interest is defined in theory, in practice it is likely to reflect the interest of the rulers. It is they who proclaim the supremacy of the Whole, and it is they who impose its will on recalcitrant individuals. Unless one assumes that they are totally selfless, it is also they who benefit from it. The rulers are not necessarily furthering their selfish ends as individuals, but they do benefit from the existing system as a class: by definition, they are the class that rules. Since the membership of classes is clearly defined, the subordination of the individual to the social Whole amounts to the subordination of one class to another. Closed society may therefore be described as a society based on class exploitation. Exploitation may occur in open society as well, but, since the position of the individual is not fixed, it does not operate on a class basis. Class exploitation in Marx's sense can exist only in a closed society. Marx made a valuable contribution when he established the concept, just as Menenius Agrippa did when he compared society with an organism. Both of them, however, applied it to the wrong kind of society.

If the avowed aim of a closed society is to ensure the supremacy of one class (or race or nationality) over another, it may fulfill its purpose effectively. But if its aim is to bring back the idyllic conditions of an organic society, it is bound to fail. There is a gap between the ideal of social unity and the reality of class exploitation. To bridge the gap, an elaborate set of explanations is needed, which is, by definition, at variance with the facts.

Getting the ideology universally accepted is the prime task of the ruling authority and the criterion of its success. The more widely an ideology is accepted, the smaller the conflict between the collective interest and the policies actually pursued, and vice versa. At its best, an authoritarian system can go a long way toward re-establishing the calm and harmony of organic society. More commonly, some degree of coercion has to be employed, and then this fact must be explained away by tortuous arguments, which render the ideology less convincing, requiring the use of further force until, at its worst, the system is based on compulsion and its ideology bears no resemblance to reality.

I have some reservations about the distinction that Jeane Kirkpatrick has drawn between authoritarian and totalitarian regimes, because she used it to distinguish between America's friends and enemies, but there is a point to it. An authoritarian regime devoted to maintaining itself in power can admit more or less openly what it is about. It may limit the freedom of its subjects in various ways, it may be aggressive and brutal, but it need not extend its influence over every aspect of existence in order to preserve its hegemony. On the other hand, a system that claims to serve some ideal of social justice needs to cover up the reality of class exploitation. This requires control over the thoughts of its subjects, not merely their actions, and renders its constraining influence much more pervasive.

The Soviet system is the prime example of a closed society based on a universal idea. There is not much point in discussing it in general terms when we have already studied it in detail. But a closed society need not embody a universal idea; it may be confined to a particular group or nation. In a way, a more narrow definition is closer to the spirit of an organic society than a dogma that applies to all of humanity. After all, a tribe is concerned only with its members. Now that communism is dead, those who hanker after the security and solidarity of an organic society are more likely to look for it in an ethnic or religious community. As I have explained earlier, those who reject communism oppose it either because it is closed or because it is universal; the alternatives are either open society or fundamentalism of one kind or another. Fundamental beliefs are less easy to justify by rational argument, but they may have greater emotional appeal exactly because they are more primitive.

When we speak of fundamentalism, Islamic fundamentalism springs to mind, but we can observe the reawakening of fundamentalist tendencies throughout the erstwhile communist bloc. They combine national and religious elements. They do not

have fully developed ideologies—indeed, they are not fully articu-
late—but draw their inspiration from a nebulous past. The struggle between the concepts of open and closed society has not
come to an end with the collapse of communism. It is merely
taking a different form. The mode of thinking currently associated
with the concept of a closed society is probably better described
as traditional than dogmatic, although, if the concept of a closed
society prevails, the formulation of the appropriate dogmas will
probably not lag far behind. In the case of Islamic fundamentalism
it is already fully formed. In the case of Russian fundamentalism
the groundwork has also been laid. *

* See Alexander Yanov, *The Russian Challenge* (Oxford: Basil Blackwell, 1987).

□ 12 □

The Boom–Bust Pattern

No Grand Design

It can be seen that open and closed societies represent alternative forms of social organization. Each is associated with its own mode of thinking in a reflexive fashion; that is to say, the mode of thinking and the form of social organization are mutually self-validating, but only up to a point. Beyond that point, each system leaves something to be desired, which can only be found in the other. Closed society lacks individual freedom and the possibility of progress, while open society cannot offer the individual the reassurance of an ultimate truth and a sense of identification with a larger and more permanent unity. They can be considered as opposite poles of social organization: mutually exclusive yet mutually attractive.

The idea of polarity is immensely enticing, because it could explain so much so simply. One is immediately led to imagine a grand pattern which interprets man's history in terms of a continuing struggle between two extremes: no sooner does one extreme attain supremacy than the forces of progress start working in the direction of the other.

THE BOOM–BUST PATTERN

When I first established my framework of open and closed societies, I toyed with the idea, but then explicitly rejected it.* I realized that the pattern is not found in history but imposed on it. The two principles of social organization do alternate, but that is not due to the interaction of historical forces—rather it is due to the fact that one has arbitrarily selected two principles and the only kind of change the pattern can reveal is from one principle to the other. There is no historical necessity in these changes, but only a logical necessity inherent in the choice of simplifying principles. The pattern tells us nothing about history, only about the pattern itself.

This conclusion is powerfully reinforced by the current historical experience. The universal closed system called communism is disintegrating. If the supposed pattern of history applied, the victory of the principle of open society could be taken for granted. But that is not the case. What follows the collapse of the Soviet system is very much an open question. We have distinguished between two alternatives: either the region will be integrated into the open system of Europe or it will break down into smaller closed units based on nationalism. Which of these alternatives will prevail is determined not by any pattern of history but by the decisions of the participants.

What remains, then, of my theory of history? There is a pattern in history, but it is quite different from the deterministic models we are familiar with from natural science. The pattern of history is not determined in advance according to timelessly valid laws; it is formed by events as they occur. The past is uniquely determined, but the future is wide open—the further one looks ahead the more open it becomes. Events do fall into patterns, but the patterns are the result and not the cause of events. They are not regular or repeatable as they would be if they were governed by laws that operate independently of the participants' decisions. We may discern some recurring patterns,

* In an unpublished manuscript, "The Burden of Consciousness" (1963).

223

but their shape and duration are not predetermined. For instance, the Soviet system lasted seventy years while Hitler's thousand-year empire endured only ten.

The Structure of Events

If we want to understand history we must study the structure of events, rather than the pattern they produce. We have discovered a two-way interaction between the participants' thinking and the actual course of events, which we call reflexivity. We have also discovered a pattern in that interaction, which we call the boom–bust pattern. It starts out with a bias and a trend that mutually reinforce each other. Eventually the divergence between perception and reality becomes so wide that it cannot escape detection. If by the time the bias is recognized the trend has become dependent on the bias, the reversal becomes also self-reinforcing, creating a boom–bust pattern. But if the bias is corrected before a self-reinforcing process is set into motion, there is no boom–bust pattern to be observed. The pattern de-scribes the interaction between trend and bias (that is, the structure of events) rather than a trend by itself (that is, the pattern of events). There is nothing determinate about it: it may never get started or it may be aborted at any point. Nevertheless it provides a valuable insight into human affairs. The boom–bust pattern is associated with far-from-equilibrium conditions: neither the participants' views nor the actual state of affairs will remain the same at the end as it was at the beginning of the process. Conversely, near-equilibrium conditions are characterized by the absence of boom–bust sequences. Whether the reflexive inter-action between perception and reality remains near equilibrium or moves away from equilibrium depends on the participants' ability to recognize their own bias. Open society is more conducive to the recognition and correction of error than closed society but it is not immune from boom–bust sequences. When does a boom–bust sequence destroy the near-equilibrium conditions of open society? That is the question I left unanswered. Before I deal with it, I want to explore the anatomy of the boom–bust process in greater depth.

Financial Markets as Laboratory

For this purpose I shall turn to the financial markets, where I have some practical experience and experimental knowledge to draw on. In contrast to the prevailing wisdom, which is based on the concepts of equilibrium and rational expectations, I regard the behavior of financial markets as a historical process in which the participants' bias plays a key role. Using the stock markets as a laboratory, I can establish a more precise criterion of demarcation between near-equilibrium and far-from-equilibrium conditions than I did in Chapter 10. Instead of studying the relationship between reality and thinking in general terms, I can focus on the relationship between the so-called fundamentals and the valuations that are placed upon them by investors. The "fundamentals" in this context refer to the companies whose shares are being valued; they include earnings, dividends, balance sheets, and the like. The market behavior of the shares themselves also enters into investors' valuations. It is usually referred to as "technical factors." Investors base their decisions on both fundamental and technical considerations.

The fundamentals are supposed to be independent of the valuations placed upon them; that is why they are called fundamentals. In normal or near-equilibrium conditions that is by and large true; but in certain circumstances valuations can change the fundamentals. How that happens will become clearer after I have given a few specific examples. Technical factors are, of course, always influenced by the investors' behavior.

I shall take two instances where the fundamentals are also influenced by valuations; both of these were discussed at length in *The Alchemy of Finance*: the so-called conglomerate boom in the U.S. stock market of the late 1960s and the great international lending boom of the 1970s. It will be worthwhile to re-examine them briefly even if it seems to take us a long way from the rise and fall of the Soviet system. The similarities in the situations will be all the more striking.

The Conglomerate Boom

In the case of the conglomerate boom, investors were willing to pay a high multiple of earnings for companies which could produce fast per-share earnings growth. This consideration, earnings growth, loomed larger in investors' minds than the other so-called fundamentals, like dividends or balance sheets; nor were they terribly discriminating about the way per-share earnings growth was achieved. This was the bias that certain companies that came to be called conglomerates managed to exploit. Typically, conglomerates were high-tech defense companies that had enjoyed fast growth in the recent past and a correspondingly high multiple of earnings. The outlook for the defense industry was unfavorable, so they decided to use their high-priced stock to acquire other companies whose stock was selling at a lower multiple of earnings. The transactions resulted in improvements in the per-share earnings of the acquiring companies. Investors appreciated the earnings growth and accorded a high multiple to the companies' shares. This enabled the companies to continue the process. Soon there were many imitators. Even a company whose stock started with a low multiple of earnings could attain

226

a higher multiple simply by announcing its intention to become a conglomerate. The boom was launched.

In retrospect, it is clear that investors were misguided in their fixation on per-share earnings growth. But the flaw in their thinking went deeper: they treated earnings growth as a fundamental that was independent of their own valuation. Until the conglomerate boom, the flaw was not exploited on a large scale, and near-equilibrium conditions prevailed in spite of a pronounced bias on the part of the investors. But the conglomerates found a way to translate the investors' bias into changes in the real world. They set up a trend in their per-share earnings that would not have been possible without exploiting the prevailing bias, and gobbled up a large number of companies in the process. The corporate landscape changed. The supposed separation between fundamentals and valuations had been breached, and a far-from-equilibrium process was set in motion. It can be seen that the demarcation line between near-equilibrium and far-from-equilibrium conditions was passed when a prevailing bias found a way to create a trend in the real world.

Other Manias

When we examine other cases, we find the same phenomenon. For instance, in the international lending boom of the late 1970s, bankers relied on so-called debt ratios to measure the creditworthiness of the borrowing countries. They thought they were using an independent measure, but actually their own lending activity served to keep the debt ratios within acceptable limits; when they stopped lending, the debt ratios deteriorated precipitously, causing the bust of 1982.

These cases are interesting because they show that the so-called fundamentals which are supposed to be "objective," that is, independent of the participants' thinking, are in fact influenced by it. But far-from-equilibrium situations are not confined to such cases. They may arise whenever market participants are more concerned with anticipated changes in market prices, that is, technical factors, than with fundamentals. The classic example is the tulip mania that gripped the Netherlands from 1634 to 1637. Tulip bulbs reached totally unreasonable prices because people were willing to bid up for them in the expectation of further price increases, forgetting altogether about intrinsic values. Similar instances have occurred countless times since. I recall a friend of mine, an otherwise shrewd investor, who proved to me what a bargain he made when he bought an Aspen condominium at an outrageous price, because his carrying cost was less than 10 percent, while real estate in Aspen was appreciating at twice that rate. Needless to say, the market collapsed shortly thereafter. Real estate is particularly susceptible to this kind of argument because of the worldwide credit expansion that has prevailed since the end of World War II; we seem to have reached the end of the road just as I write these lines. But the tulip-mania mentality is not confined to the valuation of real estate and such other assets as Impressionist paintings; it also pervades the valuation of currencies and other commodities.

Currency markets become inherently unstable when the expectation of future changes in exchange rates becomes the dominant factor in the market participants' decisions. As I argued in *The Alchemy of Finance*, the instability in a freely floating exchange rate system is cumulative for two reasons. First, the relative importance of speculative transactions tends to increase with the passage of time. Second, speculation becomes increasingly trend-following in character. In the absence of central bank intervention, price swings would become ever wider and eventually culminate in a breakdown of the system.

I would argue that the U.S. stock market has also become inherently unstable, because it has come to be dominated by institutional investors who are interested in relative rather than

absolute performance. This turns them into trend-following spec-
ulators, setting up the same dynamics that prevail in freely fluctu-
ating currency markets.

Demarcation

In Chapter 10 I drew a tentative demarcation line between near-
equilibrium and far-from-equilibrium conditions: is there is a
clear distinction between thinking and reality? I can now be
somewhat more precise. The threshold of far-from-equilibrium
conditions is crossed when a trend prevailing in the real world
becomes dependent on a bias prevailing in the participants' minds,
and vice versa, so that both trend and bias develop further than
would have been possible in the absence of a double feedback,
reflexive connection.

A prevailing bias is not enough by itself; it must find a way
to validate itself by establishing or reinforcing a trend in the
real world. I realize that the point I am making is tautological:
when there is a double feedback, we can speak of a far-from-
equilibrium situation. But the point is worth making: the participants' thinking is always biased, but it does not always translate
into a boom–bust sequence. For instance, the conglomerate boom
could have been cut short if investors had realized that their
concept of per-share earnings growth was flawed as soon as the
conglomerate companies started to exploit it.

The Question of Values

We are now ready to make a generalization about the role of
values, which applies not only to financial markets but to history

in general. In order to remain stable, that is, near-equilibrium, societies as well as markets need to rely on a set of values that do not validate themselves. These conditions would be met if people based their value judgments on fundamentals. But the so-called fundamentals may themselves be susceptible to the value judgments that are supposed to be based on them. Hence, *all* value systems are potentially self-validating; and all societies, as well as all markets, are potentially unstable. Stability depends on not allowing a self-validating process to get out of hand. How can the task be accomplished?

To give an abstract answer to an abstract question, we must ensure that a measure of separation between thinking and reality is maintained. We need a criterion by which the validity of our thinking can be judged and, to provide a stable outcome, the criterion must be independent of our thinking. But thinking and reality are not really separate and independent; they are connected by a double feedback mechanism called reflexivity. We need something absolute that can serve as a criterion for our thoughts and actions; but that something is not given: it is an illusion that needs to be deliberately preserved. Once it is recognized as an illusion or bias, the task can get awfully complicated.

Take the case of the financial markets. The illusion that fundamentals and values are independent has been helpful in fostering stability. But it is an illusion that occasionally breaks down. Since the breakdowns tend to be associated with the use of credit, they can be quite devastating. To prevent them, some kind of regulation is necessary. But regulators also operate with a bias that tends to be more rigid than the bias of market participants. Therefore, regulation also breaks down, or, alternatively, the regulators need to be regulated by a political process. Perhaps the best way to keep the bias of the regulators within tolerable bounds is to force them to interact with the market. That is what central bankers have to do, and, on balance, they provide the most efficient form of market regulation. Their presence leads to a sort of cat-and-mouse game, which can get ever more sophisticated.

In politics, the solution is to be found in a democratic form of government. People with different value systems learn to coexist. While they are guided by their own convictions, they recognize that other people have other interests and other convictions and that a way has to be found to reconcile them. Hence the system of elected governments. But the system can be undermined by politicians learning to manipulate the electorate and by the electorate allowing itself to be manipulated. The better the reflexive relationship is understood, the greater the danger that the system will become unstable. Both the leaders and the population act as trend followers, and, without any fundamental beliefs to serve as an anchor, political life will deteriorate into an aimless drift. Democracy is threatened from both sides: from a particular set of beliefs achieving monopoly and from a lack of fundamental beliefs.

It can be seen that democracy is a highly precarious form of government. Its survival cannot be taken for granted because the system is inherently flawed. Stability requires a separation between fundamentals and values, while the political system is characterized by a lack of separation. Since we have little control over the fundamentals, we can insure stability only by espousing a value system that draws a clear distinction between what is right and what is expedient. Our founding fathers had such a value system, but it is questionable whether it still prevails in Washington today. Institutions that have functioned for two hundred years may be on the point of breaking down. The survival of open society, far from being assured, depends on a commitment by its members to the idea of an open society that transcends self-interest.

The question is, can open society itself serve as the basis of a value system? I believe it can, but only with difficulty. We must recognize the flaw in human understanding in general and in the democratic form of government in particular. We

231

must understand reflexivity and all that it entails. In the end, it boils down to a choice between complexity and simplicity. If we are prepared to cope with complexity, our world will become increasingly complex. We may perceive the process as freedom, progress, and the fulfillment of human destiny. But the lure of simplicity remains, and at times, especially when the system is failing, the temptation may become too great. We may then revert to a cruder, simpler system until we discover its inferiority.

The Boom–Bust Pattern

The distinction between near-equilibrium and far-from-equilibrium conditions is very important; indeed, in my thinking, it amounts to a breakthrough. Throughout my financial career I have always sought out boom–bust sequences. I called them "reflexive" and I made a lot of money on them. I even wrote *The Alchemy of Finance* about them. But I was bothered by the fact that the process could be observed only in special circumstances. It was in some sense a departure from "normal" conditions. I can see now that I was specializing in conditions of dynamic disequilibrium.

Once I made that determination, the connection between the theory of reflexivity and the framework of open and closed societies fell into place. What I call the boom–bust sequence in the stock market is the theoretical equivalent of the revolutionary process currently unfolding in the Soviet Union. The theory of reflexivity as developed in *The Alchemy of Finance* provides a clue for understanding dynamic far-from-equilibrium conditions as they currently manifest themselves in Eastern Europe. I had been aware of the parallel, and I used the same approach in my dealings in financial markets and in communist countries. But it is only now that the two lines of thought fit together also in theory.

Let me recall briefly the distinguishing features of a boom–bust sequence, such as the conglomerate boom of the late 1960s. There is in such processes an initial bias and an initial trend. They start out as mutually self-reinforcing, but in the initial stage we cannot yet speak of far-from-equilibrium conditions. That happens only as the process evolves. The trend becomes increasingly dependent on the bias and the bias becomes increasingly exaggerated. We may call this the period of acceleration. A point comes when the divergence between belief and reality becomes so great that it comes to be recognized as a bias. We may call this the moment of truth. The trend may be sustained by inertia but ceases to be reinforced by belief so that it flattens out—let us call this the twilight period or the period of stagnation. Eventually, the loss of belief is bound to cause a reversal in the trend which had become dependent on an ever stronger bias; this trend reversal is the crossover point. The new trend engenders a bias in the opposite direction, causing a catastrophic acceleration that qualifies as a crash. That is what gives the boom–bust pattern its asymmetric shape. It starts slowly and accelerates gradually to a wild excess followed by a twilight period and then a catastrophic collapse. There are distinct stages along the way. We have identified them as the initial stage, the period of acceleration, the moment of truth, the twilight period, the crossover point, and the crash.

The Rise and Fall of the Soviet System

Let us now see how the boom–bust model can be applied to the rise and fall of the Soviet system as described in Chapter 2.

The initial bias was a fixed one—Marxist dogma—and there was a mutually self-reinforcing relationship between the rigidity of the dogma and the rigidity of prevailing conditions. The system reached its zenith in the last few years of Stalin's rule. It was all-embracing: a form of government, an economic system, a territorial empire, and an ideology. The system was comprehensive, isolated from the outside world, and rigid. But the gap between the actual state of affairs and its official interpretation was wide enough to qualify it as a case of static disequilibrium.

After Stalin's death there was a brief moment when Krushchev revealed some of the truth about Stalin, but eventually the hierarchy reasserted itself. A twilight period began, when dogma was preserved by administrative methods but was no longer reinforced by a belief in its validity. Interestingly, the rigidity of the system increased even further. As long as there had been a live totalitarian at the helm, the Communist party line could be changed at his whim. But now, that flexibility was lost. At the same time the terror also abated, and a subtle process of decay set in. Every institution started to jockey for position. Since none of them enjoyed any autonomy, they had to engage in a form of barter with the other institutions. Gradually an elaborate system of institutional bargaining replaced what was supposed to be central planning. At the same time, an informal economy developed which supplemented and filled in the gaps left by the formal system. This twilight period is what is now called the period of stagnation. The inadequacy of the system became increasingly evident and the pressure for reform mounted.

Now comes the point I emphasized in Chapter 2. Reform accelerated the process of disintegration, because it introduced or legitimized alternatives while the system depended on the lack of alternatives for its survival. Economic reform enjoyed an initial period of success in every communist country, with the notable exception of the Soviet Union itself. The Chinese reformers called this phase the Golden Period, when the existing

234

capital stock was redirected to meet consumer needs. But all reform movements are based on a misconception: the system cannot be reformed because it does not permit the economic allocation of capital. When existing capacity has been reoriented, the reform process is bound to run into difficulties.

It is understandable why this should be so. Communism was meant to be an antidote to capitalism, which had alienated the worker from the means of production. All property was taken over by the state, and the state was an embodiment of the collective interest as defined by the Party. Thus, the Party was put in charge of the allocation of capital. This meant that capital was allocated, not on economic grounds, but on the grounds of a quasi-religious dogma. The best analogy is with the pyramid building of the pharaohs. That is why the portion of resources devoted to investment was maximized, while the economic benefit derived from it remained at a minimum. It would also explain why investments took the form of monumental projects. We may view the gigantic hydroelectric dams, the steel mills, the marble halls of the Moscow subway, and the skyscrapers of Stalinist architecture as so many pyramids built by a modern pharaoh. Hydroelectric plants do produce energy, and steel mills do turn out steel, but if the steel and energy are used to produce more dams and steel mills, the effect on the economy is not very different from that of the construction of pyramids.

Our theory tells us that in the far-from-equilibrium conditions of a closed society there must be distortions that would be inconceivable in an open society. What better demonstration could one ask for? The communist system attributes no value to capital; more exactly, it does not recognize the concept of property. As a result, economic activity under the Soviet system is simply not economic. To make it so, the Party must be removed from its role as the guardian and allocator of capital. It is on this point that every reform is bound to come to grief.

Interestingly, the failure of economic reforms also served to

accelerate the process of disintegration because it demonstrated
the need for political reforms. With the advent of *perestroika*
in the Soviet Union, the process of disintegration entered into
its terminal phase because the reform was primarily political
and, as I have mentioned previously, the Golden Period was
missing. As the trend in living standards started to decline, public
opinion turned against the regime, leading to a catastrophic acceleration, which is culminating in the total collapse of the system.

The pattern is almost identical with the one we can observe
in financial markets, with one major difference: in financial
markets we have observed only a process of acceleration, whereas
in the case of the Soviet system the complete cycle comprises
two phases, one culminating in the standstill of the Stalin regime
and the other leading to a catastrophic decline.

The Fall and Rise of the Banking System

The difference is not as great as it seems. If we look hard enough,
we can identify cases of standstill in the financial markets as
well. Take the international lending boom. If we look at the
history of the U.S. banking system and go back far enough,
the conditions of changelessness approximating a standstill are
easily located. We have to go back to the Great Depression,
when a great number of banks failed. Subsequently the banking
system was frozen into inactivity by regulation and it took about
thirty-five years for it to come to life.

I wrote a brokerage report in 1972 entitled "The Case for
Growth Banks," in which I showed how the market in bank
shares had become ossified but predicted that the situation was
about to change. Banks at the time were considered the stodgiest
of institutions. A dull business attracted dull people, and there
was little movement or innovation in the industry. Bank stocks

were ignored by investors. But a new breed of bankers was emerging who had been educated in business schools and thought in terms of bottom-line profits. New kinds of financial instruments were being introduced. Some banks were beginning to utilize their capital more aggressively and were putting together very creditable earnings performances. But bank shares were selling at little or no premiums over asset value. Analysts were aware of this relative undervaluation, but they despaired of seeing it corrected. Yet many banks had reached the point where they were pushing against the limits of what was considered prudent leverage by the standards of the time. If they wanted to continue growing, they would need to raise additional equity capital. It was against this background that the First National City Bank hosted a dinner for security analysts—an unheard-of-event in the banking industry. It marked the end of the standstill imposed on the banking industry in the 1930s. I was not invited, but it prompted me to publish the report in which I recommended a bouquet of the more aggressively managed banks. Bank stocks did, in fact, have a good move in 1972, and we made about 50 percent on our bouquet.

Then came the first oil crisis of 1973, which prevented the banks from using their multiples to raise equity capital, and the big oil-recycling lending boom followed. Thus we can see the same full cycle consisting of two phases as in the rise and fall of the Soviet system, the only difference being that the phases are reversed. The rise of the Soviet system is the theoretical equivalent of the fall of the banking system.

The Two Extremes

The benefit of combining the experience of the Soviet system with the experience of the financial markets is that we can demonstrate that far-from-equilibrium conditions prevail at both extremes of change and changelessness. Closed society is the inverse of revolution and chaos; the difference is in the time scale, but the reflexive process is the same. In a closed society little happens over a long period, in a revolution much happens over a short period. In either case, perceptions are far removed from reality.

This is a significant insight. Discussing boom–bust processes in the context of financial markets, one is imperceptibly led to think in terms of acceleration. But the trend may also find expression in the form of deceleration or lack of change. Once we become aware of this possibility we have even found an actual example in the stock market: the case of bank stocks after the Great Depression. When we come to history the case of changelessness looms larger than life: Stalin's system was a far-from-equilibrium situation frozen solid.

This insight is necessary to reconcile the framework of open and closed society with the boom–bust pattern. Without recognizing that the boom–bust pattern can manifest itself in the lack of change as well as in catastrophic acceleration, we could not explain how closed societies evolve. As it is, we arrive at a theory of history based on the presence or absence of far-from equilibrium conditions. The potential for far-from-equilibrium conditions is always present, because people's understanding of the situation in which they participate is inherently imperfect. But the participants' bias may be recognized and corrected before it could engender a trend in the real world that would validate and reinforce the bias. When such a trend does arise, people's thinking may become quite far removed from any correspondence with the real world, and the divergence between thinking and reality may have far-reaching effects both on the participants' views and on the actual state of affairs. The trend may be accelerating or decelerating; thus we find far-from-equilibrium conditions at the two extremes of chaotic change and apparent standstill, with near-equilibrium conditions located in between. The boom–bust process may connect near-equilibrium conditions with one of the extremes, endangering the stability of markets (as in 1929) or of societies (as in the aftermath of World War I), or it may lead from one extreme to the other (as in the rise and fall of the Soviet system).

Limitations of the Boom–Bust Pattern

We must be careful not to overstate our case. It would be an exaggeration to claim that all historical developments follow a boom–bust pattern. It is true that the rise and fall of the Soviet system has shown a striking similarity with the fall and rise of the U.S. banking system. But that is no accident; I have chosen them specially because of the similarity of their pattern. It is only rarely that we can observe the peculiar, asymmetric yet regular shape that is discernible in the examples I have used. I could have easily identified far-from-equilibrium processes which follow different patterns. Indeed, I already mentioned one in passing: currency markets tend to follow a symmetrical wave pattern lasting several years rather than an asymmetrical boom–bust pattern. And organic society, although we have identified it as a far-from-equilibrium situation frozen solid, cannot be said to have a pattern of development.

Most far-from-equilibrium situations we can observe in reality do not have a regular shape or pattern at all. That is because reality is an infinitely complex system in which any process we may single out interacts with a number of other processes. For instance, the disintegration of the Soviet system has been profoundly influenced by the Gulf crisis. Interestingly, the great international lending boom was also connected with an oil shock. Even more interestingly, there is also a connection between the breakdown of the Soviet system and the current crisis in the international banking system. These interactions give the

239

course of events a unique, irreversible, and not-repeatable shape. It is only rarely that a boom–bust process can be observed more or less in isolation. The conglomerate boom was one of those rare cases, which is why I used it so prominently. But it would be a mistake to expect the pattern to repeat itself. For instance, the leveraged buyout and junk bond boom, which came to an end only recently, had many features in common with the conglomerate boom, yet the pattern was quite different. I have often made the mistake in my business career of expecting in vain that the boom–bust pattern would play itself out. Having "discovered" the pattern, I was like the proverbial economist who forecast ten of the last three recessions.

The disintegration of the Soviet system is almost unique in following the boom–bust pattern in such a pure form. This is probably so because it is such a momentous development that it overshadows most of the other processes with which it interacts. The size of a bust tends to be proportional to the boom that preceded it, and undoubtedly the Soviet system held sway over more people's lives longer and more completely than any other regime in modern history.

What is the use of the boom–bust pattern, then? It is certainly no basis for unconditional forecasting. Yet it provides a framework in terms of which the sequence of events can be understood. This is particularly true of the Soviet system because, for whatever reason, it seems to follow the pattern so faithfully. We have identified a number of stages in the pattern: the beginning of a self-reinforcing process, the period of acceleration, the moment of truth, the period of stagnation, the crossover point, and the crash. These stages can serve as signposts in interpreting the course of events. They can be particularly useful when the pace of events exceeds our ability to adjust to them. The distance between the various signposts is not fixed; but the sequence of the signposts is. For instance, you cannot have a crash without a crossover point or a period of stagnation without the moment of truth. The fact that one signpost has been passed does not assure that the next one will be reached: the process could be aborted or diverted at any time. But a change of course must involve a discontinuity; hence a potential discontinuity also becomes a signpost to watch for or to aim at.

Discontinuity

Indeed, the most practical conclusion to be drawn from this highly abstract analysis is the need for a discontinuity. Without it, the process of disintegration is bound to continue, and to imagine how far it may go boggles the mind. There have been many instances of anarchy in history. It is happening in Iraq even as I write. But never has it afflicted an economy that is as thoroughly integrated and interdependent as the Soviet Union. Stalin deliberately destroyed rural self-sufficiency when the villages refused to supply food to the urban proletariat because the town-dwellers had no money or goods to pay with. Stalin exterminated the kulaks and introduced a system that could not maintain itself without surrendering its output to the central agency, which controlled the tractor stations and the storage facilities. There has been anarchy and civil war in the Soviet Union before, from 1917 to 1921, but then it was still a country with subsistence agriculture.

Outside the borders of the Soviet Union the revolution is complete: the communist system has collapsed. But even there, a discontinuity needs to be introduced to reverse the process of disintegration. It was this line of argument that turned me into a fervent advocate of a radical break with the past. The system cannot be reformed, it must be transformed, was my motto. The issue arose most clearly in Poland in September 1989, when the Mazowieczki government took office. I recall my discussion with Bakka, the president of the central bank, who argued in

241

favor of continuity. Fortunately, the Balcerowicz plan prevailed. I was also urging a policy of discontinuity in Hungary at the time of the first free elections in May 1990, particularly with regard to the debt problem, but my advice was not heeded. I was convinced that a major mistake was committed for which the country would continue to suffer, but even I was surprised that the first democratically elected government actually proved to be weaker than the lame duck reform communist government that preceded it. I believe that Hungary, in contrast to the Soviet Union, will hit bottom and rebound, but the transition could have been faster and more effective if the government had engineered a more radical break with the past. Even in the Soviet Union it would have been possible to create a discontinuity and introduce a new form of integration in the midst of disintegration. That was the essence of the Shatalin Plan, and it missed only by a narrow margin. But the best chance for discontinuity was foreign intervention. As I have argued in this book and in the real world since the summer of 1988, the *deus ex machina* of Western aid was needed to reverse a seemingly inexorable process of disintegration. It is still not too late: none of the previous schemes would work, but the introduction of an internationally managed hard currency could still stabilize the Soviet economy. Naturally, the prospects for action are even slimmer than they were before.

Indeterminacy

It can be seen that the boom–bust pattern does not imply inevitability; or, more exactly, the pattern could be broken by intervention at any time. Nevertheless, it has the quality of a Greek drama: its asymmetric shape is highly dramatic, and the fact that the outcome can be predicted does not prevent it from unfolding. But in contrast to a theater, which is isolated from the real world, in reality there are a great number of performances being acted out simultaneously, and there is no way of telling how they will affect each other. The outcome may bear little resemblance to the script. In sum, the boom–bust pattern is more useful for explaining what has happened and what may happen in the absence of unexpected developments—the line of least resistance—than for predicting what will happen next. Compared with a scientific theory it is not much use at all; but it is better than nothing, provided one does not endow it with a quality of inevitability, which would render it misleading.

◻ CONCLUSION ◻

As the Soviet revolution is approaching its climax, I find myself in a calm and contemplative mood, which stands in sharp contrast with the hectic, manic state that characterized my activities during most of the last two years. I feel that I have done what I could, both as a participant and as an observer, and it was not enough.

I am full of foreboding about the future. I realize that we are approaching a complete breakdown in the Soviet Union, but I cannot quite visualize what shape it will take. It is easier to envision alternative outcomes—although there are too many to be enumerated—than the route that will lead to one of them. We are truly in a period of chaos where the element of unpredictability overshadows the element of continuity. The center of chaos is the Soviet Union, and those of us who are outside can consider ourselves observers even though our world will not remain unaffected. That is why I can afford to be calm and contemplative in the face of an impending, indeed already erupting conflagration. There is nothing much I can do about it. If I were inside, I would try to flee. But as I am outside, I can stop and gape. Of course, there is a lot to be done, but whatever I do pales into insignificance in comparison with the events themselves.

I realize that this is a passing mood generated by having spent several weeks revising this book. Soon, perhaps already next week, I shall become engaged again. I need the present moment of detached contemplation all the more, like a general before the battle. To be sure, I am no commanding general in the events that lie ahead—indeed, with the failure of the Shatalin Plan, I have been relieved of whatever position I might have held. But, equally surely, I shall continue to wage my own

245

private battle although I am far from sure what shape that may take.

I feel that my understanding has greatly improved as a consequence of writing this book. The distinction between near-equilibrium and far-from-equilibrium conditions qualifies as a significant insight, and the similarity between financial markets and history is more than a quaint coincidence. The asymmetrical boom–bust pattern is a useful aid to thinking, but it must be used with discretion. It describes a far-from-equilibrium process in isolation, but human society is an open system where no process occurs in isolation. The actual course of events is much more complex than any theoretical model, including models of complex systems.

It is amazing enough to be able to observe similarities in the patterns of such disparate developments as the rise and fall of the Soviet system and of the U.S. banking system; it would be an intolerable leap of faith to claim that the common pattern actually defines those developments. The pattern can be altered both by extraneous events and by the decisions of the participants at any time. For instance, the pattern in Eastern Europe would have quite a different shape if Saddam Hussein had not invaded Kuwait when he did. Moreover, both the Gulf crisis and the collapse of the Soviet economy are elements in another drama being played out concurrently: the crisis in the international banking system. The unfolding of that crisis impinges, in turn, on the economies of Eastern Europe and the Soviet Union. There are a number of other dramas going on at the same time which are more or less interactive.

To mention only one: Mexico is going through its own *perestroika*. In contrast to Gorbachev, Carlos Salinas de Gotari has remained in control of the process he has unleashed. The process itself has much in common with *perestroika*, because it involves the intentional destruction of a one-party system by its own leadership. It is also a typical boom–bust process in which foreign equity investors are cast in the role of providing a justification for their own investment decisions, a role that is self-reinforcing in both directions. Salinas hopes to forestall an eventual bust by creating a free trade area with the United States. If he succeeds, the foreign investors may never leave, just as the foreign capital that poured into the United States in the nineteenth century stayed there forever. It is a brilliant conception which shows every sign of succeeding, and I hope to earn back the money I am spending in Eastern Europe by investing in Mexico. The biggest threat is beyond Salinas's control: a worldwide bear market that could pre-empt the inflow of capital. The Japanese, for instance, would already be pouring large amounts into Mexico if they were not in trouble at home. This is a risk I can insure against by buying puts (or selling short) on the Japanese stock market.

Incidentally, Salinas's decision to open up the Mexican economy was prompted by his visit to the Davos conference in January 1990. He found himself talking to an almost empty room, because everyone wanted to hear Balcerowicz and Vaclav Klaus. He concluded, falsely as it turned out, that Eastern Europe will serve as a magnet for foreign capital and he must move fast if he wants to attract foreign investors. I mention this point to show how intricately the various processes are interwoven, and the external interactions are as much part of the process as the internal interaction that gives the boom–bust pattern its characteristic shape.

What is the use of the boom–bust pattern then? I believe it should be used in the same way as a conditional sentence is used in ordinary language. It defines what might happen, and it may also define what might not happen, but it does not determine anything. It can be used to explain what has happened to the Soviet system and what is likely to happen in the future. The foresight it provides is very gloomy. Not only is the Soviet Union turning into a vortex, but the vortex may also suck in

Eastern Europe, because the European Community may be unwilling to expend the effort and resources that would be necessary to prevent that from happening. The European Community itself is in danger of turning from the ideal of an open society into Fortress Europe, with its walls fortified toward the East. We may well end up with a new version of the Iron Curtain, this time erected from the Western side. This foresight is based on the experience of the last two years, when Western response has consistently lagged behind the needs of the moment. Although the amounts invested, lent, or given to the countries of Eastern Europe have increased over time, they were never sufficient to reverse the trend. But the forecast is conditional. Even today, the Soviet economy could be stabilized by introducing an internationally managed hard currency. In the case of Hungary, the economy could be turned around if my proposal for dealing with the debt problem were accepted.

It needs to be emphasized that the explanation of past events is equally conditional. The Berlin Wall would not have fallen if it had not been for Gorbachev. And, in retrospect, it is clear that there has been a failure of imagination on the Western side. The blame rests squarely with the American and British governments. The Germans rose to the occasion, and the other Continental countries did their best to keep up with them. The fact that events fit the boom–bust pattern so well is no excuse, because there is no necessity to play out every sequence to the full. The sooner preventive action is taken, the greater its chance of success. If the amounts that may be spent on humanitarian aid now had been made available in the summer of 1988, when my proposal for a new kind of Marshall Plan was greeted with laughter, there would be no need for humanitarian aid.

I have had considerable difficulty in reconciling my original framework of open and closed societies with a reflexive theory of historical change. The framework suffers from a grave structural defect: the models are timeless, but the real world is not. The way the models are constructed, open and closed societies appear as alternative systems of social organization. In fact, open society is a more complex, more sophisticated form of organization. Closed societies need only one conception—the prevailing dogma—while in an open society each participant must have his own conception. The collapse of a closed society does not automatically lead to the establishment of an open society. Quite the contrary. The evolution of an open society requires time, while the collapse of a closed society is a revolutionary event in which time is always short. There is only one way the time gap can be bridged: with active and deliberate assistance from abroad. This is the most important lesson to be learned from recent experience.

Perhaps the greatest insight of the book, and the one that gives me the greatest personal satisfaction, concerns the question of values. The question has concerned me all my life, but I did not know how to approach it. I felt that modern society in general and America in particular suffer from a deficiency of values. The idea was present in my original concept of open society, but I was not satisfied with its formulation. Having received an education in economics, which takes values as given, I felt singularly ill-equipped to tackle the problem. I was also ill at ease discussing it, because it was incompatible with my status as a hard-nosed businessman. There is something both phony and pompous about a financial speculator inveighing against the moral crisis of our age. But linking the question of values with the stability of the system resolved all my difficulties. What could be more respectable than to be concerned about stability? And it was my education in economics that was the source of my insight. I feel I have found a key that may unlock many doors. I have not yet tried all the keyholes.

It may seem ironic that the main lesson to be learned from the collapse of the Soviet system concerns the nature of open society, but it is not really so. The failure of vision in the United

States and the United Kingdom that I have mentioned before can be directly attributed to a misunderstanding about the market economy. The modern version of *laissez-faire* postulates that the pursuit of self-interest will lead to the optimum allocation of resources. What we have learnt is that self-interest is not enough; there has to be a commitment to making the system work that transcends self-interest.

INDEX

251

INDEX

Bulgaria, 72, 73
  economy in, 42, 119
  foreign debt and, 126, 127
  Soros Foundation in, 132, 135
"Burden of Consciousness, The" (Soros), 223n
Bush, George, 33, 69, 93, 94
Business education, 26

Calfa, Marian, 27, 123
Capetown University, South Africa, 5
Capital as scarce resource, 36, 37
Capitalism, 36, 235
Cargo cult, 181
Carter, Jimmy, 48
"Case for Growth Banks, The" (Soros), 236
Caucasus, 58
Causal laws, 179, 180
Ceausescu, Nicolai, 83
Central European Confederation, concept of, 77
Central European University, 26n, 129–130, 133, 136, 142
Central Intelligence Agency (CIA), 11, 13
Central Park Community Fund, 131
Central Park Conservancy, 131
Certainty, quest for, 195–196
Cerych, Ladislav, 130
Change, concept of, 175–176
Changeless society, 177–185
Chaos theory: see Complex systems theory
Charter 77 Foundation of Stockholm, 26–27, 132–133, 135
Chautauqua Conference of Soviet-American Friendship, 18
Chen Yizi, 11–13
Chernyshov, Sergei, 22
Chevron, 55
China, 83
  economic reform in, 37–38, 40, 41, 44, 52, 235
  Fund for the Opening and Reform of China, 10–13, 45, 141, 158
Chinese revolution of 1989, 14
Circular reasoning, 152–155
Civil Forum party of Czechoslovakia, 26
Class exploitation, 219, 220
Classical economic theory, 162, 197

Closed society, 62–64, 70, 218–221, 248–249; see also Soviet Union
  dogmatic mode of thinking and, 182, 211–217
  economic reform and: see Economic reform
  nationalism and, 57
Cognitive function, 153, 167
Cold War, 66
COMECON, 39, 78, 80, 82, 125
Common interest, 218–219
Common law, 184–185
Common Market, 76–77
Communism, 35, 36, 56, 71–72, 220, 221, 223, 235
Competition
  and control, 88–89
  effective, 198, 203–204
  perfect, 196–198, 200, 203
Complex systems theory, 150, 152, 155–163, 170–171
Computers, 157–158
Conglomerate boom, 226–227, 229, 233, 240
Constitution of the United States, 89, 202
Cooper, Richard, 108, 113n
Coordinating Committee on Export Controls (COCOM), 20
Council for Mutual Economic Assistance, 39
Creative urge, 195
Crimea, 138
Critical attitude, 189–190, 195
Critical mode of thinking, 176–177, 181, 186–196, 212, 213, 215
Critical process, 188–189
Croatia, 72
Crosby, Robert, 158
Cultural Foundation of the USSR, 16–17, 20
Cultural Initiative Foundation, 11, 18–24, 99–100, 133, 136–137
Currency, 58–59, 67–70, 248
Cybernetics, 158
Czechoslovakia, 56, 72, 73, 75, 120
  Charter 77 Foundation in, 26–27, 132–133, 135
  East European Payments Union and, 81, 82
  economic reform in, 42
  Gentle Revolution (1989), 26–27, 66

INDEX

Open society, 62–66, 70, 92, 131, 248–249
  alternatives available in, 206–208
  critical mode of thinking and, 176–177, 181, 186–196, 212, 213, 215
  deficiency of purpose in, 209–211
  economic reform and: see Economic reform
  freedom in, 202–203
  goal of, 128, 138
  instability in, 199–202
  nationalism and, 57
  perfect competition in, 196–198
  private property in, 203–204
  social contract in, 204–206
  U.S. commitment to ideal of, 89–91
  values in, 208–209, 231
Open Society Fund, 4–7, 140–141; see also Charter 77 Foundation; Cultural Initiative Foundation; Fund for the Opening and Reform of China; Soros Foundation; Stefan Batory Foundation
Order out of Chaos: Man's New Dialogue with Nature (Prigogine and Stengers), 158
Organic society, 177, 182–186, 205, 206, 218–220, 239
Organization for European Cooperation and Development, 105
Orwell, George, 208

Paris Club, 31, 123
Participants' bias, 162–163, 167, 170, 172, 238
Participating function, 153, 167, 168
Pavlov, Valentin S., 29, 109, 111, 136–137
Pavlychko, Dmytro, 22
Peace Foundation, 21
Pelczynski, Zbigniew, 14
Perestroika, 43, 54, 56, 58, 59, 236
Perfect competition, 196–198, 200, 203
Perfection, 169
Permanence, 169
Petrakov, Nikolai Y., 30, 101, 106, 107, 111
PHARE, 129
Philosophical Investigations (Wittgenstein), 178n
Philosophy, 147–164, 191

Photocopy machines, 8, 135
Pleasure principle, 209, 210
Poland, 56, 72, 75, 241–242
  Czechoslovakia and, 123–124
  East European Payments Union concept and, 81, 82
  economic reform in, 31–33, 42, 73–74, 143
  foreign debt and, 42, 73, 126, 127
  inflation in, 40
  nationalism in, 122
  political evolution in, 122–123
  Stefan Batory Foundation in, 14–16, 31, 132, 135
  Western assistance to, 69, 74
Political evolution, 71, 122–124
Popov, Gavriil, 100
Popper, Karl, 156, 170, 172, 192
Pozsgai, Imre, 121
Pralong, Sandra, 134
Pravda, 138
Prigogine, Ilya, 158
Private property, 45, 183–184, 203–204
Privatization, 73–74, 110, 119
Prodi, Romano, 108
Professionalism, 142
Protectionism, 201
Purpose, deficiency of, 209–211

Rapaczynski, Andrzej, 36n, 184n
Rasputin, Valentin, 18, 19
Raushenbakh, Boris, 18
Reagan, Ronald, 87, 201
Real estate, 228
Reality; see also Reflexive theory of history
  thinking versus reality, 148–152, 160–162
Recursive loops, 157–158
Reflexive theory of history, 165–174
  bias, 166–168
  boom–bust pattern, 167–170
  complex systems theory, 170–171
  static versus dynamic disequilibrium, 171–174
Reflexivity, concept of, 63, 85, 152–155, 172, 173, 177, 230–232
Relativity theory, 150
Religion, 191
Romania, 56, 66, 72, 73, 75
  economic reform in, 42
  Soros Foundation in, 132, 134–135

256

INDEX

Rousseau, Jean-Jacques, 205
Rukh movement, Ukraine, 137
Russell, Bertrand, 149
Russian Challenge, The (Yanov), 221n
Russian republics, 22–23, 57, 58, 60, 136–137
Russian Revolution, 113, 116
Ryzhkov, 29, 105, 106, 109, 113
Ryzhkov Plan, 109–111

Sachs, Jeffrey, 31–32, 108
Sacrifice, 202, 203
Sakharov, Andrei, 16, 17
Salinas de Gotari, Carlos, 246–247
Saratov Province, 57
Scholarships, 5, 8, 14, 83
Schwarzenberg, Prince Kari, 27
Scientific method, 149, 157, 190–194, 197
Self-interest, 90–91, 200, 201, 203, 250
Self-organization, 131
Self-reference, 153, 158
Serbia, 72
Serfdom, 56
Shatalin, Stanislav S., 101, 115
Shatalin Group, 106–109, 111, 112
Shatalin Plan, 30, 46, 51, 99, 109–116, 118, 133, 136, 143, 242, 245
Shevardnadze, Edvard, 94
Siberia, 57
Silayev, Ivan, 105
Simplifications, 186, 187
Sitaryan, Stepan A., 106
60 Minutes, 23
Slovakia, 72, 137
Sobchak, Anatoly, 100
Social class, 206, 219, 220
Social contract, 204–206
Social Darwinism, 88, 90, 92
Social science, 162, 191, 192, 195
Solidarity, 14–15, 122
Son of the Revolution, The (Liang Heng), 10
Soros, Susan, 18
Soros Foundation, 6; *see also* Charter 77 Foundation; Cultural Initiative Foundation; Fund for the Opening and Reform of China; Stefan Batory Foundation
in Bulgaria, 132, 135
in Hungary, 5–10, 25–26, 45, 131–133, 135–136, 141, 142, 147

in Romania, 132, 134–135
in Yugoslavia, 133
South Africa, 5
Soviet-American Foundation Cultural Initiative, 11, 18–24, 99–100, 133, 136–137
Sovietskaia Russiya, 137, 138
Soviet Union; *see also* Gorbachev, Mikhail
boom–bust model applied to, 233–236, 240
collapse of system, 34–61
confederation concept, 66–67, 71, 80
Cultural Initiative Foundation in, 11, 18–24, 20, 99–100, 133, 136–137
currency issue, 67–70, 248
economic reform in, 34–36, 41, 43–45, 50, 52–57, 67–69, 99, 106–116, 234–235
empire of, 56
evolution of civil society in, 23–24
nationalism in, 56–61
perestroika and *glasnost* in, 24, 43, 54, 56, 58, 59, 92, 236
Shatalin Plan, 30, 46, 51, 99, 106–116, 118, 133, 136, 143, 242, 245
task force on market-oriented open sector, 28–30
trade and, 78–81
U.S. and collapse of, 84–86
Speculation, 228–229
Stalin, Joseph, 34–36, 48, 50, 56–57, 66, 92, 116, 117, 172, 173, 234, 241
Stankevich, Sergei, 100, 101
Static disequilibrium, 172, 174
Static equilibrium, 197, 200
Stefan Batory Foundation, 14–16, 31, 132, 135, 136
Stengers, Isabelle, 158
Steps to an Ecology of Mind (Bateson), 158
Stock markets, 9, 89, 168, 228–229, 238
Subjective aspects of reality, 153–154
Summers, Larry, 108
Superpower status, 84–88, 91, 93, 94
Survival of the fittest, doctrine of, 88, 92, 166, 201
Sverdlovsk, 23

Tarasov, Artem, 54–55
Tardos, Marton, 29, 108

257

INDEX

Tempus program, 130
Thatcher, Margaret, 76, 104, 120, 201
Thinking; see also Reflexive theory of history
 as complex system, 159–163
 critical mode of, 176–177, 181, 186–196, 212, 213, 215
 dogmatic mode of, 182, 211–217
 vs. reality, 148–152, 160–162
 traditional mode of, 176–183, 189, 196, 211–213, 215, 216
Tiananmen Square massacre, 12, 13, 44
Timofeyev, Lev, 17
Tirgu Mures, riots of, 72
Tractatus Logico-Philosophicus (Wittgenstein), 149
Trade, 78–81
Tradition, 181–182, 186, 214
Traditional mode of thinking, 176–183, 189, 196, 211–213, 215, 216
Transcendental meditation, 161
Transylvania, 135
Trcziakowski, 31
Trend, 168, 224, 229, 233
Trianon Treaty, 74
Tulip-mania mentality, 228
Twain, Mark, 156
Tyminski, Stanislaw, 122

Ukraine, 22, 75
 nationalist movement in, 58
 Ukrainian Renaissance Foundation in, 22, 133, 138
Ukrainians, 57
Umpleby, Stuart, 158
Uncertainty principle, 150, 170

United Nations, 50, 66, 85, 87, 89, 94
Utopia (More), 208

Values, 208–209, 229–232, 249
Vasarhelyi, Miklos, 6, 10, 22
Vatra Romanesca, 72, 134, 138
Versailles Treaty, 74
Vienna agreement, 88
Volunteerism, 142

Walesa, Lech, 122
Wall Street Journal, 33, 68
Warsaw Pact, 28
Wealth, 210–211
West Germany, 74, 120
Whitehead, John, 20
Whittome, Alan, 105
Wittgenstein, Ludwig, 147, 149, 150, 178n
World Bank, 105, 112
World War I, 89
World War II, 89

Yakovlev, Alexander N., 52, 105–106
Yanov, Alexander, 60n, 221n
Yasin, Yevgeny, 112
Yavlinsky, Grigory A., 105–107, 112–115
Yeltsin, Boris, 51, 99–109, 112
Young Pioneers, 12
Yugoslavia, 36, 37
 economic reform in, 42, 72–73, 121
 nationalism in, 72–73, 121
 Soros Foundation in, 133

Zaslavskaya, Tatyana, 18
Zhao Ziyang, 11, 12, 40, 52
Znamya, 22

258

PublicAffairs is a nonfiction publishing house founded in 1997. It is a tribute to the standards, values, and flair of three persons who have served as mentors to countless reporters, writers, editors, and book people of all kinds, including me.

I. F. Stone, proprietor of *I. F. Stone's Weekly,* combined a commitment to the First Amendment with entrepreneurial zeal and reporting skill and became one of the great independent journalists in American history. At the age of eighty, Izzy published *The Trial of Socrates,* which was a national bestseller. He wrote the book after he taught himself ancient Greek.

Benjamin C. Bradlee was for nearly thirty years the charismatic editorial leader of *The Washington Post.* It was Ben who gave the *Post* the range and courage to pursue such historic issues as Watergate. He supported his reporters with a tenacity that made them fearless, and it is no accident that so many became authors of influential, best-selling books.

Robert L. Bernstein, the chief executive of Random House for more than a quarter century, guided one of the nation's premier publishing houses. Bob was personally responsible for many books of political dissent and argument that challenged tyranny around the globe. He is also the founder and was the longtime chair of Human Rights Watch, one of the most respected human rights organizations in the world.

. . .

For fifty years, the banner of Public Affairs Press was carried by its owner Morris B. Schnapper, who published Gandhi, Nasser, Toynbee, Truman, and about 1,500 other authors. In 1983 Schnapper was described by *The Washington Post* as "a redoubtable gadfly." His legacy will endure in the books to come.

Printed in the United States
129848LV00002B/266/A